The First Lions of
RUGBY

The first British Lions and their dramatic 1888 tour of Australia & New Zealand

FRONT COVER IMAGES: top: Andrew Stoddart (left; © Frédéric Humbert), Bob Seddon (right; © John Griffiths), British Lions team (bottom; © Frédéric Humbert)

The Slattery Media Group Pty Ltd
1 Albert St, Richmond
Victoria, Australia, 3121

Text copyright © Sean Fagan 2013
Design copyright © The Slattery Media Group Pty Ltd 2013
First published by The Slattery Media Group Pty Ltd 2013
All images reproduced with permission.

All rights reserved. No part of this publication may be reproduced, stored in a retrieval system or transmitted in any form or by any means without the prior written permission of the copyright owner. Inquiries should be made to the publisher.

National Library of Australia Cataloguing-in-Publication entry
Author: Fagan, Sean, (Sean Patrick), 1964- author.
Title: The first lions of Rugby / Sean Fagan.
ISBN: 9780987500274 (paperback)
Subjects: Rugby Union football–Australia–History.
            Rugby Union football players–Australia.
            Sports–Australia–History.
Dewey Number: 796.33380994

Group Publisher: Geoff Slattery
Editor: Nick Tedeschi
Cover Design: Guy Shield
Design and typeset: Kate Slattery

Printed and bound in Australia by Griffin

Every effort has been made to verify the source of each image. Inquiries should be made to the publisher.

slatterymedia.com

The First Lions of
RUGBY

The first British Lions and their dramatic 1888 tour of Australia & New Zealand

SEAN FAGAN

visit *slatterymedia.com*

'A dribbling rush': A popular tactic of the time, one side's entire pack of nine forwards would come charging up the field with the ball at their feet, short-kicking it soccer-style towards the goal line and diving on it for the try.

LE FOOTBALL RUGBY, PUBLISHED 1900; SOURCE: FRÉDÉRIC HUMBERT

NO game was ever yet worth a rap
For a rational man to play,
Into which no accident, no mishap,
Could possibly find its way.

IF you hold the willow, a shooter from Wills
May transform you into a hopper,
And the football meadow is rife with spills,
If you feel disposed for a cropper.

THERE'S danger even where fish are caught
To those who a wetting fear;
For what's worth having must aye be bought,
And sport's like life, and life's like sport,
'It ain't all skittles and beer.'

Adam Lindsay Gordon

(excerpts from *Fytte IV: In Utrumque Paratus*, published 1867)

Of Scottish descent, son of a British army officer, educated in England, emigrated to Australia; acclaimed as Australia's first poet of note. In tribute a statue stands near Parliament House, Melbourne, and a memorial bust in The Poets' Corner of Westminster Abbey, London, which is inscribed—"Adam Lindsay Gordon, Poet of Australia. Born 1833. Died 1870."

ABOUT THE AUTHOR
Sean Fagan

Sean is a sports historian and writer. His previous books include *The Rugby Rebellion: The Divide of League and Union*, which explores the initial split between the codes in Australia, and *The Master: The Life and Times of Dally Messenger*. He has written for daily newspapers, websites, and sports magazines, including *Inside Sport*, worked as a consultant and script writer on a number of sports television and radio programs, and appeared in television documentaries including *A Century of Rugby League* and *Beneath The Māori Moon: A History of Māori Rugby*.

Further reading: *sfaganweb.com*

NOTE

Some of the quotes and letters used in this book have been truncated, combined &/or converted to dialogue for reasons of length, grammar and ease of reading and comprehension within the context of the narrative. The substance of the original material has not been altered and sources may be obtained from the author.

The First Lions of RUGBY

Contents

INTRODUCTION

A Football Expedition 11

THE FIRST LIONS OF RUGBY

1 Stoddart's Team 13
2 The Wellington Unpleasantness 20
3 The Gate-Money Game 33
4 With a Jealous Eye 46
5 Drop a Tear and Bid Adieu 60
6 'He Is a Dead-Head' 65
7 Surviving the High Seas 72
8 A Devilish Track 82
9 The First of Many Hearty Welcomes 92
10 Friends and Foes Alike 96
11 Having Heard Strange Tales 108
12 Too Much Whisky, Too Many Women 121
13 Make the British Lion Bite the Dust 130
14 Whistle and Rifle 142
15 Clowes' Case Under Discussion 152
16 The Unprosperous Trinity 159
17 Brave the Lion in His Own Den 170
18 A Complete Transformation 181
19 Southern Cross or Union Jack ... 195
20 How Do You Like Our Game? ... 204

21	Bare the Marks of War	217
22	Noble Guests of Football Fame	228
23	The Great Game of Life Itself	232
24	Three Hearty Cheers and a Tiger	248
25	A Trip Through Maori Land	257
26	Lots of Kangaroo Tales to Tell	269

APPENDICES

I	A Record of the 1888 Tour	278
II	Post-tour Timeline	281
III	The First Anglo-Australian Football Team	285
IV	British & Irish Lions Tours	287
V	The Two Games Explained	288
VI	Bibliography	295
VII	Acknowledgements	297

A.E. Stoddart—the celebrated international must have many caps:
By the time of his retirement from major sport, Andrew Stoddart had amassed 16 Test cricket 'caps' for England, and another 10 for the England team in rugby. This was in addition to his appearances in rugby for the British Lions, the Barbarians, Blackheath and Harlequins, as well as Middlesex in county cricket.

ARENA, PUBLISHED 1912; SOURCE: FRÉDÉRIC HUMBERT

INTRODUCTION
A Football Expedition

THE following is an account of *The First Anglo-Australian Football Team* of 1888—a touring party of Rugby footballers who have come to be retrospectively recognised as the very first in the celebrated 125 years history of the British and Irish Lions Rugby team, an elite group of players selected just once every four years from the Home Unions—England, Ireland, Scotland and Wales—to tour Australia, New Zealand and South Africa.

The scale of the remarkable and lasting influence of the 1888 team on the development and popularity of Rugby football in Australia and New Zealand cannot be understated. To the Rugby communities that lived in those now faraway times—from the old-timers who shook their heads in bewilderment to the then youngest child, who in the 1950s was still lauding the tourists to anyone that took the time to listen—they were universally adamant that 1888 was a seminal year for the sport. Before 1888 there were the old ways of Rugby. After 1888 there were the exciting and revolutionary new ways of Rugby. People would arrive before a game believing one Rugby philosophy and leave two hours later mesmerised by an entirely new understanding of the possibilities. There was no going back to old ways, there was no slow evolution. The game dramatically, radically, and irrevocably changed for the better—for both the player and the spectator.

But rather than contentedly rest basking in these well-won plaudits, the 1888 tourists then turned their hands—and feet—to tackling the top club sides and expert footballers of Australian Rules football in Melbourne and Adelaide, taking on a code they knew of in Britain only by reputation. They aimed high, challenging first no less than the redoubtable Carlton FC. Over 26,000 Melburnians flocked to the MCG to see how these Britishers would fare, to see if such a daring transformation was even possible.

The pioneers of 1888 departed scorning authority and, after heartbreak and sorrow, they returned home in glory, having gained pride of place as the first of all British Lions teams … a team with a unique story to tell.

Sean Fagan
June 2013

Stoddart's Team

"A.E. Stoddart is the finest Rugby footballer as a three-quarter back in the world. He is as fleet as a greyhound, as active as a cat, and endowed with courage and stamina."
'Scrimmage' in Rockhampton's *Morning Bulletin*, August 18, 1888

Poor old 'Stoddy'. Died by his own hand. Shot himself through the head. The third of April, 1915.

The news of his dreadful end came as a great shock to not only his friends but the wider sporting world of the British Empire. By all accounts he was the most jovial and congenial fellow one could wish to meet. It was with mind-numbing disbelief that people took in the story of his tragic end. "It was a great pity that he should get into difficulties," they said. "Everyone always thought of him a very lucky sort of chap."

Andrew Stoddart—'Stoddy' or 'Drewy' to friends and the public alike—was a 52-year-old former stockbroker, undertaking the position of secretaryship of the prestigious Queen's Club, a multi-purpose sporting club and facility once famous for its Rugby ground but now better known for the London tennis championship that bears its name. Stoddart seemed to have everything to live for. But, of course, the world without is oblivious to our world within. The mind is an amalgam of experiences, love, joys, pleasures, accidents, grief, fears and hopes. It sometimes falsely directs us along the wrong path. The newspapers reported that Stoddart was discovered by his wife, found lying dead in a bedroom of their Maida Vale home, one of London's most desirable residential suburbs, just a short walk to the Lord's Cricket Ground. He had apparently shot himself with a revolver after considerable silent worry and burden arising from financial difficulties.

At the inquest his widow stated Stoddart had resigned the secretaryship of the Queen's Club on account of a nervous breakdown. He had been out of work since and further, lost investment money through the war's impact on the stock market. The medical evidence showed that Stoddart was on the verge of an attack of pneumonia, an illness that often increased the likelihood of depression.

Late on that fateful evening, sitting at a table with his wife Ethel, he pulled out a 'long pistol' from his coat pocket, placing it down in front of them both. "I'm going to finish it," Stoddart said in a quiet but sure voice. She implored her husband to consult his friends for help. A brief struggle then ensued between the two for possession of the weapon, Stoddart wresting it from her hold. Knowing the gun was not yet loaded, Ethel grabbed the accompanying box of cartridges. She would not let him have them. Stoddart put the pistol back inside his jacket and went to their bedroom. Later, Ethel found her husband on their bed, dead. Stoddart, it was now apparent, possessed another box of cartridges. A verdict of "suicide while of unsound mind" was returned.

Despite it being a time of war—the Gallipoli landing of ANZAC and British forces would occur just three weeks later—his death was headline news, for Andrew Stoddart had been one of the most famous sportsmen in Queen Victoria's empire. The most brilliant of sporting careers had come to the saddest of ends. One of the greatest batsmen and a champion footballer, he earned the distinction and the rare feat of captaining England at both cricket and Rugby. If all the Rugby and cricket caps awarded to Stoddart could be placed upon his head, it would have topped that stovepipe hat 'Old Abe Lincoln' made famous. As a tennis player he was above the average;

he excelled at golf; as a roller skater he was in the front ranks; at billiards he could make his 30 or 40 breaks; and upon horseback he was rarely far behind the lead huntsman. He would also prove to be more than capable as an Australian Rules footballer.

In his pomp in the mid-1880s he looked every inch the English sporting gentleman athlete and rising stockbroker that he was. Standing 5 feet 10 inches and weighing 12 stone, he was extremely good looking with dark hair, brown eyes, a late-Victorian era trademark moustache, a clean-shaven chin, and a modest and retiring manner. Away from the sporting fields he was sometimes referred to as 'The Masher'—a trend where a gentleman was given to keeping impeccably dressed in a suit with starched neck-cloth so high and stiff they could barely turn their head and 'shooting the cuffs' of the shirt out so you couldn't help but see his swell cuff-links. It was complemented with brushed-up shoes, a top hat (but not too tall) and a walking cane with the capital conversationalist basking in the sunshine of feminine adoration given the opportunity. Stoddart had the good looks, the education, the moneyed family, the London stock market job, the leisure time and the range of athletic skills to carry the role of 'gentlemanly masher' role off with aplomb.

Through the 1890s Stoddart not only succeeded the famous W.G. Grace as England cricket captain, but rivaled him for national prominence and reverence as the prolific and daring batsman and astute leader. He was a member of four English cricket teams that toured Australia, and most famously led the England XI to an Ashes series victory in 1894/95.

> Then wrote the Queen of England,
> Whose hand is blessed by God
> I must do something handsome,
> For my dear victorious Stod.
> —*Punch magazine, London, 1895*

Stoddart was probably one of the most tireless men who ever lived. On one occasion, playing for Hampstead against the Stoics, he knocked up an astonishing 485 runs in one innings, completed in one afternoon. The night before he made this famous score he never went to bed. He had been out, as the story goes, to a dance. He and some others started playing poker in the early morning, just half an hour for fun. 'Stoddy' had the good (or bad) luck to win, and keep on winning. They were only playing very small, so that no great harm was done. Soon it was 6.30 in the morning, and it was no good turning in. So they had hot baths and changed and came down again. Someone suggested a swim, and they immediately went off to the pool. Stoddart arrived at Hampstead in time for the match, and was soon called upon to bat—he compiled what ended up as 485 runs. Stoddart was out five minutes before stumps ended the day's play, trying to reach 500. Later that evening he played in a doubles match at lawn tennis and then went to the theatre and a supper party. "After that," said Stoddart, "I got to bed all right, and it wasn't nearly three!" He did not think that he had done anything physically beyond the ordinary.

On the Rugby field his deeds won an equally formidable reputation of excellence and flair, "of brilliant and dashing play". His mere presence would lift any team from mediocrity into preeminence. Stoddart began playing Rugby at the Reverend Oliver's School in St John's Wood. After school in the early 1880s he turned out for Harlequins and then Blackheath, and would later become the first captain of the famous Barbarians touring club. As a three-quarter back evincing extraordinary powers of side-stepping, he was utterly unselfish, with tremendous pace and unequalled dash. "Stoddart was the best in-and-out dodger whilst going at full speed," a contemporary wrote of him. He moved into higher honours with the Middlesex county and the South of England representative teams. His brilliance was fully recognised in 1885 when he received an invitation to represent his country in the international matches, making his debut against Wales. From then until his last appearance in 1893, some of his greatest feats came while wearing the red rose-adorned jersey of England.

Many lovers of the game journeyed miles to witness Stoddart in action.

Most assuredly these moments were well worth seeing. "Here he is now," they would say, calling up a memory, "dashing towards a regular host of the enemy through whom you might imagine a passage was impossible—a sudden dodge with a quickness almost impossible to follow, and he is away again deep into the enemy's 25-yards line, and within sight of the goal. He may run on, or unselfishly pass to an unmarked support." What they so admired in Stoddart as a centre three-quarter was his artistic and clever play, all without ever resorting to anything like roughness. He seemed to have reduced Rugby football to a science.

As a footballer he was a risk-taker, sometimes a bit of a showman—he had been known to jump clean over a man stooping to tackle or charge at him, to the utter astonishment of not only his opponent, but the other players and the spectators watching upon the unfolding scene. Yet it was known by everybody as an absurdly dangerous play, for if the tackler suddenly stood up, or threw up an arm, the jumper could be—and twice in Stoddart's career he was—flipped completely over, landing on his head, carted away to hospital with a concussion.

His power drop-kicking the ball—with either foot—was of a value impossible to gauge, particularly as early in his career victory was awarded based upon the number of goals, with unconverted tries of no relevance except as a tie-breaker. Indeed it was after Stoddart in 1886 landed a long range drop goal for Middlesex to sink Yorkshire's three unconverted tries that the code's law-makers changed the entire paradigm of Rugby as 'foot' ball, introducing point values that led to teams working towards tries instead of goals.

Like many young footballers, Stoddart had his larkish side on the Rugby field as well. Writing in *Rugger My Pleasure* in 1957, A.A. 'Alex' Thomson recounted a story handed down to him: "Once, playing for Harlequins against West Kent on Chislehurst Common, Stoddart dashed towards the enemy line in his usual steam-engine fashion, only to find that the area behind goal was deep—not inches but feet—in water. Without an instant's hesitation he dived in, head first, like a tufted duck, and was an unconscionable time in coming up again. The referee had almost decided to have the pond dragged, when Stoddart reappeared, smiling, having scored what was probably the first submarine try in rugger history."

For all who had that rare delight of witnessing him flying upon the grassed field of battle, it became a treasured memory. In Australia and New Zealand the opportunities to watch Stoddart on the cricket oval were legion, but the pleasure of seeing him on the football field came just once—in 1888 with the visit of the first British Lions team, organised by his English cricket compatriots Arthur Shrewsbury, Alfred Shaw and James Lillywhite.

Many of the tributes to Stoddart—and in the telling of Rugby history in newspapers, books and word ever since—have acclaimed the 1888 tourists who established the Lions touring tradition and had such an influence upon Rugby development in the Australasian colonies as being 'Stoddart's team'.

There is no denying how popular and fine an impression Stoddart made during that tour. He was admired wherever he went, and of course figures prominently in the tour's story. Near the long and arduous campaign's end in New Zealand, at a match against a Combined South Island XV at Dunedin, Stoddart gave yet another "splendid exposition of football" in a hard-fought victory. In those days the football team dressing room was often the town hotel. After the game the Lions and the home players, travelling on horse-drawn carts, were accompanied by a vast cheering crowd all the way back to the hotel. However, once the players had retreated inside, the gathering refused to disperse, calling out demands for Stoddart to re-appear to take one special round of applause. He finally emerged at a first-floor window, taking his final bow amidst the appreciative shouts and hand-clapping.

> Till '88 we played a kind
> Of ancient game of scrum and maul,
> Where muscle triumphed over mind,
> And heavy feet chased tortured ball—
> Indeed a very stupid game
> Till '88 when Stoddart came.

STODDART'S TEAM

Although Stoddart, the gentleman amateur rugger from London, was the star back of the tour, almost all of the other players were working class men from Yorkshire and Lancashire, the hot-beds of English Rugby in the mid-late 1880s.

This team had elected another England international as their captain. This wasn't Stoddart's team at all.

It was 'Seddon's team'.

The Wellington Unpleasantness

"The Duke of Wellington once said that it was on the football fields of Eton and Rugby that the battle of Waterloo was won."

Apocryphal ascription, late 1800s

———

Here they came. Another wave of attack from the red-and-blacks. Given heavy drizzling rain was making the ball greasy to handle, it was textbook wet weather Rugby. All nine of the home team's forwards thundering in a pack towards the Lions' goal line, the ball at their toes, dexterously dribbling it with their feet, soccer-style. Left behind in their wake, Britain's captain, Robert 'Bob' Seddon, and his fellow forwards could do nothing but watch on as their three-quarters and full-back attempted to stop their opponents.

Unfortunately, the back men were without Stoddart, who was in the stands looking on, nursing an injured ankle.

Then, in a flash, a red-white-and-blue jerseyed man, swooped in on the scene—too fast to credit who this plucky fellow was. Without curtailing his speed, he stooped down before the ongoing phalanx of doom, picked up the rolling leather from their very boots, and was away across and then

THE WELLINGTON UNPLEASANTNESS

back upfield. It relieved the team of danger, and probably saved a try. A smart, crowd-thrilling move, it was also one of self-preservation—the alternative of diving on the ball and laying there being particularly unwise, as the opposing forwards would ruck and kick through and over the fallen in their attempt to free the football. Only when certain the ball could not be extricated from beneath the now lifeless hero, a scrum ('scrimmage' or 'scrummage') would be ordered. Attempting to instead take a 'flying kick' at the ball was equally reckless, with a broken leg or knee injury likely from any collision with the on-rushing forwards.

Through a swift interchange of passes, the British backs carried the ball past Seddon, and he followed in support. A quick short pass saw the ball in the skipper's hands, and he ran towards the opposition's territory.

The English newspapers had described the Lions' captain as:

> A 'Lancashire lad,' and standing, as he does, within an inch of 6ft, with fine broad shoulders, he fills the eye at once as an ideal Rugby footballer and leader of men. He has the perfect physique of a true temperate Briton; aided in no small part by his abstemiousness from hard liquors. One at once puts him down as a keen hard worker. Amiable in disposition, elevated in principle, a most genial and kind companion. Born in Salford in 1860, though both his parents have now passed on, he has four brothers, two sisters, and any number of nieces and nephews that he loves to put on his knees and sing jovial songs to. He was educated in Manchester, and on leaving school entered into a large woollen mill. By industry and business tact, he was soon raised to a position which involved great responsibility in the warehouse. An enthusiastic lover of all manly sports, he has long held a reputation as one of best exponents of the Rugby game of football, crowned in 1887 when he was awarded a place in the England forwards against Scotland, Ireland and Wales. Once of the famous Broughton Rangers club, last season he threw in his lot with

Swinton, another strong Rugby club in Manchester, and was immediately elected captain. No sooner is conversation begun than Seddon displays his perfect knowledge of the science of Rugby football. Always in the thick of the struggle, he has never been known—unlike some other Rugby players—to have ever taken a mean or unfair advantage of an opponent, but works hard to win victory with that determination which his looks predict, and which all his companions know he possesses. Make no mistake, he plays the game very hard, but his manly conduct guides his play; he has been seen many times to render assistance to a suddenly disabled footballer during the game, no matter who they were, whether an opponent or not.

In 1888 the captain and his word was law both on and off the field. All responsibility and directions in regard to team matters rested with him. There were no coaches in Rugby. When made an offer to be part of the first British football team to visit Australia and New Zealand, Seddon had very quickly and cheerfully accepted, looking forward to the adventure of it all immensely.

The British and Great Britain—or, as was the custom when referring to most matters pertaining to Great Britain until after World War II, "the English" and England—were now a fortnight into their tour, the opening New Zealand leg. Their long itinerary next included Rugby games in New South Wales (NSW) before a switch of codes would see the team play Australian Rules matches against the top clubs in Victoria and South Australia.

Their opponents here in this match were a mixed team of local Rugby players from Wellington and thereabouts. For the sake of posterity, they were declared to be 'Mr. Roberts' XV' in honour of their captain and chief organiser, Harry Roberts (who had 'repped' for New Zealand in 1884). A fair gathering, by local standards, of over 2500 made their way to the Basin Reserve to see the contest. Large flags in Wellington and Union Jack colours were flying at all points around the ground. A brass band, dressed in military style garb and stationed in front of the packed grandstand, were playing appropriate musical pieces to mirror the mood of the on-field play. Despite the threat of rain, no one was dissuaded from enjoying their opportunity to see Seddon and his band of touring footballers from Britain, the very first of their kind.

Seddon's run beyond the half-way line was ended by an opposing three-quarter bringing him down in a tackle. The skipper rolled away, leaving the ball on the ground, and quick as you like, teammate Harry Eagles kicked the leather onwards, but a little too hard—the opposition's half-back now had the ball in his hands, then smartly drop-kicked it upfield, and out over the touch-line. At the ensuing line-out one of the home team knocked the ball to ground, and once again their forwards were off on another 'dribbling rush' assault deep into British territory. This time the horde was not to be denied. Lions defenders endeavoured to get to the ball, but each in his turn fell by the wayside. Near the goal line a young Maori forward, Tom Ellison, with cool and sure hands took hold of the ball, and amidst great cheers from the onlookers carried it in under the posts for a try, and the game's opening points.

Despite being in front of the goal, the conversion attempt flayed wide and missed. A short time later, the ball was kicked long towards towards Harry Speakman, a fast-improving young three-quarter who played for Cheshire County and Runcorn, and had impressed a growing number of judges through the 1887/88 Northern hemisphere winter. 'Speakie,' when he found himself isolated, rarely took the conventional escape route of kicking for touch. Instead, he chose the rather naughty Rugby habit of diving at the ground, just in front of the onrushing opponent about to tackle or charge him. From a distance it gave the impression that he had been tackled, and that the ball could not be dug out from under him, meaning play would be called 'dead', and a scrum would be held. Sometimes he would be a bit trickier, extending his ruse to try to catch sleepy opponents out: if no scrum had yet been called, or he realised none was forthcoming, he would suddenly roll over and pass the ball or get up with it and take off on another run.

This time though he was confronted by a giant forward—Edmund Whatman, captain of the Wairarapa RU rep team—about to launch a full charge upon him. Seeing Speakman drop to the ground in front of the oncoming opponent, Fred McShane and Jack Lawlor, two Victorian footballers accompanying the team to train the players in Australian Rules, could barely get out "Rabbiting!" before an almighty "crack!" sound choked off their shouts. Whatman had fallen heavily across the top of Speakman, his leg violently striking the Englishman's shoulder. His left leg had been broken just above the ankle. One account stated: "The limb snapped like a twig. The leg broke with a report which was distinctly heard by many of the spectators, and the bone actually protruded through the skin." Another said "the noise of the broken bone was like the crack of a whip". The band, playing their instruments, didn't fully hear the dreadful sound. Seeing the man down though and the game stopped, the conductor had the members struck up the familiar sombre refrains from Handel's *Dead March in Saul* and Chopin's *Funeral March* triggering much laughter and whistling along from among the crowd, many unaware of the seriousness of the injury.

Though undoubtedly a game of many lurking injury risks, it was not yet the norm, even at major Rugby matches, to have ambulancemen present. Nor were stretchers to be found, even at the big cricket grounds in Melbourne and Sydney where the chief football games were played in winter. Fortunately this time among the spectators there was a local doctor, and entirely appropriately in the eyes of the code's critics, the British squad also carried its own medical men, the Edinburgh University trained Dr. John Smith and Dr. Herbert Brooks.

With Whatman in excruciating hurt, but given nothing for the pain relief other than the standard Rugby fortifier of a good four-finger nip of whisky, the doctors roughly re-set and braced the broken limb on the spot, using two walking-sticks bound tightly with handkerchiefs. It was equally important to get him up off the damp ground as quickly as possible to avoid giving him a chill to the kidneys (many players also wore wide and tight belts around the waist, believing they needed to protect their kidneys from impact in tackles and other jostling).

A few industrious men in the crowd wrenched a nearby gate from its post and hinges to act as a makeshift stretcher. The players watched as Whatman was carried from the field and carefully placed on a horse-drawn drag (open wagon), which then slowly disappeared in the general direction of Wellington Hospital. Later that night word got about that the fracture was clean and would heal readily. In the end it was six weeks before Whatman could even get onto crutches, and another six before he returned to work on his farm. He never played Rugby again.

In standing about during the long break, offering a comforting word to Whatman and Roberts, the opposing captain, even the normally placable Seddon was showing signs he was exasperated. None regretted Whatman's accident and injury more than the visitors, especially after the unjust way in which they had been charged with causing all the rough play in the game against the official Wellington XV two days earlier. He was relieved it wasn't this time one of his own men, but feared he and his Lions team would be again vilified for what the local press called their "unnecessary roughness and reckless brutal play". It was seemingly the final straw in a despairing and frustrating past few days. In many respects it was a miracle that the team had ever left England and reached the Australasian colonies at all. So many hurdles had been put in their place by those that wanted to see the venture fail, those that said it could never be done. But now, at this moment in Wellington, Seddon thought those doomsayers might have been right.

The first difficulty had begun four days earlier, trying to get to Wellington. The steamship *Te Anau* they intended to board in Lyttelton was held over for a day due to heavy fog meaning they would not arrive in the capital until the Saturday morning, which was match-day. When they did finally get on the ship, they found it had been over-booked. "Everybody made for the cabins, only to find there were five bunks for 26 of us," explained Seddon. Most of the team was forced to camp out on the deck, and very few got any sleep that night at all. "This was not at all a pleasant position, considering we had to meet Wellington, one of the strongest teams in the colonies, the following day." The ship eventually arrived at Wellington dockside at 10am and the players were welcomed by a large and enthusiastic crowd.

"After getting our luggage together," said Seddon, "two waggonettes (horse-drawn) took us to our hotel, most of our men retiring to rest for some hours. The afternoon turned out beautifully fine, and great crowds of people were pouring through the entrances as we drove to the ground, which had a grandstand down one side; this was simply packed with ladies, who showed their feelings by wearing the colours of their favoured team."

The colony's premier and chief justice were among the crowd that numbered 7000 spectators. The teams entered the field of battle, Wellington in black, contrasting with Britain's tricolours. The air was so still and unseasonably warm that, as a local put it, "the very chilliest mortal could stand about without feeling the need of an overcoat". This was highly unusual for the city often known as 'Windy Wellington'. The pleasant setting didn't extend to the match itself. The home team had been laying-in-wait, training the same men in fitness and tactics for six weeks in readiness. So much for the 'Corinthian spirit' of amateur sport in the colonies!

"The least said about this match the better," explained Seddon. "Stoddart, disabled at Christchurch, was unable to play. From the commencement it could plainly be seen that rough play was the order, for before half-time four of our men had to be carried off. The match eventually ending in a draw— a try each—I was not sorry when it was all over, for I felt, as two or three of our men remarked afterwards, 'I'm glad I'm alive!'".

According to the *Bay Of Plenty Times* reporter, "the Englishmen state the game was the roughest and most quarrelsome they have played for years, and at one stage the English captain threatened to withdraw his men from the field. Bumby, Banks, Stuart, and Haslam got tolerably severe injuries." The casualty toll had mounted steadily as the game went on, each necessitating a lengthy stoppage in the contest, and with replacements not permitted, none of the men were anything but reluctant to leave the game and place their side at a numerical disadvantage. Walter Bumby received a kick on the neck trying to pick up the football at the feet of the charging Wellington forwards. Somehow in a scrum Angus Stuart was given a severe knock to the groin, and had no choice but to be taken from the field. Tom Banks then took a heavy blow to his knee, and as he slowly limped off, a slightly recomposed Stuart hobbled back on again. Tommy Haslam too was *hors de combat* for a time.

"I then thought that it was getting too serious," said Seddon. He called the Wellington captain King over. "I will take my men off the ground if this 'game' is to be continued," warned Seddon.

"You should give and take in matches of this kind," King curtly replied.

"Of course that is all very well for your side, when you can put a fresh team into the field if necessary, however my men have got to last out four or five months," retorted Seddon. "I am quite willing to play the true Rugby game—we do not care one button how rough your team makes this affair, as long as they do not infringe the laws of the game."

Arthur Shrewsbury, who along with fellow promoter of the tour James Lillywhite was travelling with the team, wrote in a letter home: "Wellington players went in for a lot of bullocking and tried all in their power to injure our players." Salford's Jack Anderton added: "If there was one club more than another who play what you might call an unrefined game it was Wellington. 'Great Scot!' they can tackle. They meant it! While Banks and Stuart were lying on the grass disabled, King, the captain, was heard to say, 'Go on, Wellington break their b__ necks.' Not very nice to hear was it? But still, I should not say they played rough, though I can think it!" As far as Seddon and the tour party were concerned, it was scant courtesy to show a team of men that had travelled all those thousands of miles to play *friendly* games of football with their colonial brothers.

Some in the crowd were not so friendly either. "As the injured Englishmen were brought to the bank, in succession, a Maori watching the play and whose war whoop was "Kia kaha Ake! Ake!" cried out gleefully "Kapai kill them! Kill them!" noted the *Bay Of Plenty Times* report. A fair bit more humorously, years later the *New Zealand Truth* revealed that at this game the sisters of Davy Gage (one of three prominent footballers of Maori blood in the Wellington team, the others being Joe Warbrick and Ellison), "were in the little stand on the Basin Reserve, and one of them got so excited in the second spell on the collaring of an Englishman that she stood up and clapped her hands and called out, quite oblivious of her surroundings: 'That's right, Wellington, kill them, kill them all!' For a moment the spectators in the stand quite forgot the game which was going on and laughed most heartily at the lady."

On the whole, the game was a poor one for the spectators—frequent and lengthy scrums, a very heavy tackling game, little successful offloading of the ball, interminable appeals to the match officials, and squabbling between the players, along with the numerous delays through men being down hurt. The much heralded and anticipated fast and exciting game of the Lions never got going. According to local press—entirely dispassionate in their accounts, of course—the match "certainly exhibited the Englishmen in a worse light than they have yet appeared".

In the town on the Saturday night, as told by a local newspaper, "there was a great deal of enthusiasm shown over the fine fight made by the local players; the Wellington men fully deserved the praise they got, as they played a fine game, and evinced during the second spell a marked superiority to the visitors at all points". The tourists' travel woes were also dismissed: "A good deal of nonsense was talked about the unfitness of the Englishmen for a struggle so soon after the voyage, but the sea during the *Te Anau's* passage here was as smooth as a mill pond, and the footballers on board seemed the jolliest of the crew."

The Lions weren't amused, as shared by a *Star* reporter: "I am told that the Englishmen showed great vexation last night at not having won the match. Of course during the last quarter-of-an-hour they were heavily handicapped

THE WELLINGTON UNPLEASANTNESS

by the injuries suffered by two of their men." The team opted to spend the evening at the local roller-skating rink, leaving captain King and his Wellington men and their supporters to entertain themselves at the official post-game dinner. "Most of our men feeling hurt, both in body and mind, did not care to accept the Wellington RU's invitation" said Seddon.

Though most of the team were disporting black eyes, bruised limbs and the other fresh marks of this game, Sunday morning initially seemed brighter, bringing laughter and friendly jibes among the players when captain Seddon "received a beautiful bouquet of red, white, and blue flowers" with the following letter:

> Bouquet worn by a colonial lady at the match today, presented to the captain of the English football team as a token of appreciation of the pleasures enjoyed by watching the play of the visitors.
> *Wellington, Saturday, May 12, 1888*

The mood soon turned dark very quickly when the team were shown the contents of the Wellington's Sunday newspaper, the *New Zealand Times*, which stated: "In practising 'ways that are dark and tricks that are vain' the Englishmen are, unfortunately, a little too proficient. Indeed, they play very largely on the 'win, tie, or wrangle' principle, and cannot by any stretch of imagination be considered well-mannered. If any advantage is to be gained by off-side play, they will gain it; they will appeal [to match officials] whenever they lose ground; use, in some instances, or at any rate did on Saturday, most disgraceful language, and in point of conduct generally in the field, are by no means desirable models for local players to copy. They started on Saturday to play a rough game, in which 'hacking' (kicking opponents' legs) and 'scragging' (tackling around the neck) were the most noticeable features, and were deservedly hooted in consequence. We understand that they complain now that the local men play roughly, but if that really was the case the visitors brought it on themselves, and if New Zealand is to have any more visits from English teams, it is to be hoped that the players who come here will be a little better behaved and a little more given to fair play than most of the members of the present team appear to be."

"Considering that up to half-time four of our men had been carried out of the field, I think the roughness was on the other side!" roared Seddon after reading the report. The *Daily Telegraph* stated the Britishers "complain bitterly of the report in the morning paper, which attributes all the rough play to them". The entire party resolved not to send any newspaper reports of the match home to Britain, believing they were so one-sided. The Lions though found an ally in the Auckland-based *New Zealand Herald* when they weighed into the growing controversy, writing: "From our recollections of the ungentlemanly conduct of the Wellington footballers during their last visit to Auckland, and on their return to their city, we are not surprised to learn that the English visitors have been roughly used at the metropolis. They (Britons) say it was the roughest play they had had for years; and though the Wellington players, with characteristic disingenuousness, assert that the Englishmen began it, there is no place in the colony outside of Wellington in which the verdict will not be that the roughs were true to their character."

Meanwhile the *Evening Post* put to the Lions' forward from Scotland, Robbie Burnett, a growing rumour getting about the city that some of the team "had been dissipating for a day or two before the Wellington match". Burnett admitted that three or four of the team had "enjoyed" themselves in Christchurch with some friends, but he denied that they played intoxicated or hungover. "Little or no drinking was indulged in on the voyage from Lyttelton, but want of sleep told on the team, and in Saturday's match they did not play so well as they would have done if the *Te Anau* had arrived here on the Friday."

So much bad blood had emerged during and after the game that a pre-arranged second match on the holiday Monday was called off by the Wellington RU officials. The Lions suggested the "Wellington men, having made a draw, are content to rest on their laurels and prefer to let well alone"

THE WELLINGTON UNPLEASANTNESS

rather than face the chance of being defeated. Had the same sides met again, it would not have taken much to ignite the simmering discontent.

The tourists though were still eager to play a game against someone—certainly their managers hoped to do so in order to earn another few pounds of gate-money from the Wellington sporting public. A number of leading gentlemen involved in Rugby met on the Sunday at one of the city's pubs, along with local footballers and those from nearby towns, where it was unanimously resolved to form a team to play the visitors, in spite of the wishes of the local Union (who went so far as try to have the council declare Basin Reserve unavailable). "This was better than nothing as it put £75 our way," noted Shrewsbury, with the team's accounts ever playing upon his mind. Once the injury to Whatman occurred, 'Mr. Roberts' XV' were always at a disadvantage, playing a man short, and though the home side had scored the opening try, Seddon's team crossed for two in the second half, and took victory.

The tentative tour plans had pencilled in for a return visit to New Zealand, but no one at this stage was sure which cities and towns would be on the itinerary. Dr. Brooks was in no doubt about the players' preference: "The scandalous reports about us in Wellington there can be no excuse for—they will never be forgotten by us. As far as the team is concerned we would not care to play in Wellington again."

In Melbourne, anticipation for the visit of the British team was building and had triggered an ongoing newspaper debate about the merits of Rugby compared to the Australian code. Reports of the dramatic events in Wellington were closely scrutinised and commented upon. *The Argus* immediately cited the injury toll from "the Wellington unpleasantness" as evidence that the local Melbourne game in comparison is played "without subjecting the teams to the same risk of injury as at Rugby, it strains the physical capacity of players to the utmost". The same commentator added that examining the published heights and weights of the Lions players—generally bulky frames—revealed "Rugby is more a matter of brute strength" and that as much of the sport's reporting of games and follow-up was about injuries, this provides "a very fair idea of the character of Rugby play". As to further illustrate the view that Rugby had failed to evolve into a football game of science and skill, citing the Speakman-Whatman collision, the writer added: "'Stooping before the charge' so graphically described as the cause of a broken leg, was once known as 'rabbiting' in Australia, but has long since been prohibited as unfair and unmanly. No better testimony in its favour (Australian Rules) could perhaps be given than the printing of the report of one of our premiership matches side-by-side with such a game as that of England *v.* Wellington."

Coming on the top of the earlier injury to Stoddart, *The Argus* appeared to share the view that Seddon expressed to King: "It becomes really a matter of some concern to Victorians whether, in the face of such a list of casualties a sufficient number of the Englishmen, free from bruises and fractures, will reach us to make a team. Wellington has indeed, as the local papers put it, 'made a record in disabling more opponents than Otago and Canterbury put together,' though no doubt both the latter teams made their work in the same direction." Shrewsbury, with his and fellow promoters' money and reputation on the line, was particularly worried that the team would not be in a state to draw the big crowds in Victoria. "We should require 50 men if each game was played as roughly as the Saturday match," he said.

The Gate-Money Game

"Where cricket in the colonies attracts its hundreds now-a-days football will draw thousands, which is a reversal of the former order of things."
The Daily Telegraph, Hawke's Bay (New Zealand), April 24, 1888

The names Shaw, Shrewsbury and Lillywhite ran across the British and Australian sporting landscapes bigger than any others in the 1880s, particularly when it came to organising and promoting cricket tours. Shaw brought out the sixth English cricket team to Australia in 1882/83. Three Australian summers between 1884/85 and 1887/88 saw the triumvirate of Shaw, Shrewsbury and Lillywhite bring England cricket XIs down under. "No game, either amateur or professional, ever produced finer men than Shaw, Shrewsbury and Lillywhite," wrote *The Referee* in the 1930s, a long-standing Sydney sporting newspaper. It was these three cricketers that organised and financed, in 1888, the inaugural British Rugby team. "If cricket in Australia owes much to those men, Rugby owes much too."

Professional cricketers had long playing careers in that era and few could rival the standing of these men—come the end of their touring days, each had expended well over a year of their life at sea travelling the globe as full-time cricketers and organisers. By 1884 all three had been England captains in Test cricket. Lillywhite was a member of a now long forgotten team of English cricketers that visited North America in 1868, playing sides in Boston, New York and Montreal. In Melbourne in 1877, he was England's skipper in the first ever Test match. In that same game Shaw took the honour of bowling the first delivery in Test cricket. Shrewsbury, who was 32 years old in 1888 (14 years younger than the other two) continued to play Test cricket into the 1890s, and was praised by *Wisden* as "the greatest professional batsman of his day".

These tours fulfilled a vital symbiotic role to Shaw and Shrewsbury's main business, which was operating a "cricketing and athletic outfitters" manufacturing and wholesale sporting goods business. They afforded the men enormous profile and good will, giving them means to canvass and nurture sales opportunities, not only where they personally visited, but throughout Australasia. Cricket bats, footballs, tennis rackets, boxing gloves, fishing tackle and even a fox terrier could be procured for you if so inclined. Whether the tour itself ended in profit or not wasn't necessarily a measure of how valuable it had been to the promoters. During the football tour Shrewsbury wrote to Shaw saying he estimated the sales he was generating during his present stay would reach between £20,000 and £25,000; "I am not joking when I say it is worth that; I am opening business with all the best houses in the Australian colonies, which should lead to great business."

Their London showroom was at 147 Aldersgate Street, near the current location of the Museum of London, and what's left of the London Wall, a relic of the barrier the Romans built around the perimeter of the city just under 1800 years ago—'Aldersgate' was one of the guarded openings in the wall. It is repeated in many British journals over the last decades of the 1800s that "football came over to England with Julius Caesar" and his Roman armies, who brought their rough ball-carrying game 'harpastum' to Britannia. This became folk (mob) football, such as that played on Shrove Tuesday, which in turn was modified within the public schools, most famously at Rugby School.

The popularity of cricket at all levels was on the wane throughout Australasia by the mid-1880s, especially in New Zealand, while that of football was ever increasing. The idea of the colonies battling for victory in cricket against the Mother Country initially held great appeal with the public. However, with England XIs dominating over combined Australia and individual colonies, as well as too many tours taking place, the public and player interest began to decline.

"English cricketers of late have not had much monetary success in the colonies," wrote *The Daily Telegraph*, "for which they themselves are to blame, as the gate-money game has been overdone, with the result, that club cricket is not half so popular as it was a few years ago." The desire to harvest income from colonial Australians and New Zealanders interested in cricket reached the absurd situation in the summer of 1887/88, when two England teams visited at the same time. The Melbourne Cricket Club (MCC) had negotiated with one group, 'gentlemen amateurs' led by Middlesex cricketer George Vernon (whose party included Stoddart), while the trustees of the Sydney Cricket Ground (SCG) had been working on a team of 'professionals' with Shaw, Shrewsbury and Lillywhite.

While the Melbourne and Sydney cricket authorities were still drawing daggers at each other well into the Australian spring of 1887, it didn't seem to bother the two teams of cricketers much—both groups sailed to Australia on the same ship. The presence of two parties, along with the fact four England teams had visited over the past six summers, filled the public "with ruinous indifference" to watching cricket. It confirmed a downward trend in gate-takings that had set in during the previous England team's tour in 1886/87.

Many modern sources tell us the 1888 British Lions venture came about as an attempt by Shaw and Shrewsbury (Lillywhite is invariably forgotten) to recover financial losses from their 1887/88 cricket tour. It is clear though from Shrewsbury's letters and the newspapers that the planning for the football tour had been well underway, even before the cricket team had first left England in September 1887.

In Melbourne in November 1887, Shrewsbury and Lillywhite went public with news that the three cricket-playing promoters were turning their hand to a football tour, particularly against teams of the local Australian Rules kind. "When we were here with our last team (1886/87) we heard a lot of talk about the great crowds that went to football matches," explained Lillywhite. "It struck us as we were on our way home that it would not be a bad idea to bring 20 men out. There was no question about it that cricket was 'played out' in Australia, and it did not seem as if anything could be done to revive it. I'm sure we did our best to create an interest, but it was no use. Well, when we got to Colombo [Sri Lanka] we wrote to Melbourne, and asked for a copy of their rules. Dozens of copies were sent, and they reached us shortly after we arrived in England, and a little examination showed us that there was not a great deal to learn that our players did not already know, so we decided to go in for it."

Of course they did a bit more investigation than that, with all three independently making inquiries with people who were likely to know the prospects for success of the venture—financially and competitively—and became convinced that Rugbeians would be able to play the Australian game well enough to make a contest of it. They obtained advice from gentlemen such as Tom Horan (aka 'Felix'), the sporting editor of *The Australasian*, and H. Hedley of *The Age*. The question of having the Rugby players take on soccer was also raised, but Shrewsbury very early on dismissed the idea: "Very little Association Football (soccer) is played here, and if our side learn the Victorian game (Australian Rules), we should have no time to play the former game."

The codes, both in Britain and in Australia, weren't yet so far apart that swapping from one to the other was seen as foolhardy for an individual—indeed many had succeeded. The football columnist in Melbourne's *The Argus* in January 1888 wrote: "Though the English games are wider apart than our game is from the Rugby, it is still the case that the same player finds no difficulty in following both Rugby Union and Association, not playing one of them in a mere perfunctory fashion." However, an entire team crossing over for a lengthy tour against the best sides of a game none of them had ever seen, nor even read the rules of, was something else.

In explaining another code, it was often easier to illustrate from the perspective of the audience, using the game they already understood. In Perth in the mid 1880s, where Rugby was dominant and Australian Rules only beginning to emerge, the *West Australian* told its football readers: "The Victorian game may be described in general terms as the Rugby Union game divested of its 'off-sides' and 'scrimmages,' and with a rule added that the ball if carried in the hands, must be bounced on the ground every few yards." The Melbourne correspondent for the *Morning Bulletin* in Rockhampton (Queensland) wrote: "In the Victorian game the ball must be continually bounced when it is being run with, whereas in the Rugby game it may be taken up at any time, and ran with until the player is stopped. In the Eton [college in London] or Association [soccer] game no running at all is allowed, and this game is, as its name implies, purely 'foot' ball. The Victorian game is a capital blending of the two; it is not so rough as Rugby, not so tame as Eton."

Given so many cricket teams had been brought to the colonies, one could surmise that a football team making a tour would not be an innovation or organisational difficulty. Yes, English and Australian cricket teams had been exchanging visits across the great oceans since the 1860s, but they were small troupes of 12 full-bearded gentlemen of the leisured classes, where finances of such tours were more manageable. A football tour—where there was a greater risk of injuries occurring, particularly in Rugby—and where Australian Rules required 20 men a-side, it meant a party of around 25 players would be needed. A football tour thus necessitated twice the expenditure outlay in travel, food and accommodation. It would take many more matches and many sizeable gate-takings to make the venture pay its way at all, let alone turn a tidy profit. Securing players would also be more difficult as many would refuse to take part as they had to learn and play a new code. Most crucially, unlike cricket, the large bulk of footballers were working men, who couldn't fund their own way on a tour and provide for their families while away for something like 10 months.

The notion of bringing a football team to the colonies was not new. It had been around for a decade at least. In late 1879 current Rugby international and Richmond FC captain Frank Adams made extensive negotiations with Rugby Union and Australian Rules bodies in the colonies that went on for months, before it was finally accepted the financial risk was too high and the plan was abandoned. Efforts to send a team the other way also arose. In 1880 one of Sydney's most prominent Rugby footballers, John MacNamara of the Waratah FC, took up the idea of sending an Australasian football team to Great Britain, writing to as many football clubs and bodies as he could identify: "Doubtless you have heard 'ere this that I am forming a football team from the Combined Colonies to match their strength against the players at Home. It is my wish to make it as much colonial as possible by obtaining men from each of the colonies if possible." His plan was for the team to play Australian Rules in Melbourne and Adelaide and then sail to England to play Rugby through the Northern winter of 1881/82. He succeeded by interviews, letters and telegrams in building a team of interested and competent footballers, including three New Zealanders to join with those from NSW and Victoria—a feat in itself—but it never took the field, nor left Australia.

In July 1883 a letter writer to *The Argus* in Melbourne ignited a round of newspaper debate throughout the colonies by suggesting Victorian footballers ought to start practising soccer if they ever hoped to see Australasia send a team to Britain. Most felt the concept of an Australasian football touring team could not be pulled off unless all the colonies banded together as a Rugby team, built around players from Sydney and New Zealand. It was the only hope of competitiveness in Britain. In 1885 the English FA [soccer] issued a tour invitation to its fledgling counterparts in Sydney. The idea, which ultimately failed, was to send to England a team of Australia's best footballers, who would play the round-ball code against the clubs of the FA.

However, great offence was taken in Melbourne that a combined colonial football team would not "consist of men who represent the football strength of Australia" as these "nearly all play the Australian game and [they] will not be induced to discard it in favour of one which certainly does not possess equal attractions". The criticism against the tour was so pronounced that the Victorians argued that the Australian soccer team, given the standard the game was played in the colonies, should never be permitted to leave our shores "for the sake of Australia's athletic prestige". However, more than one sports editor was prepared to point out that "the Australians will wait a long time before they will be asked to send Home a team to play the Victorian game".

The consensus was that football tours, in either direction, were for some time yet an impossibility. In May 1886 the Rugby columnist for the *Otago Witness* wrote: "I am permitted to make the following extracts from a letter received by the last Home (UK) mail. The writer is a well-known authority on football. He says if a team does go from here to New Zealand, which I very much doubt, it will not contain the leading players of the day. I am acquainted with men in all the leading southern clubs Blackheath, Richmond, London Scottish, Queen's, Middlesex Wanderers, West Kent etc., and speak by the book. I had a long talk with Rowland Hill, who is a thorough football enthusiast. He fancies that a good team will never be able to leave England, as it is so difficult for men to get away, and apart from that, footballers as a class are not a wealthy lot."

Hill was more than an "enthusiast" being secretary of the English Rugby Football Union (RFU) since 1881 (a position he would hold until 1904, when he became president). In October 1886, Hill oversaw the implementation of "professionalism" laws banning financial compensation to players by their clubs for anything beyond bare expenses, which made the prospect and undertaking of tours even more of a difficulty for the working class players. Men of influence in Rugby had seen the soccer code swamped by professionals, where teams full of amateurs were no match for their trained and collected expert opponents. The view in Rugby circles was that the FA allowed professionalism not after some long examination of the most prudent path, but because it was too late to stop its growth. When it came to Rugby, Arthur Budd wrote in the 1886's *Football Annual*: "The Rugby Union Committee, finding themselves face to face with the hydra, have determined to throttle it before it is big enough to throttle them" and "no mercy but iron rigour will be dealt out".

England's *Land and Water* predicted the expenses issue would prove the Shaw-Shrewsbury-Lillywhite football tour's downfall before it even sailed for the colonies: "With their full and ample powers the RFU have only to declare all the players going to Australia professionals to at once smash the whole scheme, which can only result in failure and defeat, and, as far as we can see, a pecuniary loss to the promoters."

On the other side of the globe Lillywhite was promising to Melbourne reporters that "it is going to be just as hot a team as we can get together in all England, Ireland, Scotland, and Wales". However, to live up to their box-office billing, and draw the much needed gate-money, the Rugby players would need to be trained and schooled in the colonial rules of the football game.

'Goal Post' in the *South Australian Register* put it in context: "Those enterprising entrepreneurs, Messrs. Shaw, Shrewsbury, and Lillywhite, have made many plucky ventures, and they are embarked in a most risky venture now. They are spending about £12,000 in taking a team of English footballers round the colonies. The venture is so risky, because the Englishmen have to learn our game (Australian Rules) and it is extremely problematical whether they will pick it up quickly enough to combat crack Australian teams."

While Lillywhite and Shrewsbury had come to Australia as part of the cricket team, and would stay on to negotiate for matches and manage the football tour, Shaw remained behind in England to keep their London business operating while at the same time carrying out the necessary preparation and organisation of the football team. They were all equal partners in the enterprise, though Shrewsbury and Lillywhite, settling the arrangements, and then accompanying the team, would have a lot more work to do than Shaw. Indeed, he had even less to do after they engaged Henry Turner, secretary of the Nottinghamshire County Cricket Club with the heavy task of seeking out suitable footballers in Britain, and coming to terms with them to agree to join the team. Using Turner was considered necessary as he was closer to the Rugby centres in the North, and, unlike Shaw, had knowledge of the game and established connections. "His instructions," explained Lillywhite, "were to pick the best men—get them from England, Ireland, Scotland, or Wales. The players will be selected not only for their ability at the game, but carefully chosen as well from a social point of view."

Not long after arriving in Australia, Shrewsbury wrote to Shaw: "We require average £300 a week to pay expenses as we calculate the cost of the tour to be about £6,000. Of course, we tell everyone it will cost £8,000 or £9,000, you may tell them (newspapers) even more." He also suggested they should give serious contemplation of taking a team of colonial footballers back with them. "The big draw," he wrote, "would be for us to bring a New Zealand team home, which we intend doing—this must be kept very secret." They could keep their plans hush-hush, but once a team came from Britain, it was immediately apparent that one going the other way was no bigger a leap. Joe Warbrick, the Maori footballer, saw potential and opportunity right away, seeking out investors and interested footballers.

"An exceptional interest will be given to the next football season in Australia by the visit of an English team," *The Argus* told its readers in Melbourne. "Lillywhite, the cricketer, is one of the promoters of the team, which will consist of 22 of the best football players that can be got together in England. The team will be specially organised to play the Australian game, which they will practice constantly during the present winter under the instruction of a competent Australian coach. They will play matches in Australia during the months of May, June, July and August. While in the colonies, Lillywhite will arrange a programme of matches, and settle all details in connection with the tour."

"The proposed visit of an English football team to Australia is bolder than it seems on the surface," claimed London's *The St. James's Gazette*. "The Rugby game is played in New Zealand very extensively to the practical exclusion of the Association [soccer] game. But in Australia, Rugby is not a favourite, except here and there. In Victoria the Association [soccer] game is not even played, as the enterprising Victorians have 'improved' upon it. The Melbourne Association rules (Australian Rules) are peculiar, and may be called more Association than the Association (soccer once allowed the 'fair catch' in its early rules). Some idea of it may be gained by the technical name of one of the positions in the game; namely, 'goal sneak.' So that, although the chosen 22 are to be under the training of an Australian player, they are likely to be handicapped in some of their matches at least. Even Association [soccer] players would feel at a loss in Melbourne, and much more so Rugbeians."

The Rugby supporters in the colonies saw the visit of a British team as reinforcing that their code was an international game, with the prospect of tours to and from other nations. "Should such a team come out," explained Lillywhite, "there is not the slightest doubt but that they will meet with a grand reception in NSW, Queensland, and in New Zealand, and financially also, I am sure, the tour would be a splendid success. The benefit to the Rugby game in the colonies in consequence of such a visit would be almost incalculable, and it is to be hoped that favourable arrangements will be made."

The Australian Rules community saw it as the opportunity to widen the growth of its game, and hoped the tourists would take the code back home, the first beach-head in establishing it in Britain. The promoters were quick to feed that dream in the hope it would reinforce support for the tour. "It is quite on the cards," said Lillywhite, most enthusiastically to the Melbourne reporters. "From all I have heard it is a wonderfully fine game, and if the team take a liking to it, as I have heard every one say they will, it is quite possible that when they go home they will play some games to show English people what it is."

Shrewsbury added: "I have heard that once a man plays the Australian game he will never play any other after, and if there is anything in that the visit of this team means a big future for Australian [Rules] football. We have had diagrams of the football field (player positions) in the Australian game prepared by players here, and they have been sent Home for the team to study. The team will have a coach in England, so that they are not likely to let anything escape them. Besides, there are plenty of men at Home who know all about your game, and they will give assistance in teaching it."

"We have arranged for the team to leave England on or about March 10, with the mail steamer that calls at Hobart and goes on to New Zealand, for at the latter place we intend the men to play first. Then, in the meantime, we could get a coach or two here, and send them on to join the team at Hobart, and teach them well, while they are down in New Zealand, all the ins-and-outs of your game. They would get down to Dunedin towards the end of April, and thence they would make their way through the colony, coming over to Sydney about the beginning of June, and after a game or two under Rugby rules come down here, where we propose to spend the most of our time if the [Victorian Football] Association agrees to help us, as I hope they will do. I believe the interest would be enormous, especially after the first match or two, when our men had got well into the swing of the game, and had shown the stuff they were made of. They want us to go up to Queensland, as far as Rockhampton; but we will have to see about that."

"It has to be considered what the expense will be," added Lillywhite. "It's going to cost an awful lot of money, for their passages out here mean a pretty big sum. Then their expenses will not be under a £5-note a week, and this, if you calculate it up for six months, is something to think about. They are not paid, of course, but some of them will have to leave men in charge of their businesses, and that has to be settled. They'll be no mean lot, I can assure you, for they will be a score of about as fine a lot of athletic young fellows as ever you set your eyes on. There will be some, no doubt, from the universities.

It is there you find the pick of footballers, and, as I said before, every man will be an international player."

Shrewsbury sensed the Melbourne reporters were doubtful, speaking in a very dry fashion: "Really, I think that they will astonish your fellows. It is not as if we proposed to bring men who had never played football. Those who come out will have been at it all their lives, and as they will all be international footballers—and that means something at Home, as, I daresay, you know—Australian [Rules] footballers will have all they can do to beat them. I have heard some people say that they would be no good at your game, but they can kick, and mark, and run, and, believe me, that when they land here, there will be very few of the wrinkles (smart plays) of the game they do not know something about."

As positive as all of that may have sounded to the public and the press, the prospect of news that cricket professionals were intending to bring together a party of British Rugby footballers, to undertake a pioneer tour Australia and New Zealand, where they would be also playing another code, did not commend itself to the officials of the RFU in England, nor indeed the Victorian Football Association [VFA] in Melbourne.

The promoters would soon seek the endorsement of both the RFU and the VFA—but whether they shared the same enthusiasm for the pioneer expedition would be answered soon enough. Choosing to go ahead with the tour even without the patronage of one or both bodies was not impossible, but it would land a very serious blow.

More immediately troubling for Shrewsbury and Lillywhite was their cricket tour was now a failure moneywise—their available financial resources were exhausted, and at this point they must have come very close to taking their return passage to England, and giving up on the idea of a football venture. "You must know," Shrewsbury informed Shaw by letter, "that it has taken us all our time to keep this scheme going. As we have been terribly short of funds, we have to leave bills unsettled at our hotel. I can tell you we have had to act with great caution and diplomacy."

The only thing that seems to have kept the tour concept alive was others reassuring the promoters an entire team of Rugby footballers successfully crossing to Australian Rules was possible. For two cricketers from England investing their own money in a football scheme in the colonies, it was an act of faith reliant upon the expertise of others, and what they were telling them. After a special trial game between Geelong and Melbourne clubs was played at the Melbourne Cricket Ground in March, held so the promoters and visiting cricketers could witness Australian Rules between two proficient teams, Stoddart said "there is nothing in the game that our men cannot pick up in half an hour". Stoddart might have been basing that upon his own prodigious sporting skills, but Victorians were telling Shrewsbury the same thing, including McShane, one of the Melbourne footballers he had engaged to coach his team. "He, along with other good judges appear to think the team will learn the new game very quickly, and if they can do this, and play good matches against Victorian clubs, there is money in it," said Shrewsbury.

With a Jealous Eye

"It should be distinctly understood that the team is not exclusively English. It is a British organisation of a representative character and the colours worn will be red, white and blue, and on a cap to match will be a suitable inscription."
Plymouth, England—dockside announcement at embarkation
of the team on *Kaikoura*; March 9, 1888

"The team has been formed under discouraging circumstances. It comprises a very fair lot of players, but can scarcely be described as representative of the football strength of the Kingdom," *The Argus*' London correspondent explained to football enthusiasts in the colonies. "The hostile attitude of [the English] RU has proved most discouraging to the promoters."

Bringing together the team had been a tortured path. Many differed in their views as to whether the touring party was a true representation of Rugby in England. In early 1888 the only meetings of the best English footballers were the two annual North v. South contests at Manchester and Blackheath. London's prominent clubs—Richmond, Blackheath and the Universities—usually supplied the bulk of the South team, while the Northern XV was invariably centred upon Yorkshire and Lancashire players.

Traditionally this selection trial game produced an England team for the annual international series against Scotland, Ireland and Wales. However, the latter three nations had at a meeting in Manchester in December 1887 formed an international association (the International Rugby Board), and while England's RFU were invited to take part, they felt it was unfair that each of the nations should have equal voting power given the great bulk of Rugby players and clubs resided in England. Since its founding in 1871, the RFU had been accepted wherever the game was played as *the* authority on Rugby matters and laws. For two seasons England did not play, until in 1890 it was agreed that the RFU be given six seats on the IRB with the other nations receiving two each.

The first 1888 North *v.* South game was held at the Whalley Range ground in Manchester. It was fully expected that a crowd of 12,000 would attend, and while the grandstands that ran the length of each of the long sides of the ground were full, behind the goal ends was sparsely populated. When only 6000 turned up, the finger of blame wasn't pointed at the ongoing international discord, nor inclement weather, but the opening on Manchester's racecourse that same afternoon of *Buffalo Bill's Wild West* travelling show. Bill Cody and his troupe showcasing America's gun-slinging west was an extraordinarily popular draw. Unsurprisingly, many of the players themselves did not wish to miss out, and they too caught up with the show over the following days.

Did the prospect of a trip to Australia hold out the same enthusiasm for young Britons as that of Cody's American frontier? In the 1880s, aside from the Australian cricketers and the occasional professional rower, Australia and New Zealand were rarely in anyone's mind. A few colonials gained international caps at Rugby in the 1880s: Melbourne-born James Alfred Bevan was Wales' inaugural captain (1881), NSW's Charles Wade (Oxford University) played eight times for England, while former Geelong FC Australian Rules player Reggie Morrison (Edinburgh University) was picked for Scotland in 1886. If Britons knew anything at all about the colonies, it was a vague idea that Australia was possessed by the sons and daughters of convicts, gold hunters and desperate bushrangers and held little of note beyond sheep-runs and kangaroo haunts. As far as anyone could gather, New Zealand was home to fierce Maori warriors and bones of the extinct giant moa bird, might have a volcano and apparently nothing else worth mentioning. A rough estimate of the 1891 census shows 86 per cent of Australians were of British blood, with a third born in Britain.

A trip away travelling around the world—six weeks by sea, a holiday adventure into the great unknown, all the while playing football and being fed, clothed and housed—must have sounded appealing. For any young man, it was claimed, a long travel journey was a form of education. It was suggested by a footballer with colonial experience that: "A team of Rugby players with spare cash at disposal could count on many a good game under the Southern Cross. Great hospitality could be met while picturesque scenery would 'be on view' and gate-money would be liberally given to meet expenses." Despite these immediate attractions, progress in composing a touring party was going ahead at a snail's pace and the promoters were still trying to sign players in the first week of March, when the team was meant to be packing their bags.

London's *Sportsman* wrote: "The team for Australia seems to gather but slowly, and we view its formation with feelings of the most conflicting character. It gathers so slowly that, as yet, we know of only one man, Mathers, late of Leeds St. John's, who has actually signified his intention of going, though it is true that Bonsor and one or two others are giving the suggestion favourable consideration. This is one of the reasons for our conflicting feelings. There is no sign of a really first-rate team being raised, and if the team is not first-rate, we have no desire to see it leave our shores. We should like to see a team go out which should be in every sense of the word entitled to call itself representative of England, but we believe such a team can only be got together if the leaders of football give the suggestion their countenance and active support. We trust they will do this and that they will keep careful watch that nothing is done to give the team the faintest semblance of professionalism."

Shrewsbury had written to Shaw early on, instructing him to seek the RFU's granting its much needed imprimatur on the tour project. Without the RFU sanction, the scheme would be more difficult to achieve—and more costly. "If you could obtain their patronage, all the better as the Association (VFA) here would at once—which they are sure to do—give us their patronage and support," he wrote. Shrewsbury even hoped that if the RFU sanctioned and selected the team, the RFU's laws against professionalism could be used to the promoters' advantage as some difficulty may arise if the players require a large share of takings. "If the Rugby Union can get players to come out without paying them anything, all the better for us. It would be much better if the Union would select the players."

The RFU's committee formed to consider the request, kept true to the sport's increasingly strong stance against professionalism and money-making and "declined to award their patronage to a team which was manifestly being organised and conducted for the benefit of individual promoters". That the team was also to play a series of games under another code for gate-money and no other reason, gave the RFU a ready-made out—it was irrefutable evidence it was intended "as a means of making money for the promoters rather than as the visit of an English international team desirous of measuring its strength against fellow-sportsmen in Australia and New Zealand". The RFU issued the following statement:

> The Rugby Union Committee wish it to be known that, in response to a request from the promoters to give their support and approval to the projected Football Tour to Australia, they decline to do so. They do not consider it within their province to forbid their players joining the undertaking, but they feel it their duty to let gentlemen who may be thinking of going to know that they must be careful in any arrangements made that they do not transgress their laws for the prevention

of professionalism. The committee will look with a jealous eye upon any infringement of such laws, and they desire specially to call attention to the fact that players must not be compensated for loss of time.

—Rowland Hill, Hon. Sec., Rugby Football Union

The RFU would continue to state it was holding a neutral stance to the venture, insisting it wasn't interfering or trying to stymie it, but the warning to potential tourists against professionalism was a very big weight hanging over players' decision-making. There is little doubt it was endeavouring the stop the tour going ahead, but without actually declaring it couldn't—not merely to end this scheme, but to dissuade any future attempts.

Shrewsbury was incensed when the news was cabled to Melbourne. "This action on their part puts us between the devil and the deep sea, as the VFA will not recognise us because we come without the patronage of the English Rugby Union. I cannot possibly see what the Rugby Union has to do with players when their season is over," he said. Remaining defiant, Shrewsbury instructed Shaw: "You must bring a team out in spite of them if possible."

The RFU's threat was very real, and some players were dissuaded. Others weren't though and the promoters certainly pushed on. Turner got to work from his Nottingham office, contacting likely candidates who were also able to remain trusted. Shrewsbury had written to him: "You must obtain as good players as possible, at the same time should like them to be men with every respectability and who know how to behave themselves."

From the available reports, it appears Turner's *modus operandi* with the working class men was to arrange a meeting with the player—usually a few miles away from their home and work—and put an offer to them of an all-expenses paid trip to the colonies to do nothing but play football. They would be banqueted by hosts along the way, plus receive £75 on top, with an immediate advance of £15 once they agreed. In some cases the money appears to have been paid to a family member, to keep the player's hands clean should the RFU investigate.

From examining Shrewsbury's correspondence it is revealed that Welsh international Willie Thomas was able to negotiate a payment that totalled £90. That many players declined the offer was evidence of the RFU's warning that the players risked becoming professionals. According to some equally strong evidence, it was also an indication that some clubs were compensating amateur footballers very well if they had players prepared to walk away from such liberal offers. Indeed it was one of the wonders that clubs could have such big paying crowds and have no official player wage costs yet finish the season with very little to show in the club's bank account.

Of lesser reason was "a considerable number of players did not fancy the idea of learning a new set of rules" to play the Australian code. That so few knew what the Australian game was didn't help. Nor did an article in the respected *Sportsman* which inferred the colonial game was merely Rugby in its pre 15-a-side form: "They will sometimes have to play under the strange condition of 20 players on each side. What an enormous change this makes in the play can only be appreciated by those who remember our old club games when that was the prescribed number." A good description of the game in Melbourne could be found in C.W. Alcock's *Football Annual* but few seemed to avail themselves of it.

Shrewsbury was particularly desperate for "gentlemen players" from the "higher stations" usually found in the teams of the prominent London clubs and the universities. "Should have liked some South players—good ones—among the team," he wrote. "Amateurs give tone to the team and you may be able to get them to come for their expenses."

It became clearer later that Stoddart had agreed to join the team on terms of at least £200. During the tour, New Zealand's *The Evening Post* interviewed Lillywhite and then added: "As a good deal of curiosity exists as to the remuneration of the team, we may say that we have reason to believe that each man has been guaranteed £200 and expenses for the tour."

In 1908 a Rugby journalist in *NZ Truth* claimed one of the players told him during the tour he had signed a contract for £150 and "the job hoodwinking the fossilised Rugby officials of the Old Dart" was easy. Shrewsbury may indeed have been willing pay even higher amounts, telling Shaw in a letter "you have got the players cheap".

From that North-South game the only players Turner signed-on were Bob Seddon and Harry Eagles—the two men were great friends, having known each other since before their teens. The perpetually smiling and moustached Eagles was already locally famous outside of football, having been awarded a medal in 1882 by 'The Humane Society for the Hundred of Salford' for, in two different instances, saving individuals from drowning. Eagles, along with Percy Robertshaw, became anomalies in the record books after that North-South trial, recognised as official England 'reps' when the RFU chose an England team and handed out caps and jerseys, even though they had no opponents to play.

To the disappointment of Seddon and Eagles their North teammate and friend from the Bradford club, French-born half-back Fred Bonsor, chose at the last minute not to join the tour. He was an established member of the England team and a big loss to the promoters, as were other internationals that were seemingly "on the boat" but in the last days opted not to sign or rescinded. These included Robertshaw, as well as Dewsbury's international pair of Dicky Lockwood (England) and William Stadden (Wales).

As time went by with little mention of any 'gentlemen players' possibly joining the team, Shrewsbury became more agitated. "Have not got names of many amateurs in football team … should have been cabled out before now," he wrote. He took matters into his own hands—with Stoddart on board he then began to work on three other cricketers from Vernon's XI: George Brann, Tim O'Brien, and Charles Aubrey Smith. If he could secure their services, the combination would appear more socially impressive (even though all were amateur soccer players and of little real use until the Australian Rules games).

As can be seen from the final team list, the players were for the most drawn from clubs in the North of England, though Wales, Scotland, Ireland and the Isle of Man were all represented, as were the Universities. The team also included numerous club and county captains, as well as future international captains in Stoddart (England) and Thomas (Wales).

The First Anglo-Australian Football Team

Backs

More familiarly called full-back, this player stands at the rear of the field, primarily to defend his team's goal posts and goal line. He must be a good tackler and possess strong drop and punt kicking abilities for clearing kicks to touch or upfield. Speed, as always, is an advantage.

Tommy HASLAM (Batley; Yorkshire; North of England). The crack back of the North of England and one of the best in England. A clever drop-kick, using both feet with equal facility; picks up in a remarkably clean manner, and his tackling is of the surest description; possesses good pace and plays with great dash; 25 years of age; 5 feet 9 inches, 11st 10lbs.

Arthur PAUL (Swinton; Lancashire). A splendid back, but also plays well as a three-quarter, and is a brilliant forward. Successful at kicking goals. Born in Belfast (Ireland), played several years with the Isle of Man FC; is very strong and muscular; a first-class cricketer; 23 years of age; 6 feet, 14st 7lbs.

Three-Quarters

There are three three-quarters in a team; they stand in a line spread apart across the field, mid-way between the half-backs at the rear of the scrum and the full-back. The best of a team's three-quarters is placed in the 'centre', always positioned on the open-side of the scrum, and must be an expert and long-range drop goal exponent. Two faster men will do for the 'wings'. These players must be very strong individual and forceful runners, knowing how to end their run with a drop-kick at goal or offloading the ball to a trailing forward or three-quarter. With so much open field to defend alone, they must be deadly tacklers. Interchanging of passes between the three-quarters is increasingly being adopted by the best clubs in England and Wales, and some are adding a fourth three-quarter with one less forward.

Harry SPEAKMAN (Runcorn; Cheshire). Best centre three-quarter in the country; possesses good running powers; is a capital dodger; picks up splendidly; collars safely as well as being a good drop-kick; Commenced his football career about nine years ago with a club in the small village of Weston, near Runcorn, where he played half-back. 24 years of age; 5 feet 8.5 inches, 11st 12lbs.

Dr. Herbert BROOKS (Edinburgh University; Durham). Another good three-quarter; steady, cool; also good at the Association [soccer] game. First played Rugby aged about 16 for Darlington Club in 1874 as full-back. Has played well in county matches this year; kicks and tackles well; a difficult man to collar when fairly started. Has captained the Edinburgh University team, elected captain of Durham County this season. 29 years of age; 5 feet 8 inches, 12st 6lbs.

Jack ANDERTON (Salford; Lancashire). Good-natured fellow, extremely popular among supporters of the Salford club. A very useful three-quarter, has represented his county and club successfully. Not to be confused with the Anderton of the Manchester Free Wanderers club and North of England player. 22 years of age; 5 feet 7 inches, 12 stone.

Andrew STODDART (Blackheath; Middlesex; South of England; England). Second to none in England as a three-quarter; high class drop-kick exponent; good tackler; passes with judgement. He is a grand runner and dodger—"like bloomin' dancin' master" the Cockneys describe him. First appeared for England in 1884-85 season, and the best scorer England has. 25 years of age; 5 feet 10 inches, 12 stone.

Half-Backs

Two in each team, one stationed either side (left or right) of the scrum. Needs to be a darting runner with good sharp kicking skills as well as a fast moving defender who can floor an opponent before he gets moving. Feeds the ball into the scrum, and throws the ball at line-outs.

Walter BUMBY (Swinton; Lancashire; North of England). A dangerous half-back; has represented his county; plays three-quarter also and possesses good turn of speed and wonderful dodging powers; has been a consistent scorer; backs up well, and works very hard; 26 years of age; 5 feet 9 inches, 11st 13lbs.

Johnny NOLAN (Rochdale Hornets). Half-back and a "demon" scorer; excels at all points, tackling, dribbling, running, and passing; a wonderful man to follow up; very fast and strong; has gained 114 tries in nine seasons. Very dangerous when near the line. 24 years of age; 5 feet 7 inches, 11st 8lbs.

Willie BURNETT (Hawick; Roxburgh). One of the best three-quarters in Scottish Borders and also a brilliant half-back; can play anywhere behind the scrum; he is a sure tackler and good dodger, careful passer, powerful kicker, and fleet runner. 23 years of age; 5 feet 9 inches, 11st 7lbs.

Forwards

Forwards are constantly on the ball wherever it may be. Most teams will have nine forwards in the pack, though generally few have a particularly assigned position, with scrums forming "anyhow" based on which forwards arrive first; the most used scrum arrangement is 3-2-3-1, but there is no regulated form. If a back leaves the field injured, a forward will most likely be called upon to move out of the pack to replace them. Must have good soccer-style dribbling ability with the ball, and be a good passer and receiver of the ball in interchanges of passes between the forwards. Need to follow-up three-quarters and support.

Charlie MATHERS (Bramley; Yorkshire; North of England). This player ranks among the most prominent forwards in Yorkshire, invariably will be found contesting for the ball. He has played in 14 county matches, and twice this season for North of England, distinguishing himself highly. 27 years of age; 5 feet 9 inches, 12st 8lbs.

Sam WILLIAMS (Salford; Lancashire; North of England). A speedy forward, very useful at the outside of the scrum, good on the line-out, dribbles very cleanly. Played for his county, being the most successful try-getter in 1886. Captain of his club in its most successful era yet. 26 years of age; 5 feet 9 inches, 11st 7lbs.

Tom BANKS (Swinton; Lancashire; North of England). Has played for Lancashire regularly since '84. A very useful player, smart at half-back, a quick three-quarter, and a very consistent forward who does a lot of work in the scrimmage; never tires. Particularly strong and vigorous tackler. 29 years of age; five feet 8.5 inches, 13 stone.

Robert SEDDON (Swinton; Lancashire; North of England; England). One of the best dribblers in the game, a very good passer, can kick with either foot. As grand a forward as one would wish to see, one of the finest players in the north of England, has played for Lancashire County for six years, and represented England against Scotland, Ireland, and Wales. Captain of his club. 28 years of age; 5 feet 11 inches, 12 stone.

Harry EAGLES (Salford; Lancashire; North of England; England). A sterling forward who played for his county last year, and scored frequently; also scored for North of England and won his England cap this year. A grand all-round player especially good at dribbling and backing up. 26 years of age; 5 feet 6.5 inches, 11st 12lbs.

Willie THOMAS (London Welsh; Cambridge University; Wales). Played for Wales for the past three years in international fixtures, and also represented his university; steady, hard-working forward and a fine all-round athlete. 21 years of age; 5 feet 11 inches, 13st 7lbs.

Jack CLOWES (Halifax; Yorkshire). A very fast forward; good tackler, and expert dribbler. Played for his county this season. One of the most promising players in the north of England. 21 years of age; 5 feet 8.5 inches, 11st 7lbs.

Tom KENT (Salford; Lancashire; North of England). A player of great dash and untiring energy, and a consistent scorer; stops rushes well and is a sure place-kick. Has played for his county and North of England. Until recent move to Salford, was captain of Radcliffe FC for many seasons. 24 years of age; 5 feet 9 inches, 12 stone.

Angus STUART (Dewsbury; Yorkshire). A dashing forward, formerly of Cardiff FC before switching to Dewsbury, can also play with success at three-quarter; tackles well, and scores frequently; considered the best forward player in the Yorkshire *v.* Cheshire match last season. His speed is undeniable. A dangerous sort of opponent. A Scot by birth. 27 years of age; 5 feet 8 inches, 12 stone.

Alf PENKETH (Douglas FC, Isle of Man). Club captain, his team has this season played 14 matches, some against first-class English teams, won 13, drawn 1. Originally a three-quarter back. 25 years of age; 6 feet, 12st 12lbs.

Alex LAING (Hawick; Roxburgh). One of the fastest forwards in the team; a good dribbler, and a splendid tackler, very dangerous near the goal line. Has represented his county and South of Scotland. Club captain this season. 23 years of age; 5 feet 10.5 inches, 11st 11lbs.

Robbie BURNETT (Hawick; Roxburgh). Older of the Burnett brothers, was until this season captain of Hawick Club. Has played for his county. A fine sterling forward, a hard worker in the scrum and always turns up fit. 26 years of age; 5 feet 10 inches, 12st 8lbs.

Dr. John SMITH (previously Edinburgh Wanderers; Edinburgh University; Scotland [non-capped reserve]). Full-back or three-quarter; very tall and strong individual. Played for Scotland 10 times in the Association [soccer] game. Will umpire the team during the trip. 32 years of age; 6 feet 3 inches, 15 stone.

The London correspondent for Melbourne's *The Argus* declared: "On the whole the team is a fairly strong one, and ought to be able to hold its own against any of the New Zealand Rugby clubs, but it must not be regarded as a representative British Rugby team, for in the opinion of many players, a good club, like Richmond, Blackheath, or the London Scottish, would not find much difficulty in defeating the international team."

Asked by a newspaperman about the ability of the team, Dr. Smith replied: "Oh I think we have a rattling team, especially forward. We have three international men, one Welsh (Thomas) and two English (Seddon and Eagles), and then, almost without exception, the team are county men, the average weight forward being about 13 stone, and I feel certain we shall make a good show against the colonials."

Beyond reading that the tourists would be formidable enough, in the colonies they were just pleased to know the team was on its way. A New Zealand football columnist wrote: "Though the team will not be all internationals, it is clear that a strong lot is being brought out. Probably their form will be about midway between that of the best county team and an international 15. If so, our men here will have to play their best to have a show at all. Whatever the issue of the matches, however, there will be good lessons to be learned from the visitors' play. If the team can hold their own against our players, they will be able to walk over the New South Welshmen, but what possible chance can they have against South Australia and Victoria at a new game?"

The Argus thought they had a better chance than soccer players: "To Victorians and South Australians, not less than the footballer of NSW and New Zealand, it will be good news that nearly all the members of the team are Rugby men—for in New Zealand and NSW they will at the outset meet foemen worthy of their steel, while Rugby men are much more likely to become familiar with the points of the Australian game than the Association [soccer] player, who is not under any circumstances, except when acting as goal-keeper, permitted to handle the ball. Some feeling has apparently been created in England by the fact that the team has been chosen almost entirely from Northern players, but this is a matter with which we have little to do, though it is just possible it may explain to some extent the attitude assumed by the Union (RFU)."

Though the team had been announced and passages booked, the RFU was not yet done with. "The ghost of professionalism still seems to dog the progress of Messrs. Shaw and Shrewsbury's scheme for taking a football team to the antipodes," wrote the *Leeds Times*. The RFU was about produce something far more dangerous and corporeal than a ghost.

Drop a Tear and Bid Adieu

*"For England and Ireland, and Scotland and Wales,
Are bound fast together by friendship's strong nails."*
From *Little Jack Sheppard*—a comedy musical
by H.P. Stephens and W. Yardley (1885)

The enthusiasm of the farewells for the footballers as they left their home cities and towns revealed just how much public interest there was in the men about to set off upon their great adventure. Maybe London was indifferent to it, but the North wasn't. At Manchester and Leeds, and on a smaller scale with Scottish players leaving Hawick, extraordinary scenes took place reminiscent of the departure of great Victorian era explorers, expeditionaries and military contingents. Sport and its participants, especially football, was an important part of northern life.

The *Huddersfield Chronicle* reported of "animated scenes" at Leeds railway station. The *Manchester Courier* recounted: "The Central Station in this city was the scene of great excitement on Wednesday at noon, when some thousands of persons assembled to witness the departure for Australia of the Lancashire, or rather Manchester, contingent of Messrs. Shaw, Shrewsbury and Lillywhite's

Australian Rugby Football Team." The footballers had been provided by the Midland Railway Company with their own private saloon carriage for the journey south, which was attached to the Nottingham Express.

Bob Seddon wrote later that the "enthusiastic feeling shown by the great crowd to see us off seemed to pierce the gloom cast over most of the players at leaving many friends who are very dear. Many felt proud that although the Rugby Union have tried to discourage the public opinion regarding this tour, the followers of football in Lancashire know better how to treat its representatives."

Though the railway platform's entry barriers at Manchester were closely guarded, many hundreds of locals streamed across from the adjacent platforms, over the railway lines and swarmed around the front of the train engine, pushing on to where the players were trying to board their carriage. "The men were surrounded on all sides by admirers desirous of wishing them God-speed," wrote one observer of the chaotic scenes.

With barely minutes until the scheduled departure time, several of the players were "held" in anything ranging from romantic embraces to fond farewells with the large crowds of onlookers pooled around them. Seddon bade one last long goodbye to his teary-eyed sweetheart—they were to be married at year's end after the team had returned. He joined with Harry Eagles, and as they made headway toward the saloon's door were met at every turn by a constant flow of eager hand-shakers and well-wishers "for a safe journey!"

Dewsbury's Angus Stuart and Rochdale's Johnny Nolan made their way through practically unnoticed, but when Salford's popular Jack Anderton was spotted, his "appearance was the signal for a tremendous outburst of cheering".

> *"I've come to say good-bye, Jack, I've come to say good-bye,"*
> *A ragged little urchin said, as he slowly 'piped his eye';*
> *"They say to-day you sail away to foreign lands afar,*
> *So I've come to say good-bye, Jack, and I've brought you a cigar."*
> —excerpt from poem in Salford newspaper, March 1888

Tom Kent and Sam Williams, like all of the Salford players, were easier to spot courtesy of the handsome travelling bags with their names, painted in white letters outside, which the club members had presented to them at a farewell dinner. They boarded the carriage, quickly followed by Runcorn's Harry Speakman, fending away as politely as he could more clutches.

Right on time the station master's whistle shrilled its warning to stand clear, doors were slammed shut, steam hissed out across the platform, and the train began to slowly move out. However, all the players were not yet on board. Eagles couldn't get past his admirers at all, and in the confusion of loud shouts, pushing and urgency, was bundled into the only open door within reach … the luggage compartment! Bumby, Banks and Paul finally made it into the saloon, and after a quick head count, there was a last moment cry of "Where's Seddon?" He had been so greatly occupied saying goodbye to his many friends, that with the train now beginning to gain momentum, his teammates held the door open, shouting him onwards. Forced to sprint along the platform to catch up, Seddon was "followed by a running and hurrahing crowd". He jumped inside and the door was quickly shut behind him. An inauspicious start!

As the train steamed out of the station, a volley of laughter rose up as each section of the crowd saw Eagles' smiling face pass by, peering out through the ventilation holes in the door of the luggage compartment. He looked as if he enjoyed the joke as much as anyone.

The train took them down to Nottingham where Shaw and Turner were waiting, along with the Leeds and Hawick contingents. Eagles rejoined the team. The *Nottingham Evening Post* reported there too a large crowd had gathered on the platform to see off the team for London. Before boarding the train, the players were each presented with two jerseys and a cap, "both being much admired" recorded Seddon. "The cap is red, white, and blue velvet, trimmed with gold braid and tassel, in the front being a shield in cardinal silk with the Union Jack crossed." Shrewsbury had set Shaw the task "to get [a] nice outfit—especially made for them. Something that would be good material and yet take them by storm out here [in Australasia]". The triple-hooped long-sleeved jersey in the British flag's colours with neat white collar and neck buttons seemed to fit the bill nicely.

The team arrived at the Manchester Hotel, London, soon after 6pm. A large formal farewell banquet was provided for the team courtesy of Shaw, Shrewsbury and Lillywhite. Of course, only Shaw was present, along with Turner and Dr. Smith, who was managing the team while on the steam-ship to New Zealand. The dinner's chairman was the Right Hon. Lord Newark, M.P. It's not recorded how many of the men were still in the room to hear Lord Newark propose a toast to the health of the team, nor "success to the team" given by Turner. Seemingly only Dr. Smith.

"It could easily be seen that the minds of the players were set on something more lively than listening to speeches on their last night in London," recalled Seddon. "One after another asking to be excused, for only a minute mind, just to speak to a friend outside. Each of those gentlemen in every case forgetting to return! Anyway, not the same evening! What a bad memory some of our team must have! I wonder if in some of our matches they should have a chance of a clear run-in they would so easily forget to touch it down and secure a try. I don't think so!"

Where each individual or small group was off to one can merely speculate. An evening in London had much to offer. Unfortunately, if a Gilbert and Sullivan comic opera was on one's mind, the Savoy Theatre had none on show, with *Ruddigore* finished its run and *The Yeoman of The Guard* not debuting until near year's end. At least we do know it was still relatively safe to walk London's streets at night, with the first of the infamous 'Whitechapel Murders' not for another four weeks and 'Jack the Ripper' a few months thereafter.

Not even Seddon—who made notes during the tour—revealed what he himself got up to that evening. We know he preferred the sober lifestyle—always tactfully declining to accept when a glass of wine or whisky or pint of beer was offered to him—but he never stood in the way of others having a good time.

"Breakfast being ordered for 9.30am, we were presently surprised to find the whole team once more together," wrote Seddon with some astonishment. The great day of excitement and anticipation of leaving home shores had finally arrived, but the mood of all was about to quickly change.

Seddon added, "Mr. Turner had for us some important news".

'He Is a Dead-Head'

"Perhaps they will prove the pioneers of many teams, who, in years to come, will visit England and Australia under more happy auspices."
The Field, sports magazine, London, March 1888

After breakfast Turner stunned the team with news that at a RFU meeting held in Leeds overnight, Jack Clowes of Halifax, one of their touring party, had been classed as a 'professional'. The immediate effect was not only dire for the 21-year-old's football career, but if he was to play during the tour, the RFU would declare the whole of the team, and indeed their opponents, as professionals as well. Moreover, on closer inspection of the full resolution of the RFU, it had serious implications for the playing future of every member of the team—if not now, certainly when they returned back from the colonies. Some surely must have been tempted to turn around and go back home there and then.

"We called together a meeting of players to consider what had better be done in the matter," said Seddon. "Most of the team objected to move a step further [towards the ship] unless something was done."

The RFU had resolved:

> The Rugby Football Union has decided, on the evidence before them, that J.P. Clowes is a professional within the meaning

of their laws. On the same evidence they have formed a very strong opinion that others composing the Australian team have also infringed those laws, and they will require from them such explanation as they may think fit on their return to England.

The RFU had adopted its "Laws Against Professionalism" at a meeting in 1886, the provisions of which can be summarised as:

It is illegal for any player to receive from his club, or any member of it, any money consideration whatever, actual or prospective, for services rendered; to receive any compensation for loss of time; to be trained at the club's expense; to transfer his services from one club to another on consideration of any contract, engagement, or promise of employment being found for him; or to receive any sum in excess of the actual amount disbursed by him in hotel and travelling expenses in connection with the club's affairs. No money can be received by a playing member for services rendered as secretary, treasurer, or in any other capacity in connection with his club. Surely it will be impossible for the "cloven hoof" of professionalism after this to find any foothold in Rugby football.

Leeds Times, October 9, 1886

The specific finding against Clowes being:

That J.P. Clowes, of the Halifax club, having received £15 from Mr. Turner of Nottingham for an outfit in connection with a football tour in Australia, has thereby received money consideration for playing football, and, in the opinion of this committee, is a professional football player according to the Union rules as to professionalism.

The matter of Clowes had come to the attention of the game's authorities via a complaint lodged by Mark Newsome, president of the Dewsbury club. It seems that along with Stuart, who was now in the touring party, Turner had been given some indication that it may be worthwhile making approaches to two other Dewsbury players, Dicky Lockwood and William Stadden. Stuart

'HE IS A DEAD-HEAD'

and Lockwood signed the agreement to join the team, and were duly sent their £15. It was a very liberal amount of money for what it was purported to cover. Stadden, apparently not happy with the financial terms on offer, declined to sign. Lockwood then withdrew his acceptance. Stadden gave his copy of the unsigned tour agreement to Newsome, and told him Stuart had shown him a cheque from Turner for £15.

None of these happenings had anything to do with Clowes, except that his Halifax team had been about to play Newsome's Dewsbury club in a knock-out Yorkshire Cup contest. It was evident from the names appearing in the newspapers that it was widely known in the Rugby community which players were joining the touring team, and that each was receiving a £15 expenses payment for his outfit [suit] and preliminary expenses. Had Dewsbury been playing another club with a player signed by Turner, it is likely they would have been Newsome's target instead of Clowes.

On match day Newsome had the Dewsbury team take the field without their tour-man Stuart. The unsuspecting Halifax would play theirs, Clowes, as normal. Newsome's plan was ready—they may win the game, but now they could not lose it—if Dewsbury were beaten in the do-or-die game, the club would appeal to the Yorkshire RU, to have Clowes declared a professional and as Halifax had used the services of a professional player to have the game nulled and replayed.

The match was played, Dewsbury lost, the complaint was lodged. After being called to a hearing to explain himself "Clowes acknowledged in an open manly manner that such was the case, and he admitted having spent the money in providing himself with clothes and other articles necessary for the trip". Turner made representations to the RFU in a letter:

> Shaw and myself most positively deny that anything has been done in any way or shape to break any of the Rugby Union laws. I told you at first we should not do so, and we have not done so. As regards Clowes, he was recommended to us by Mr. Duckett, of the Yorkshire County RU, who states in his

letter "Clowes wants to go out if he can have bare expenses". This is the agreement with him: out of £15 sent him he had to pay railway fare to London, hotel expenses, and insurance. We consider this a reasonable amount and fail to see anything in it breaking the Rugby Union laws. If he spends it in outfit, then he must pay the other expenses out of his own pocket.

In an attempt to bring into question the integrity of the Dewsbury players, whose evidence was being used to damn Clowes as well as the promoters and the whole tour enterprise, Turner may well have used the truth of how much he was in fact willing to pay players. Francis Marshall in *Football: The Rugby Union Game* (published 1892) said: "The case is remarkable as disclosing the agreement made between Messrs. Shaw and Shrewsbury and the members of the team." Turner was also adamant Stadden could not have seen Stuart with a cheque for £15 (perhaps as it seems he was sending payments in cash):

We understand Stadden says he saw a cheque Stuart received for £15. This is a positive falsehood. I further hear he stated he had been offered £75 for incidental expenses to go out, and that Lockwood said he was offered £50 and outfit. I think I scarcely need deny these statements as a look at these two men would convince anyone that if either of these men had been offered such a sum, to have a free holiday in Australia for six months, they would not have refused it.

Turner again reminded the RFU that the tour promoters had repeatedly sought their involvement, and argued it was wrong to have ignored that offer and then to punish the team for failing to meet its requirements:

The promoters appointed the tour in good faith, and in proof, as you know, offered Rugby Union selection of teams, and all arrangements. We wish you had accepted the offer. We appeal in all fairness to you not to injure our team by putting a term upon it of which it is not guilty and of which the promoters have studiously avoided running any risk of.

'HE IS A DEAD-HEAD'

The Yorkshire RU, and then the RFU itself, found that Clowes had breached the laws against professionalism and that the cup match was to be replayed. So now the touring team—on the very morning of the day they were to sail—had to very quickly decide what to do about Clowes, and indeed what to do about their own futures as Rugby players in Great Britain. The RFU made it plain it would be going in search of answers when the players returned home. Turner took them through the case, read to them the submission he had made to the RFU and asked the players what they wanted to be done.

"After some argument," explained Seddon, "it was decided that, as Mr. Clowes had made all preparations for the journey, we should ask him to write a letter to the Rugby Union saying for what purpose the money was sent him, along with a letter signed by every member of the team, stating the agreement under which we are going out, and asking them to reconsider their previous decision. Should they refuse we agree to let Clowes take the tour, but not as a playing member of the team. Seeing that the Rugby Union had left over their decision until the very eve of his departure we had no other course left open to us." The team letter was in fact prepared and signed in quadruplicate—not only was the English RFU sent the document, but also the Irish, Scotch and Welsh Rugby Unions.

Given Clowes was younger than the rest of the team (other than Willie Thomas, who was the same age), there was a lot of compassion for his plight. "I think the Rugby Union have dealt harshly with him," Seddon told the press. "Had he known he would become a professional for accepting a comparatively small sum of money for his outfit he would not have taken it. He wanted to give the money back through the secretary of the Union."

"If I am called upon I will ignore the matter altogether," said Seddon in response to the question as to whether he was a professional. "They must prove me to be a professional. I do not think I ought to be called upon to prove I am not. One of their rules is simply that clubs can pay travelling and hotel expenses for their players, and what more has been done in this instance, I do not know. So far as I can judge not one of our players has received any money for his services. I have not, and I know for a certainty others have not."

"Why should the English Rugby Union object to the tour? I do not know why they should object. Shaw intimated his willingness that they should pick the team and manage it altogether and they said they could not get up a team. He said he would get up a team and place it in their hands. They objected to the various propositions."

Dr. Smith told the London *Star* that morning the promoters were not paying players for loss of time away from work: "No such idea was ever promulgated by the promoters, and even if it had, I think the authorities would have been better occupied in stamping out the professionalism that actually does exist in connection with certain Rugby cup competitions than in interfering, on only a theoretical basis, with the first venture in Anglo-Australian football".

The doctor was hinting at the well-known circumstances of Dewsbury in 1886 gaining the services of Stuart and Stadden from Cardiff FC—both had claimed that they moved from Wales seeking work, which just happened to be found at Newsome's mill factory.

The alarming conclusion from many independent observers, including the respected English journal *Sporting Life*, was what consequences the RFU's resolution would have upon the tour: "When this fact is cabled to Australia it will cause a wholesale cancelling of the fixtures, as some of the men who are going for expenses, and a cheque for pocket money, are [thus] professionals." Another added: "It would appear that the majority of them are northern professionals, on gate-money acquisition, very materially bent."

How the Rugby bodies in the colonies would react wasn't clear. In Melbourne though, the VFA had already made it plain that it would not be willing to recognise the team if its own body in England was not prepared to sanction it.

The Halifax club undertook to make an appeal to the RFU to have its decision on Clowes overturned or the punishment removed. The club also decided to make its own complaint against Lockwood for signing the tour

'HE IS A DEAD-HEAD'

contract and accepting the £15 payment. All poor Clowes could do was hope that someday during the tour a telegram would come with the good news that he could again play. Maybe when their ship reached the Cape in South Africa there would be a cable waiting.

The longer unknown was whether Clowes' frustration at not being able to play might eventually lead to the team and management feeling sorry for him and relenting, letting him play during the tour irrespective of the RFU's warning. Nor did anyone know what it all meant for the Australian Rules matches. As far as Shrewsbury was concerned though, Clowes ought never have been put on the ship, or even be sent straight back when he arrived in New Zealand. In a letter to Shaw, which in itself confirmed Clowes [and by inference the other players] were paid more than the RFU allowed bare expenses, he wrote: "It was a great pity you [have] sent Clowes out here, as he won't be able to play a single match and we shall have all his expenses to pay. When he looked like being disqualified you should have obtained a substitute. We shall have to try and make some arrangement with him to come (return) home, or only pay his bare expenses. Of course, if you can get the Union at home to cancel what they have done, you could then cable out to us that he would be able to play. He is a dead-head, and of no use at all."

The popular English sporting journal *The Field* offered the team a parting consolation of how, in time, their tour may come to be regarded, writing: "We have felt it our duty to point out thus plainly the drawbacks to the expedition and we commend the Rugby Union for taking up its present position. On the other hand we are sure that the men engaged will enjoy their visit as much as the cricket XIs of previous years, and will receive the same cordial greeting from those they meet in the antipodes. They will no doubt give a good account of themselves at the game, for they are all players of some reputation; and perhaps they will prove the pioneers of many teams, who, in years to come, will visit England and Australia under more happy auspices."

Surviving the High Seas

"And white waves heaving high, my lads, The good ship tight and free; The world of waters is our home, And merry men are we."

Allan Cunningham, Scottish poet & author (1784-1842)

"After this unpleasantness (Clowes and the RFU) had been got over all was bustle and hurry to catch the 12 o'clock train from London to Gravesend," Seddon explained. The team then headed for Fenchurch Street Station to take the 90 minutes rail trip to Gravesend where their ship was waiting. The New Zealand Shipping Company's new steam-and-sail ship, *Kaikoura,* would take them down the English Channel to Plymouth on England's south coast, re-coal at Tenerife in the Canary Islands, then journey southwards along Africa's west coast, making port again at Cape Town. From there the steamer would head across the vast expanse of the Indian Ocean, landing in Tasmania, and then onto their destination, New Zealand

The football tour contingent was a larger group than the well-wishers at the Gravesend dockside gathering. Perhaps an indication of what general feeling pervaded British Rugby upon the first Lions departing their home for lands far away, can be gained by noting less than a handful of newspapers are known to have referred to the farewell. One was an unattributed cutting which recorded: "Among those present to see the men off were Alfred Shaw (one of the promoters of the tour), W. Scotton (the Notts cricketer), F.W. Burnand (Harlequins), and H. Thompson (Kent Rovers). The attitude of the Rugby Union in discountenancing the tour doubtless kept many away and the fact that the team did not include a single south country player also contributed to lessen the attendance. All the football players who are making the trip were present and they seemed in the best of health, although the lack of enthusiasm may have damped their spirits."

A picture of the players on board the ship was published in *The London Illustrated News*, but the accompanying text bordered upon an apology to its readers for the impoliteness of having the team appear before their eyes: "We give an illustration from a photograph taken on board the steamer by Mr. A. Willis, of Gravesend, of the Rugby players who started on the ninth for Australia. In doing so we desire to express no opinion one way or the other on the question of the amateur status of the team, which will doubtless be further considered by the Union at the proper time." The image shows the men proudly adorned by the tour caps they received at Nottingham. Some are smoking, almost all disport the fashionable trimmed moustache, the full-bearded Ned Kelly style faces of the generation of men before no longer in vogue.

Arthur Conan Doyle's first *Sherlock Holmes* publication had appeared in a London journal just a few months before, and the detective, along with Dr. Watson (who it is revealed in *The Adventure of the Sussex Vampire* was a Rugby player with Blackheath FC), would have fitted right in among the footballers in their day wear. Indeed Doyle himself could have too, given in all likelihood he knew one or both of the team's Rugby-playing doctors (Smith and Brooks) as they were all of a similar vintage at Edinburgh University studying medicine and playing Rugby and soccer.

Arthur Paul's brother, the Reverend Paul of Nottingham, came to see him off.

The reverend handing to each member of the team a copy of the *New Testament*, which he "hoped would not be forgotten" during the adventures that lay ahead.

Seddon, probably with the send-offs in the north more in mind than the modest gathering before the players now, said: "Allow me to thank sincerely the many friends and supporters of Rugby football who showed their good feeling towards us by the hearty manner and good wishes with which they sent us on our long journey." From the ship the players gave three cheers for each of the gentlemen who had come to see them off, and to bring the short formalities to a close, three cheers for merry England.

The men headed to their berths to make them as homely as possible, and in Seddon's words, "we now began to think our long journey had fairly commenced".

Ironically, for many travellers, indeed no doubt members of the touring team, conditions on board a passenger ship were often far better than day-to-day living at home. Work was no longer an issue, and while it must be admitted you were bound with the same group of people for an extended period, you were also free from the responsibilities and drudgeries that many faced every day on land.

The coal-burning steam-powered *Kaikoura* was built in Glasgow in 1884, was 4474 gross tons, measured 430 feet long by 36 feet across the beam, three masts (rigged for sail if needed), one funnel, top speed of 14 knots. Under the agreement which the players had entered with the promoters, they were promised first-class accommodation, including here on the ship, which catered for 77 passengers in first, 58 in second, 230 "emigrant class passengers" and a substantial hold for goods, mail (on this run, the count was 4295 bags of mail for the New Zealand colony) and its coal stores. The *Kaikoura* had a generously sized deck area large enough to run about on and undertake exercises and games. All parts of the ship had electricity for lights, and it also included a dining room, a smokers' lounge, piano and library.

Life on board a passenger steamer was not as stale as many imagine, particularly so when the usual number of voyagers was swollen by a team of lusty-lunged footballers in good physical condition. The state of things is then generally very lively.

"After dinner, which is at 6pm, we had a little dancing and singing, Willie Thomas being both a good *pianoforte* player and singer, although only a short head in front of Dr. Brooks, both gentlemen rendering some first-class songs, much to the enjoyment of the passengers," said Seddon. "The team, so far, are defying the enemy (sea sickness) with wonderful success, perhaps with one exception, Tom Banks, who has taken an unfair advantage by starting a day before everyone else!" The short run from Gravesend would be tamer than what was expected once they left Plymouth.

A New Zealander who came upon the tourists at Plymouth wrote to the *Auckland Star* (noting his correspondence, travelling by the faster mail-steamer, would beat the *Kaikoura* to New Zealand) repeated a point that would be made numerous times during the tour about the team's composition: "I was down at Plymouth yesterday, and witnessed the embarkation of the fine team of English footballers, who should arrive in your colony per *Kaikoura* a few days [after receipt of this]. It should be distinctly understood that the team is not exclusively English. It is a British organisation of a representative character and the colours worn will be red, white and blue, and on a cap to match will be a suitable inscription."

Leaving Plymouth ended communication with the outside world. Ship-to-shore and ship-to-ship radio telegraphy were things of the future. Since the 1860s undersea and overland cables had meant that news could be flashed within minutes around the major centres of the world (Australia was connected through Java in 1872) but the ships that traversed the great oceans in-between were alone.

For now, the tourists and all the souls aboard the *Kaikoura* might as well be on their way to the moon as far as it came to being able to connect with them; it is an isolation that is foreign to our global life of today. The outside world could not contact them, could merely guess where they may be at any day, and the team members had no way knowing what events, whether personal, football, gossip or political, were transpiring in their absence. Depending upon wind and sea conditions, as well as mechanical issues, ships could arrive at their destination port days early or worryingly overdue for those waiting with no news other than speculation. Ships of all sizes in the late 1800s sometimes vanished without trace due to storms, on-board fire or treacherous coasts. In March 1890 *RMS Quetta*, a similar steamship to the *Kaikoura* that operated between Australia (mostly Brisbane) and England, was wrecked on rocks trying to traverse Torres Strait—just under half the 292 passengers and crew were drowned in the disaster.

During the Lions' voyage out Seddon had written in a letter to a friend that he had almost been swept overboard from the *Kaikoura*, adding "I don't think I was born to be drowned" (from the then popular saying that followed any escape from a watery grave, "He that's born to be hanged need fear no drowning"). In many aspects of life most people put fate and faith in God's will ahead of real or imagined risk and danger, and in the case of travel, went to sea anyway. After all, it's not as if steam train derailments and runaway horse-drawn vehicles were an uncommon occurrence moving about on land, nor the many sudden illnesses and untreatable infections such as typhoid or septicemia that continued everyday to take many away without warning. Even playing Rugby had its risks.

In mid-February 1888 as the *Kaikoura* was heading towards England on its most recent passage from New Zealand, the ship, its passengers and crew had a most terrifying experience, as Captain Crutchley dramatically re-told the footballers: "Between Tenerife and Ushant (entering the English Channel) she met with furious squalls of wind, rain and hail, and shipped several very heavy seas. Two days after leaving Tenerife, the chief officer and part of the crew were engaged securing the jib, for which purpose the ship's head had been let off to the wind. While so engaged, the vessel came up again to the wind, plunged her head into a heavy sea, which poured on board, completely swept the decks, and washed the chief officer and seven of the crew clean off the forecastle. The chief officer, besides sustaining other injuries, had one of his hands crushed and cut, six of the men were badly bruised, and the seventh was carried overboard by a huge wave. Another wave washed him back on the deck immediately afterwards, and he was then found to have dislocated his thigh. He was attended to by the surgeon of the ship; and on the *Kaikoura* arriving at Plymouth, he was landed and taken to the hospital."

In addition to carrying the first group of British footballers to the colonies, the *Kaikoura* didn't have a berth to spare. Among the 'passengers' in the hold were some 300 stoats and weasels, intended for the destruction of rabbits in New Zealand. Not far away in a specially built 'ice chamber' were 400,000 salmon ova packed in moss in 'insulated transport' boxes. These "lively little midgets" were under the careful care of Sir Thomas Brady, the Irish Fisheries Commissioner. From the River Erne, the salmon were to stock the principal rivers of Tasmania to create a viable export trade.

As predicted, once the *Kaikoura* hit the swell of open sea, many of the team were very soon turning green and other hues, as John 'The Big Doctor' Smith detailed in a letter to a colleague:

> It is just a week today since we left you in Gravesend lamenting. Our lamenting came after we left Plymouth and got into the chops of the Channel and the Bay of Biscay. For the first 24 hours we only registered 185 miles, as we were practically 'lying to' during our first night from Plymouth, the gale and sea being exceedingly boisterous. In my long career as a sailor I never felt so collapsed before. I was completely done up on Sunday and Monday, and it was Tuesday before I felt fit to do any justice to my meals. I have this comfort, if such it could be called, that others were worse, the principal sufferers being the Burnett brothers, Seddon, Clowes, Nolan, Bumby, Eagles, Banks, and Williams. Nolan was very bad. He said, "If I was only back in Rochdale, neither Shaw, Shrewsbury, nor Lillywhite would ever take me out again, and if Dr. Smith will let me I will go back!" Some of his remarks were such as I have mentioned and I believe it was very comical to hear him.

"Could they only have taken the train back again the team would have arrived in New Zealand minus some 15 of the selected players," said Seddon.

It seemed that the ride back to England would not have a full complement either, with one of the first discussions after all gained their sea-legs revealing that many of the men were going to stay behind, either as a result of the RFU's declaring they would have to explain themselves upon return, or as they had decided when first signing-up that it may be a way to gain free migration to the colonies. "Paul, Kent, Mathers, Clowes, Haslam and Stuart all have declared their intention of giving Australia a fair trial before coming back again," Seddon revealed.

The players were each given a copy of the playing rules of Australian Rules football, but no one appears to have shown great interest. Shrewsbury had instructed Shaw to send him three footballs with the team so he could use them as samples to gain more orders, and suggested the men could take to the ship's deck and use them to master bouncing the ball as needed in Australian Rules.

After a week at sea the *Kaikoura* reached Tenerife about 10pm. As the captain intended 'coaling' the ship (a very noisy, bumpy and dusty experience for those on board), the passengers were advised they had six hours on shore, of which all the football tourists availed themselves. "Much fun and amusement was caused by the natives trying to make themselves understood, the extent of their English being 'Haf of a shilink,' of course, meaning half of a shilling," Seddon noted. "Considering the cheapness of the wines and the quantity consumed, I was pleasantly surprised next morning to see all of them (the players), or rather to hear that they were all aboard again, many preferring bed the next day; cigars, cigarettes, oranges etc. being found all over the ship."

Not long after leaving Tenerife the ship had a breakdown, and remained at a standstill in the ocean for six hours until repaired. As the *Kaikoura* headed south the days became hotter and more oppressive; the temperature reached 105 degrees Fahrenheit, only tempered for the passengers by finding shade where they could on the deck and an occasional breeze.

On March 19 the players finally had a meeting to elect "officers for the team," which resulted in "Seddon [being] selected captain without opposition". Dr. Brooks was elected vice-captain; and the team's management and selection committee, in addition to Seddon and Brooks, being Dr. Smith, Willie Thomas, Sam Williams, Jack Anderton and Tom Banks. The captain of a Rugby team, as in Test cricket until recent times, decided all matters concerning the team once it was put in his hands—while the promoters could sever any player's contract or withhold payments, and obviously must be able to work with the captain, it is the captain that chooses and enforces what style of game, methods and tactics the team will use in the field, the choice of team selections, arranging training, keeping up enthusiasm, and, importantly, player behaviour on and off the field.

"We made lots of sport and kept ourselves in good health by the exercise," Seddon said. Shrewsbury's sample footballs never made it to the colonies, as Harry Eagles recalled:

> On the outward journey the men engaged in a variety of exercises, with the object of keeping themselves in condition. Football, on a somewhat restricted scale, was indulged in with rather disastrous results, for three of the balls were kicked into the sea and lost. Canvas balls, made on the vessel, were then substituted for the leather ones, but these shared the same fate as their predecessors.
>
> The men were in the habit of assembling every afternoon about four o'clock for practice, the exercises engaged in including boxing, skipping-rope, club drill, and jumping. Sports were also organised on board ship, the programme consisting of three-legged races, sack races, cock fighting, wheel-barrow races, high jumping, skipping-rope contests, and "chalking the pig's eye" (for the ladies).
>
> There was also a tug-of-war, 'Footballers v. Sailors' in which the latter were easily beaten. Though these sports were organised by the team, Mr. East, the chief officer, took an active

personal interest in the matter, and worked hard in bringing the athletic festival to a successful issue. The various races were joined in by the passengers, crew, and footballers, though the prizes in almost all the events went to the members of the team.

Ship life fell into a routine. At night concerts were held among the passengers and crew, with singing, piano playing, and recitals of stories and jokes. Knowing whether at land or at sea you would be expected to contribute an item, most people had at least one 'performance' they could deliver. However, a long sea journey could exhaust the résumé (and the audience) of the keenest of social performers. Still, before long all would know each others' songs, and there were then no more solo acts. Games were popular, particularly card games, such as whist.

Alcohol was a popular distraction. It seems that when Turner negotiated terms with each of the players, the matter of paying for drinks, which really would have only been availed, in cricket terms, by the 'gentleman players' of the team, was overlooked. Shrewsbury got a shock at the invoice after the voyage, writing to Shaw: "You don't say who are to have drink; you leave this I suppose to Dr. Smith—the bill on board the ship came to £68!"

After three weeks on the briny ocean thoughts turned to Cape Town where hopefully the local Rugby footballers had arrangements well in hand for a game against the Britishers while their ship was in port for a few days. It seems the Cape Town ruggers had the same notion, initially resolving "to endeavour to detain the steamer *Kaikoura* for a few hours to enable the Englishmen to play a match". However, one or more of the mail steamers from England slipped by the *Kaikoura* and arrived first with reports of the RFU's declaration about Clowes and the team itself. So the footballers arrived instead to the news that "under all these circumstances the committee of the Western Province RFU, which wisely recognises the stringent rules laid down by the English Union for the suppression of professionalism, have decided to be on the safe side and to abandon all idea of the proposed match, even if the brief stay of the vessel rendered it practicable".

SURVIVING THE HIGH SEAS

Rumour reached the Australasian colonies that the RFU had in fact interdicted by telegraphing the RU authorities in the Cape, and warning them of the consequences they risked by taking to the field against a team of professionals. The tourists were disappointed, but admitted playing while still on their "sea legs" wouldn't have seen them at their Rugby optimum either. So the first Lions game in South Africa would have to wait until London Scottish RFC's Bill Maclagan led a British touring team there in 1891.

Very soon after leaving The Cape and turning eastward into the Indian Ocean, the *Kaikoura* and its passengers encountered "severe gales" and a "very rough passage" that made life on board miserable. There would be no let up in the conditions the entire two-week journey to Tasmania. In the depths of this melancholy period, Seddon wrote one brief sentence.

"Did not see the sun or stars for seven days."

The *Kaikoura* log suggests Seddon was mistaken. He must have lost track of time. It was in fact nine days.

A Devilish Track

"Cricket and football, which are, so to speak, the sun and moon."
The Living Age magazine, 1888

———

Stoddart had taken one quick, indifferent look at the Sydney Cricket Ground (SCG) wicket, shrugged his shoulders loose, and freely struck out with his bat in his elegant style, hitting the ball clearly and well. A moment later it was beyond the boundary. With Lillywhite watching on from the ground's newly opened double-storey members pavilion, Stoddart and Shrewsbury had strode out to the centre of the grassed sward, opening the batting for the England XI. In what was proclaimed as "the great cricketing event of the current season," this was a match between a combined XI chosen from the two visiting English teams against an "All Australia" line-up brought together by the SCG's Trustees. In the cricket history books, this game stands alone as a one-off Test that also constituted an entire Ashes series.

It was held late in the Australian summer of 1887/88, while faraway in the cold of northern England, the first British Rugby team was in its final weeks of preparation and then boarding the *Kaikoura* for the colonies.

The wicket, being uncovered in those times, had been exposed to heavy rain the day before and was all but unplayable. The Australians—who included famous run-accumulator Charles Bannerman and Victorian footballer-cricketers Jack Worrall and Pat McShane—closed the day eight wickets down for a mere 26 runs. That was after England had been bowled out earlier for a very modest 113. Stoddart and Shrewsbury were the top scorers for the visitors, who went on to win by 126 runs.

All going well, Shrewsbury and Lillywhite would be back at the SCG in winter watching Stoddart among the British XV playing Rugby against NSW. Since the start of the summer, when Shrewsbury and Lillywhite announced their forthcoming Lions tour, they had been mixing cricket responsibilities with their endeavours to organise the football venture. Shrewsbury was still working at signing Smith, Brann and O'Brien. These cricketers were precisely the 'gentleman players' that Shrewsbury had been pressing Shaw in England, to give the team "tone". Of course, like Stoddart they were desirous of being paid substantial "expenses" money, and were holding back committing until the names of "men of similar stamp" were confirmed as joining the team.

The easy way to reveal a cricketer's station was to look at the team list. If he was referred to as "Mr" you knew he was a 'gentleman amateur' and almost certainly getting more money than those merely mentioned by their surname alone. This left the cricket writer for *The Capricornian* (Rockhampton) asking: "A slight conundrum will perhaps impart a chastened cheerfulness to the subject of travelling cricket shows. Here it is: What is the difference between a professional who gets weekly wages and an amateur who gets a lump sum for an engagement? Give it up? So do we."

O'Brien's name quickly dropped from the scene, while Smith and Brann began hedging, not only over who of note was coming from England, but wanting the same £200 plus expenses Stoddart received. At this point Shrewsbury was prepared to pay it, but in England cricket officials had begun exerting pressure on Smith via cables from his father, playing up the extent of his mother's ill health. It naturally troubled Smith, and he said he ought to be going home. At this news, Brann announced he felt his previously broken leg could not stand the rigours of a football tour. But when Smith got news his mother wasn't that dire after all, Brann's leg concerns went away. Their "humbugging", as Shrewsbury put it, ended with news they had both left on a ship bound for England.

As events transpired, instead of playing Rugby in Australasia, Smith secured a substantial financial arrangement to lead an England cricket team on a tour of South Africa. This time he stayed after the tour, taking up stockbroking before getting involved in amateur stage shows. After returning to London he worked in the West End theatre productions and then the film industry when it started up. By the 1930s he was in the USA as Hollywood's go-to man for "*the* upper-class Brit", playing in many well-known films such as *Cleopatra*, *The Prisoner of Zenda*, *Little Women*, and *Lloyds of London*, the latter with Tyrone Power. There is a star on Hollywood Boulevard in his honour. None of which may have happened if Smith had stayed in Melbourne to join the Lions team.

Shrewsbury's notes reveal he was in the end happier Smith and Brann had gone, saying it saved him up to £600. "I am pleased both went home as they ran our cricket expenses up frightfully, which they also [would] do in football, and what is more set the example to the rest of the players," he said.

Meanwhile Shrewsbury was approached by immigrant Melburnians that had played Rugby in Britain, but only two were of sufficient merit to be of use to the tour. The first was recent Halifax player and captain Tom Scarborough. Seddon knew him: "Scarborough used to play for Yorkshire County (1885-86) [and] was a very good dodger and runner."

Unfortunately, Scarborough's approach had come after the team had already sailed, prompting Shrewsbury to write to Shaw: "Wish he had written us before, we could then have done with one player less from England." Shrewsbury told Scarborough "to learn the Victorian game, so that he can take part in our matches in Victoria and Adelaide". No doubt the promoter despaired even more when Charles Chapman, a Cambridge University rugger now teaching at Melbourne Grammar School, announced his presence very late in the picture—he had played three-quarter back for not only Cambridge University, but in 1884 for England against Wales.

Chapman, who had already been trying to come to grips with Australian Rules in games at the school, was encouraged by Shrewsbury to join the Lions when they arrived in Melbourne. Chapman had played for England alongside Charles Wade, the Australian who had been studying at Oxford University, and some early reports speculated he too would become part of the tourists. However, anyone that knew Wade at all suggested that was exceedingly unlikely—he was so was fiercely patriotic to his birth-place that while at Oxford he played in their famous dark blue Rugby jersey with a badge cut in the shape of a kangaroo.

Of more immediate alarm to Shrewsbury were the growing financial losses of the two English cricket team tours. The costs of his own scheme were one thing but the Melbourne Cricket Club (MCC) decided that their losses from Vernon's team could and would be blamed squarely upon Shrewsbury, Lillywhite and Shaw. On the pettiness level, the two sides squabbled over who should pay Stoddart's fare home—Shrewsbury argued the MCC brought him out to Australia, so it was only right that as with the rest of the cricketers they pay his way home. But the MCC said their obligation to Stoddart ended when he joined the Rugby team. It is a measure of the growing bitterness that much of Shrewsbury's letters to Shaw are taken up with this one point alone. In reality, bickering over Stoddart's ticket was merely the festering sore on the outside of a very deep wound. Shrewsbury increasingly began to fear the MCC was intent on gaining some revenge, exerting influence in Melbourne upon the VFA, football club officials, and the cricket clubs (who owned and managed the grounds) in the hope of either forcing the football tour to be abandoned or extracting what they believed they were owed.

The promoters' most pressing task was to contact each of the football authorities in the cities and towns they intended to visit. The NSWRU negotiated games for its NSW team in Sydney but left the minor matches up to the promoters to arrange. In New Zealand the NZRU had not yet been founded (1892), so individual provincial Unions were approached. Interest was also expressed from Queensland, South Australia and Tasmania. Requests for games soon began to come in from football bodies in the towns situated along or nearby the route the team would be travelling along. Terms offered were generally that the promoters got 80 per cent of the gate-takings, the hosts were responsible for all expenses in putting the match on, and in the smaller towns an additional minimum guarantee of usually £70 was set. Recognising the large costs the promoters had put into the venture, and that there was more to be gained for a city or town by having the team visit than merely profit, everywhere bar Melbourne fell into line.

The VFA management committee called a meeting to consider a letter from Lillywhite requesting sanction of the tour and arrangement for matches. He also stated that the venture might result in introducing Australian Rules into England and eventually the exchanging of tours.

The meeting was chaired by Henry Colden Harrison—a man who upon his passing away in 1929 was referred to across the nation as "the Father of Australian Football and the originator of the Australian game". It was an honour bestowed for his almost single-handed "12 rules" codification of the game in 1866, which brought uniformity, stability and then growth to the game. Harrison was also a long-time official of the MCC committee and the Melbourne Cricket Ground (MCG) once had a grandstand on the southern side of the oval named in tribute of him.

In more recent times the palm of recognition as the game's founder has been, in popular understanding at least, transferred to Harrison's cousin, Tom Wills—who after returning to Melbourne from Rugby School wrote a letter published in *Bell's Life in Victoria* in 1858, suggesting a football club be formed to keep cricketers fit in winter. "If a club of this sort were got up," Wills wrote, "it would be of a vast benefit to any cricket ground to be trampled upon, and would make the turf quite firm and durable; besides which it would keep those who are inclined to become stout from having their joints encased in useless superabundant flesh." There was in fact a group of

A DEVILISH TRACK

men along with Wills who met and wrote the Melbourne FC's first rules in 1859 at Jerry Bryant's Parade Hotel. The meeting began with Wills suggesting "the Rugby rules, but nobody understood them except himself" according to Cambridge graduate William Hammersley. Also at the gathering were Thomas H. Smith and James Thompson.

In 1908 when the code was celebrating its 50th anniversary, *The Argus* recalled Harrison's ultimately unsuccessful attempt to have the game trialled in England in 1884:

> Mr. Harrison went to England on a holiday tour with the Australian XI. He interviewed the authorities of both the Association [soccer] and Rugby games, with the idea of arranging an exhibition match under Australian Rules, and offered to devote three weeks to coaching the teams in the main points of the game. Mr. Alcock, then secretary of the Surrey County Cricket Club, was a leading official in Association football and he had heard so much from English cricketers visiting Australia about our game that he offered the use of Kennington Oval (The Oval) for the match, and agreed to find an Association team to play in it. The Rugby people were, however, less cordial. Their standpoint was "this game of ours is 150 years old [and] if one of us has to adopt the other's rules, the obligation is surely upon you—the younger people—to adopt our game". It was not in one sense an unreasonable view and had Rugby been the only game played in England at the time the argument would have been unanswerable. But England had its rival game, and though Mr. Harrison's suggestion appeared to be in some sense audacious, it at least offered a compromise between the two as a universal game, putting Australian interests on the matter quite upon one side.

Here four years after that attempt in England, Harrison was now chair of a meeting of VFA club officials considering a proposal from Englishmen that many suspected was a 'Trojan horse' aimed to help Rugby's colonisation of Victoria. "We have fought hard to keep up the interest in football, and it would be foolish to assist anything that would destroy that interest," said J. Simpson (Fitzroy FC). "If the clubs continued to fight against one another, the game would continue as popular as at present." F. James (Ballarat FC) suggested "the coming of an English team will undo all that has been done to popularise our game and do much to introduce and improve the Rugby game here and in the other colonies". J. Morris (Melbourne FC) was favourable to "the granting of the Association's patronage on condition that the English team played none but our game in Victoria".

Carlton FC's Theo Marshall, VFA secretary, objected as "an English team would have no chance against a Victorian 20 in a match according to Victorian rules". Harrison wasn't so sure, saying "it has been urged that it would take seven months for the Englishmen to acquire a knowledge of the Victorian game, but as I have always urged it is so simple that children could master it in a few hours".

The VFA committee members voted 10-3 "to refuse its patronage to the proposed team of English football men". *The Argus*, in an extraordinarily long and severely critical article for a football matter (even by Melbourne standards), took the VFA to task, dismantling each of their objections as mere smokescreen:

> If our game is absolutely the best—and good judges who have seen all phases of football say that it is—we should be anxious to encourage Englishmen to play it, if it is not the best the sooner we are brought to realise the fact the better. If Englishmen beat us at our own game—and they propose to play no other in Victoria—it will be a useful lesson. If they are badly beaten the loss in prestige as well as in money will be theirs and not ours, for Australians will not attend matches where the result is a foregone conclusion. If Lillywhite proposed to bring 20 cricketers or lawn tennis players to meet us at football, the objection as to the impossibility of learning the game might apply. Had it been at once stated that each

delegate fears that the visit of an English team might interfere with the engagements of his club and lessen its income for the season, the real motive for the resolution would have been stated. And it might just as well have been so stated, for all the effect the fictitious reasons so gravely debated by the VFA have had in blinding those acquainted with the game as to the real reasons for the resolution.

Many Rugby supporters were convinced that the VFA decision would result in not just the Australian Rules games being abandoned, but the entire tour. Others theorised that as Rugby was bound to advance as a result of the tour, killing off the voyage was the VFA's intention, even if it meant forgoing meeting the British at the Victorians' own game.

Melbourne's *The Argus* suggested over two articles that the tour's potential to advance the growth of Rugby was the sole valid reason any supporter of Australian Rules could have against the visit, and that while the Rugby colonies speculated the entire venture would have to be called off, Victoria had let slip a rare opportunity:

> The visit of the Englishmen to NSW will, no doubt, give the Rugby game in that colony "the lift" it has during the last couple of seasons stood as much in need of, and in this respect only have Victorians any need to feel antagonistic towards the Englishmen. Year by year the Australian game has steadily gained upon the Rugby in NSW, and last season the advocates of the former claimed that their matches had drawn much larger audiences than the best of the Rugby games, so that, in spite of its being handicapped by the fact of its originating in Victoria, it has made wonderful advances there. It may be further pointed out that in the event of the Association adhering to its decision, and the clubs also declining to arrange matches with the Englishmen, the latter will play the Rugby game solely, and confine their attention exclusively to NSW, Queensland and New Zealand, the fewer men required under

> these circumstances considerably lessening the expense of the undertaking. The natural consequence of the colony (Victoria) being shut out entirely from international football cannot but have an injurious effect. May not the decision of the VFA react upon themselves in a manner they have not foreseen?

Shrewsbury was convinced that the MCC were behind the voting actions of some of the VFA members. In public though Lillywhite was still playing a straight bat to the VFA, telling Melbourne's *Daily Telegraph*: "Well, it was a bit of a staggerer when we heard that they had refused their patronage. Yes, we did fret a little, for you know how we receive teams of cricketers at home, or anybody else who comes; while, if a team of footballers went, no one would be able to make too much of them. But I wrote to the [VFA] secretary, and asked him if they could not reconsider their decision, and I see that they have been good enough to arrange to do so."

A good many number of the delegates changed their minds but not sufficient to overturn the original decision—the motion was put and lost by 13 to 10. The VFA would not be granting their patronage. *The Argus* (who seemed increasingly well informed on football matters in England) fired another broadside shot at the VFA, now as a matter of influencing the clubs individually and the public, given the VFA were finished with the matter:

> Would it not have been more honest to say at once that Australian [Rules] footballers fear, not the consequences of an English visit, but the consequences of defeat? Do they pretend to believe for a moment that had we beaten the Englishmen at cricket on every occasion of meeting there would have been any stagnation in the game today? The lack of interest is the consequence of a lack of success and the Association may be discreet if chicken-hearted in saying: "We are afraid of the English footballer." Their case for the Association, put in plain words, is this: "We have the finest game of football and the finest players in the world, and we are so satisfied upon this

point, that we have no desire to put it to the test by playing against the representatives of any other country, even when they challenge us and are prepared to meet us on our own grounds. We don't know why we should be braver and better and less mercenary than anyone else in the wide world, but we are."

The promoters then turned to negotiating directly with individual clubs and quickly got another rude shock. Looking at the events from the neighbouring colony, the *South Australian Weekly Chronicle* revealed that: "Most of the clubs [in Melbourne] showed an exceedingly parsimonious spirit, and were at first averse to granting anything like liberal terms to the visitors. They nearly all demanded one-third of the proceeds and to cap all the MCC demanded a similar portion for the use of its ground (the MCG). This left the remaining third for the Englishmen. Such terms were very extortionate, as the visitors have to bear heavy travelling expenses for the better portion of a year."

The Leader in Melbourne was particularly robust in its comments: "The intending visitors have not asked for any especially favourable terms, although their expenses will be enormous. They know that Victorian clubs 'go for the gate'—which unfortunately 'nobody can deny'—and are prepared to be reasonable. As matters now stand the footballers of Victoria occupy a most unenviable position in the eyes of their neighbours and of the world at large, and it will redound very greatly to the credit of the first committee or club which undertakes to set matters right, for as they now stand the meaning of the word 'sport' is disgracefully prostituted."

Shrewsbury and Lillywhite decided, with reluctance, to accept the less generous terms from the Melbourne clubs and got on with arranging a schedule of matches in country Victoria and Adelaide.

What was clear to all was the Lions were now sailing under their own black flag, rejected by the both the RFU and the VFA, and without support from the British newspapers. Faced with opposition at home and in the colonies, Lillywhite opined: "It cannot be expected but that some people will look on the gloomy side and predict failure."

The First of Many Hearty Welcomes

"Our attitude towards football is like that of the Scotch toper toward whisky. The toper opined that he had never tasted any whisky that was bad; all whiskies were good, only some were better than others. So do we think of football."
Murray's magazine, 1890

The *Kaikoura* made land-fall at Hobart in the early evening of 18 April. The stay would be about 12 hours, leaving mid-morning the next day; long enough to coal, long enough to offload Sir Thomas and his precious salmon ova. The news cables flashed throughout the colonies. Naturally, wiring the news that practically all 100 per cent of the salmon ova were alive and well took precedence at the top of the reports conveying word that, despite a most ghastly crossing from the Cape, all the passengers—"among whom were the English footballers"—were no longer green about the gills, appeared as a closing afterthought.

Despite the ship being hours overdue, a large muster of hardy local footballers were on the wharf to greet the team, shouting and cheering. "Three cheers for the English football team! Hurrah! Hurrah! Hurrah!"

A most resounding welcome. These were all Australian Rules footballers of the Southern Tasmania Football Association. Rugby was not played in the island colony. They, of course, had been for days planning to show the visitors all the Hobart sights and to have a kick about of the football at their Cornelian Bay ground. But the lateness of the ship's arrival meant day was now night and the brevity of the stay meant there would be no time to fit any of the touristy things in. Nor was there any opportunity to learn some Australian Rules tips from the local footballers, nor any chance to give an exhibition of Rugby to the Hobartians.

Just as the excitement on the wharf cooled down a letter was handed to Seddon: "It's asking us to dine with the mayor in his parlour at the town hall!" A roar went up, and before anyone could ask the hows and wheres of finding and preparing for the mayor's parlour, the local footballers had all the team up in four-and-drags galloping at break-neck pace into the town. After the mayor had given the team an effusive welcome, and wished them success throughout their tour, "we were not slow in testing the quality of his champagne and cigars!" laughed Seddon.

All were back on board just after midnight. Some of the players escaped back into Hobart early the following morning—the sight of the sudden appearance of Mount Wellington as a backdrop to the city a most unexpected surprise. A few hours wandering about the city, with so many fine stone buildings, many built by convict labour, and then back to the *Kaikoura* in time for a 9.30am departure.

Today, Tasmania is renowned the world over for its salmon, while encounters with a Tasmanian rugger are slightly more common than with a Tasmanian tiger. Ironically, one of the few places Rugby posts permanently stand in Tasmania is at Rugby Park in Cornelian Bay. Almost unknown is that Tasmania can lay claim to two international rugby players: Henry Braddon, who we will speak more of when the Lions arrive in Sydney, and William Allan Stewart, who was born in Launceston in 1889. Studying at the Royal London Hospital to become a doctor, the young Tasmanian joined their Rugby team, and then, being of Scottish descent and showing aptitude for the game, moved on to London Scottish RFC. In 1913-14 he was chosen four times to play for the Scotland Rugby team. An astonishingly fast sprinter, in one game against Ireland he grabbed four tries. It wasn't just his speed that led to his try-scoring success but also his ability to snatch the ball from teammates' passes, no matter how wayward they were. *The Athletic News* was convinced this was a skill he picked up "from Tasmania, where they play a funny style of football".

The Tasmanians had adopted Australian Rules in the late 1870s. Quoted in Hobart's *The Mercury* (in 1936), Walter Conder, President of the Australian Amateur Football Council, said that "in the '70s, the Australian game was not played in Tasmania—the football played consisted of soccer, Rugby and a cross between the two games known as the Tasmanian game". This code had no off-side rules, allowed running with the ball and used Rugby posts and ball. Much earlier, at Christ's College in Bishopsbourne (northern Tasmania) through 1847-49 the boys played Rugby under the stewardship of Reverend John Philip Gell, a Rugby School 'old boy' who was the model for the character of 'Old Brooke' created by Thomas Hughes in his famous novel *Tom Brown's Schooldays*.

With everyone keen to sail from Hobart and get the final four days to New Zealand over with, the ship's engine was fully stoked. But the *Kaikoura* remained idle. She had no captain. It seems the good Captain Crutchley had some personal business in Hobart town as well; when it came time to sail he was nowhere to be found. There was delay of an hour or so until a steam-tug was seen making its way to the ship's side, bringing the missing skipper aboard. Nearing midday, the *Kaikoura* could finally be seen making her way up the Derwent River towards the sea.

None of the tour's Melbourne contingent had been in Hobart to meet the team, nor was any word received from them. Shrewsbury and Lillywhite had gone to New Zealand with their England cricket team in late March, and Stoddart met up with the duo in Christchurch a week before the *Kaikoura*

THE FIRST OF MANY HEARTY WELCOMES

was due. In a sign of how closely guarded the promoters had kept the final composition of the team a secret—probably to hide how many 'name' players had not come, not least of all to keep Stoddart 'on the hook'—Stoddart said in the *Christchurch Press* that the ship would be arriving with other star English backs on board, notably Lockwood, Stadden, Bonsor, Robertshaw and Haslam. Only Haslam was with the team. Meanwhile the Australian Rules coaches McShane and Lawlor failed to reach Hobart until the day after the *Kaikoura* had left port. They would have to catch up.

On the final evening at sea, the *Kaikoura* moved across the bottom side of New Zealand's South Island and began to head up its eastern coast towards its destination of Port Chalmers, located some 15km inside Otago Harbour. The footballers gathered to thank Captain Crutchley and his crew. Seddon presented the captain with hand-written testimonial of thanks, signed by the whole of the tour party, and gave a short speech thanking him for the safe delivery of the team. "The memory of our *Kaikoura* voyage will long live after other recollections have become dim and this is in no small degree due to your personal kindness and general disposition and to that social affability you have ever exhibited to the passengers in general and to the football team in particular," Seddon said.

Perhaps they should have waited until standing on solid earth to thank the captain. That final night at sea did not to pass quietly, for an extremely severe thunderstorm came upon the *Kaikoura*. For over two hours the ship was forced to reduce speed, barely making any headway until the storm had dissipated.

Come first light the weather had cleared and the steamer turned to enter Otago Harbour. By mid-morning, the players watching from the deck could see the throng of footballers in their various club jerseys waiting on the wharf at Port Chalmers to welcome them.

After 46 days since leaving England the *Kaikoura* was now at the end of her long journey. The first British Lions were about to set foot in New Zealand.

Friends and Foes Alike

"At a period when Federation is the password of the day this advent of the English footballers must be regarded as one of the many ties that draw the colonies and the Mother Country together."
Wanganui Chronicle, April 23, 1888

The Dunedin morning broke fine with a warm sun and scarcely a breath of wind. "A beautiful day," Seddon wrote, "great excitement prevailing throughout the place". It was evident in the town that something unusual was going to take place, for the footpaths were thronged with pedestrians. Trains from north and south brought hundreds, maybe a thousand, of country visitors to the railway station. By early afternoon everyone—on foot, on horseback, in carriage, on the trams—was going southward from city centre to the Caledonian Ground. The object was to be early to the oval to secure a good vantage point from which to witness the struggle between the 15 chosen representatives of the Rugby clubs of the Otago region and the first football visitors from Great Britain.

It had been five days since the *Kaikoura* had arrived at Port Chalmers and for the Lions, seemingly every waking moment thereafter they had been feted and banqueted as if they were the conquering heroes returning from war. The large contingent of footballers and officials that had been waiting on the dock carried the team to the train and then escorted them on the short ride to Dunedin. Leaving the station the crowd that had gathered expectantly in the streets outside was so large that "we had some difficulty in getting to the carriages that were waiting," said Seddon. "We were [then] driven to the Grand Hotel, and were formally welcomed to the colony."

Opened in 1883, the four-storey high Grand was regarded as the finest and most opulent hotel in Australasia (it is now the Southern Cross Hotel). On the back of earlier gold finds in the region, Dunedin was at the time New Zealand's biggest city, with a population near 40,000. The president of the Otago RU, Dr. Millen Coughtrey—yet another product of Edinburgh University of the early 1870s—seemed particularly happy to single out the team's Dr. Smith for special mention in his welcoming address. On Rugby in the colony, he said, "the game of football was played in New Zealand on the same lines as in the greater part of Great Britain and Ireland—under Rugby rules—and the game was played simply for sport's sake [and] I am sure the other unions in the colony will vie with the Otago Union in endeavouring to make the visit of the English team a pleasant one". He concluded by proposing "Success to football and to the series of matches to be played by the English team!" The toast was drunk in bumpers of champagne.

As many visitors from Britain notice very quickly, the Lions found many towns and villages in the colonies possessed names familiar to a Briton's ear, being bestowed by the first explorers and settlers a name in honour of a British town, individual or some other identifiable trait or place. Around the Otago peninsular almost everything seemed to have involved something from Scotland; the people of Dunedin had recently erected a statue in tribute to the long since dead Scottish poet Robert Burns. The other common trait to every place the team came upon during their long tour was a desire to entertain the visitors with banquets, scenic drives, visits to prominent local institutions, factories, town halls and all manner of other places and outings.

During their first days in Dunedin the team was placed in four-horse carriages and taken on day trips "for the purpose of showing them a little of our country" including Portobello, Mosgiel and Blueskin (named after a local Maori who was so well-adorned by his Tā moko body markings that from a distance he appeared blue). Each excursion included a formal lunch and more speeches of welcome from local dignitaries.

A visit to one of the local woollen mills one morning seems like one of the less interesting activities, especially to the men from Yorkshire and Lancashire. "We were taken in hand by the manager, Mr. Morrison who in every way did his utmost to make our visit enjoyable," recalled Seddon. It appears all the local man had to do to gain this accolade from the team was to provide access to the factory floor. "It was surprising, though quite natural, the interest taken by our men in the work being done by the girls," explained Seddon wryly. "Come time to leave, the gathering of our men together again was a very difficult task."

The evenings were just as busy. "Thursday we had three different invitations, of which we preferred a cricket club concert and an oyster supper," said Seddon. On Friday evening "we had each an invitation to the Masonic Hall [dance]. Here we were not long in finding that the ladies were quite as enthusiastic as the gentlemen in trying to make our first visit enjoyable."

Of course, as good as the attention was, the players sometimes needed an escape and found, to their surprise, that nearly every city and most towns in the colonies had been swept up in "the skating craze" and had built or converted a hall for a roller-skating rink. Though far from unknown in Britain, according to Seddon, "there were only two or three who had tried this difficult exercise before". The team found it a lot of fun and at any opportunity during the tour they would seek out the local rink (whose manager invariably welcomed them with open arms and free entry, as their presence drew in extra customers in their droves). Their first such venture came at Dunedin's Columbia Skating Rink, where a race in which, as Seddon put it, "most of our men started, but few finished" was held. Walter

Bumby won, just ahead of Stoddart. Shrewsbury and Lillywhite didn't seem too perturbed at the players' risk of injury from skating. If anything the activity and exercise helped to offset the torpid nature of the banqueting and entertaining the team were receiving.

Writing to Shaw ahead of their tour opener against the combined representatives of the Otago region, Shrewsbury said: "Our first match here looks like being a success. They (the town) are working the excitement up admirably, and expect 10,000 people present." Many of the spectators gathered in front of the Grand Hotel, waiting to see the Lions embark for the ground, carried royally in an open carriage drawn by an impressive six-in-hand team (three pairs of horses). The footballers emerged to loud cheers and flag waving. The 15 men selected to do battle for Britain that day were already stripped ready for the fray in their Union Jack coloured jersey, long down-to-the knee white flannel knickerbockers and velvet cap (most discarded their cap just before the kick-off, but some backs kept them on through a game). The Otago team gathered at the City Hotel and their carriages joined up with those of the Britishers, creating a long convoy of footballers, officials and supporters heading to the field. "Red, white, and blue flags were being waived from the windows of our supporters," recalled Seddon. "The ladies were very prominent, a great number wearing ribbon of our colours. As we drove to the ground, a great crowd of people cheered us on our way."

Plenty of investments were made with bookmakers right across New Zealand. The *Otago Daily Times* reporting that "betting has all along been greatly in favour of the English team winning" but "among good judges of the game it is thought that the Englishmen are a little overrated, and that they will not have a runaway victory". A more of a "sure thing" was tipping the final attendance, with no one in any doubt it would be the largest ever seen on an Otago football field. So it turned out to be, for the numbers that crammed the grandstand, and lined the chains around the playing arena four deep were quite unprecedented. Small boys and men who could not afford to pay clambered on to the top of adjacent fences, and one or two buildings in the vicinity of the gasworks were black with spectators. By day's end the crowd was over 10,000. Shrewsbury and Lillywhite walked about with grins from ear to ear; a start of £280 in the bank was a good first deposit. The promoters' angle was to make money from Melbourne's reputation for large crowds at football games, but on a relative scale, Dunedin would be hard to top.

To thunderous cheers and clapping from the crowd and the playing of a brass band, the Otago team made their appearance first, in dark blue jerseys, contrasting with the vibrant green of the sunlight-bathed field. Then the visitors—"prettily clad" in their red, white, and blue—filed onto the oval and the cheering was renewed, seemingly with increased vigour. The teams raised their caps aloft, then heartily and generously gave each other cheers, and proceeded to take up their positions for the start of the game.

Each team brought to the contest its own umpire, armed with a flag and dressed in civilian clothing; his team's players could appeal to him if they saw an infringement that disadvantaged their side. If their umpire agreed he raised his flag. If the other umpire concurred, he too raised his flag, and upon seeing both flags in the air, the referee would blow his whistle for the game to stop for a scrum to be formed at the place of the infringement. If only one umpire raised his flag, the game would not be stopped unless the referee agreed a breach had occurred and blew his whistle. If during the course of the match the referee saw an infringement—but neither umpire had raised his flag—he had no power to interfere and was not permitted to blow his whistle. (The modern system of a single referee, two touch judges and penalties began the following season.)

Matches normally were 90 minutes, broken into two 45 minutes halves. The length of the half-time break was agreed to by the two captains. Expressed in today's nomenclature, the points values used during the tour (apart from games in NSW) were those of the RFU:

- 3 points for a drop-kicked goal or a 'field goal' (soccer-style, but over the bar) during play
- 3 points for a place-kicked or drop-kicked goal from a fair catch

- 2 points for a place-kicked conversion
- 1 point for a try

After losing the toss of the coin, Seddon kicked-off and his forwards followed up fast, play at once centring on the Otago 25, the opposing forwards rallying around in double-quick time. With the ball firmly held under fallen bodies, and no way to extricate it, the first scrum was formed deep in Otago territory. Both teams packed quickly and firmly—and then for what seemed an eternity but was probably five or so minutes—spectators and backs alike looked on as the scrum moved about the field in the struggle over the ball. The tense silence was broken from somewhere deep in the crowd, with a solitary yell of "Blues!", then followed another, and yet another louder than the first, until the cry grew into a prolonged shout all round the field. It was difficult to say from whose side the ball finally emerged and while the Otago forwards held their own in the battle, the ball could now be seen in British hands.

A few minutes later another scrum was called for. This time the Blue forwards buckled down to some serious work, pushing the Lions pack backwards, inch by inch, yard by yard, with the crowd wildly cheering them onwards as they steadily moved the phalanx into British territory. And so the game went on, the Lions three-quarters, primarily Stoddart and Speakman, would go on their long solo runs and the Otago forwards would force the ball back. In turn each of the goals was assailed by the opposing forces, but no score came. At one point the Otago forwards, from near half-way, got a dribbling rush on and swept down the ground with the ball at their feet, "amid a perfect storm of applause". But the visitors somehow got a boot on the ball and Sam Williams, along with Harry Eagles, returned the compliment, dribbling the ball back to neutral territory.

Then, in the most unexpected way possible, the deadlock was broken. The Otago forwards again came with a dribbling rush. Within sight of the goal posts, and the ball bounding along in front of him, the team's captain, Edward Morrison, suddenly took a speculating kick at it. "Greatly, to the astonishment of everyone, it went flying over the bar between the posts," wrote the *Otago Daily Times*. "It was an astonishing piece of play, such as one might not see in a lifetime, and the Otago supporters could hardly realise that their men had scored." As the Blues went back to the centre the cheering grew louder and louder as the realisation of what had happened spread. Otago 3, Britain 0. Ironically, Morrison was in fact an Englishman, in Dunedin for a time working as the English master at the boys high school.

The home men were now urged on by "the shouts of hundreds of their supporters, who yelled 'Blues' till they were almost blue in the face themselves". Their joy was short-lived though for the score seemed only to put the Lions on their mettle and as they got down to their work it was easy to see that they meant business. Johnny Nolan came up with a splendid run and passing to Stoddart, he went on, but was pushed out over the touch-line just before the corner flag. The Lions forwards took hold of the ball from the ensuing line-out and by some smart close-in hand-passing they entirely puzzled the opposing forwards, and Tom Kent got over the line near the posts. The cheers went up for the visitors, and all eyes turned to Jack Anderton for the "try at goal"—which he duly fluffed, as one of the charging Blues forwards knocked the ball down. Otago 3, Lions 1.

Taking place-kicks at goal wasn't as straight forward as it is today with the kicking tee. Similar to what still happens in American football, one of kicker's team would lay on the ground on his belly, and hold the ball with outstretched arms in place for the kicker—and the moment the placer let the ball touch the ground, the opposing team could charge at him, the ball, and the kicker, and attempt to stop the goal. If they did knock the ball down, it was still "live" and the play would immediately go on just as if it were any other charged down kick during the game.

Tom Banks, one of the older and bulkier men in the Lions and known for his sometimes heavy-handed tackling style, caused a little sensation by 'scragging' (slinging) the smaller Otago half-back Jack Thomson over rather roughly. The problem was both were already well outside the touch-line. The crowd, quick to notice and jump on the slightest suspicion of rough play, hooted at him. Most of the newspaper reporters politely gave Banks, being a guest, the benefit of the doubt, writing it up as an unintended accident.

Nolan, playing half-back, performed a solo novelty act. Otago put up a high kick, and their forwards took off after it. Nolan got into position to catch the ball, but there was little doubt he was in great danger of being enveloped under a dark blue avalanche before he could claim a 'fair catch'— to do this he had to catch the ball without leaving the ground, immediately make a mark in the earth with his heel, and cry out 'fair catch!' Sensing that mercy rule was about provide no mercy at all, Nolan instead jumped into the air, met the ball with his forehead, and sent the pigskin flying back down the field again. A cool and clever piece of play that was loudly applauded. Some later suggested it was against the deliberate knock forward rule but the playing laws did not bear them out on that point.

Some watching on were also troubled by what they saw going on with the British in the scrum—they were employing 'heeling back' or 'hooking' the ball, so it came backwards through their forwards instead of the traditional 'shoving matches' of endeavouring by kicking and pushing power to drive the ball forwards through the opposing pack, and into the open field behind. It had long been surmised in the colonies that this 'heeling business' was contrary to the game's laws, believing that as the ball came further back in the scrum, in turn each row of forwards were in front of the ball and were thus off-side and obstructing.

After the game Seddon revealed that under a strict reading of the laws it arguably *is* unlawful, but in Britain 'custom winks' at the breach, and it is ignored. The Lions also unveiled a variation to 'heeling back' called 'screwing the scrum' or 'wheeling'. Time after time they held the ball in the second or third row, just on the inside of the scrum; then, on Seddon's shout, all would push (skew) to the opposite side; this would move the Otago pack out of the way, leaving the British forwards with a clear field in front of them and the ball at their feet, which usually became a dribbling rush. "We do not believe in too much scrimmaging and try to make the game fast and open, and therefore we try to screw the scrum in order to get the ball into the open," Seddon explained. "Why should we push through nine men when we can screw the ball out much quicker, and, besides, the play is much prettier to watch."

The "heeling back" completely changed the role of the three-quarter backs; they were no longer merely the scavengers that stood about waiting to pounce on the ball the moment it suddenly spewed forth from somewhere among the forwards, but were instead hand-passed the ball from the half-back, who had collected it from behind the scrum, leaving men like Stoddart free to run with the ball into open field or take a drop-kick at goal or for territory. It was also quickly realised that at scrum time, with 18 forwards and four half-backs all gathered in one place like bees over a honey pot, the six opposing three-quarters really had the field all to themselves—running and hand-passing the ball into the vast open spaces now offered unlimited possibilities for attacking play. Teams having today's four three-quarters and eight forwards system was a further refinement from these changes, but would not be seen in the colonies until the Matthew Mullineux-led Lions tour of 1899.

More than revolution of the scrum, what Seddon's team showed at the Caledonian Ground was a new Rugby game—of hand-passing and support play. A reporter for the *Poverty Bay Herald* was so put out by the speed of the inter-change of passing, he gave up the normal practice of identifying who passed the ball (moreover, who "chucked" the leather over his head in the midst of a tackle and hoped there was a teammate behind), instead writing: "The Englishmen playing into each others hands so well that it was impossible to distinguish the individual players." The *Star* wrote: "The Colours (Lions) had evidently learned from the first spell that they could trust each other and their combined play in the second was a treat to witness. Hardly any individual could be singled out, all playing like a well ordered machine. If one started on a run he did not wait to be collared, but directly [when] he was threatened he parted with the leather, and there were always one or two of his comrades handy. The ball thus passed across the field and back again over and over again, seven or eight players handling it. Did an Otago player get the ball and start a run, there was always one, if not two, to collar him at once, and they not only got the player but the ball also, thus invariably preventing a pass. Their splendid play was observable in other directions. Before the spectators had time to notice which particular player had started to do good work for his side another and then another had taken part in it. Such combination, such skill, and such fast play has not been seen here before."

Many agreed that any lesser team than Otago would have been soundly beaten long before the final bell, but here, with time fast running out, Morrison's unlikely 'field goal' was still trumping the Lions' now two unconverted tries. Speakman, who had already been having a fine game, particularly with Stoddart marked so closely and more ball coming his way, finished as the hero of the match, kicking two drop goals. The first came after Bumby, using 'dummy' passes that puzzled the opposition, reached to almost the goal line; there he offloaded to Speakman, who potted a smart drop goal, made difficult because he was so close to the posts. That put the Lions ahead 5-3. The win was secured via another drop goal to Speakman. "He took the pass beautifully, and quick as lightning, with a fine screw kick, he sent the ball once more flying fairly between the posts." The English reserve men and their supporters were now jubilant. Waving their hats frantically in the air, they cheered themselves hoarse, and there were loud cries of "Speakman! Speakman!" The full-time whistle sounded and the large crowd scrambled over the chains and across the ground.

The *Star* noted the Lions "were greatly delighted at the decisive victory of eight points to three, in this their first match on colonial soil, and shook hands very heartily with each other". There was no doubt from the *Otago Daily Times* how important this match was in the colony's Rugby history, declaring it "the greatest football match that has ever been contested on New Zealand soil".

"The play of the Englishmen was a treat to witness, and nothing like it has ever been seen here before. The passes were sharp and accurate, and the men rarely, if ever, failed to take them. They backed one another up splendidly. The Englishmen were heartily congratulated upon their victory by friends and foes alike, and no one grudged them their hard-earned laurels after having come 16,000 miles over the ocean to play in New Zealand."

News of the Lions victory was immediately telegraphed throughout the cities and major towns of the colony. People had stood for hours that afternoon on footpaths outside newspaper offices, post offices, tobacco shops and a countless other establishments, waiting for the half-time score and then full-time result to be posted on a window or wall. The match result and some sparse but useful details could be found in newspapers in Australia (next day) and Great Britain (two days). From London's *Sporting Life*, April 29:

> DUNEDIN, APRIL 27, 1888
>
> England beat Otago to-day by two goals and two tries to one goal. Speakman kicked both goals for England. The match caused tremendous excitement in Dunedin, and there were 10,000 spectators present. The weather was gloriously fine.

After being brought back to the Grand Hotel the team changed out of their football attire, had their bath and put on their usual street wear. With two games against Otago (the next being on the coming Wednesday), the traditional post-match function between the teams was set for the Monday evening in between, leaving the players a free Saturday night. Proving that their exertions on the field had by no means exhausted their stores of youthful energy and exuberance, the men instead went to the skating rink for a series of match races against each other.

The following days saw more trips in carriages, on horseback, taking part in a shooting hunt, even one day returning to the ship life for a few hours (generous lunch onboard supplied, of course) to view the recently completed harbour defence fortifications (cannons and other ordinance) erected upon Lawyers Head and Forbury Hill. With guns also mounted at Taiaroa Heads, this completed "the defence of Dunedin", part of a colony-wide scheme to protect New Zealand's major port cities (the result of fears in late 1870s that if Russia declared war on Britain, the colony could not rely on British forces to arrive in time to protect it).

"In the evening a banquet was given us by the Otago RU, the room and tables being decorated in a most lovely way," Seddon noted. "Our colours being red, white, and blue, everything in the room was of the same colours, table flowers, buttonholes, menu tickets, and even red, white, and blue ribbon round the wine glasses. The Otago RU presented each of us with a very handsome walking stick of native growth, having silver shields with [our] name inscribed. These are very much appreciated."

Such sticks were a very popular addition to a gentleman's outfit, but were especially a sign that the carrier was of "the leisured class". While the men were on tour, that was indeed the life they were living and enjoying. Many of them proudly carried their sticks everywhere they went. Amidst a long night of music, songs, cigars, comic recitals, food, drink and many, many speeches, Dr. Coughtrey, the Otago RU's president revealed that once they learned the tour's first game would be in Dunedin, they determined to set the benchmark when it came to hosting the guests. "You will find the country a picturesque one, and we hope you will all stay in it, bring over your sisters, cousins, and aunts, to stay with you! We compliment our visitors on their play in the match on Saturday and our local men learned several lessons from your tactics."

After much enthusiastic cheering, Seddon responded, thanking them all for "the many kindnesses shown to our team during our stay in Dunedin— I am sure the kindness received here will live long in our memory and we will never forget our visit to Dunedin".

He wrote home: "You cannot imagine in England the hospitality we have received during our stay here. I am greatly afraid, if this kind of welcome is accorded us throughout New Zealand and Australia, many of our players will be very sorry to return to the old country again."

Having Heard Strange Tales

"To Englishmen this is a great fact: New Zealand looks English at every turn—British through and through."
London *Daily Telegraph* journalist, December 21, 1888

The Otago XV had a new man for the second game, half-back Patrick Keogh—born in Birmingham, before migrating to New Zealand as a child. After debuting for Otago in 1887, he quickly became one of New Zealand's most highly regarded backs … until it all came undone. In 1891, an Otago RU investigation into match-fixing led to Keogh being banned as a professional for profiting from gambling on local Rugby matches. Here though he was helping Otago meet a British team that appeared, after a further four days of excess, a little slower in their movements. There was no score in the first half but there was little doubt Otago had the best of it.

Not long after half-time, a scrum went down near the Lions goal. Otago won the ball and following the tourists' example from Saturday, heeled it backwards through the pack. They didn't quite get it right and the ball suddenly shot out the back of the scrum like a cannon ball. The alert Keogh darted back, smartly picked up the leather, and then came straight upfield, choosing to try and dodge his way through the thick of the British forwards. It seemed an absurd move until, almost before anyone knew what had happened, there he was planting the ball down behind the posts for a try. "Then ensued a scene of wild excitement such as has never before been witnessed on the Caledonian Ground," wrote the *Otago Daily Times* of the pandemonium that erupted. "Otago supporters ran and jumped, and threw their hats and sticks high in the air, while cheer after cheer arose from the thousands of spectators who crowded the stand and lined the chains. All eyes centred on Lynch as he was called up to take the try at goal. The ball was well placed and as he sent it flying fairly over the middle of the bar, the cheering broke forth with renewed vigour. The Otago players expressed their joy by turning somersaults and [spectators'] hats and sticks were again hurled in the air. The grandstand fairly shook with the cheering, and even the ladies joined in the general excitement by waving umbrellas and handkerchiefs. The excitement subsided at last and the Englishmen kicked [-off] again."

If the scoring of a try against the Lions could cause those scenes, an Otago victory would be something to see. Unfortunately for Otago, Thomson, their other half-back, was soon seen to fall heavily in a tackle. The result was a dislocated shoulder. In those times players could not be replaced; if a man went off, the team just had to battle on. "Why should the other team have to face a fresh reinforcement?" was the prevailing argument in favour of not allowing replacements. Apart from the most obviously dire injuries, it was regarded by nearly all in Rugby as a sign of weakness—or worse, effeminacy—for a man to withdraw from the field and force his mates to battle on with one less. Despite his palpable pain, Thomson refused to shirk his duties; he got up and attempted to throw in the ball from a line-out (because that was *his* job). Though he could not do it, his teammates and nearby crowd could be heard shouting "Stick to it, Jack!" He remained at his post a little longer but with honour now having been served, he left the game.

Sensing the opportunity, the Lions stepped up. A clearing kick from Otago was charged down, but the player appealed to the umpire, claiming the

Britishers were off-side. The referee had blown his whistle in agreement and despite Seddon disputing the claim, the game went on. The crowd noticed from this point on the visitors were "playing a trifle roughly at times" while Otago, who were now with one less forward to cover the loss of Thomson, were tiring markedly. When close to the Otago goal line, Seddon ordered his team's full-back, Arthur Paul, to get in among the forwards, giving a further advantage in numbers.

The game now swung though on two brilliant long field runs. Seddon, breaking away from a scrum near half-way, came charging down the field. He passed to Anderton who went out near the corner. The rules gave the throw-in to the side that carried the ball into touch, and taken quickly, Banks gained possession and dived across for the try. From a difficult position, Anderton landed the goal, the score now 3-all. Moments later Stoddart came to the fore with a splendid run that took the action from the Lions' end deep into the Otago quarter. From there Nolan made "hot haste" and crossed for a try wide out. Paul missed the difficult conversion. With the score now 4-3 in Britain's favour, Otago strove all out in the dying minutes, but it was to no avail.

After handshakes all round, the visitors conceded the Otago XV (and Otago XIV) played a splendid game and had Thomson not been forced to retire they may have won. There was no doubt that they profited by their experience of the lesson in tactics given by the tourists on the Saturday. Here was the biggest danger to the Lions—in many places they were to visit they would be playing their opponents twice, and if the Otago men were typical, New Zealanders would prove quick learners. It was also planned for the team to finish the tour with a further round of matches in New Zealand and who knows what expertise in Lions tactics their Rugby opponents may have reached by then.

The players chose again to spend their post-game evening roller-skating. "There will be some wonderful feats done in the way of skating when we get back again to the old country!" wrote Seddon. Less may be said of Johnny Nolan's fall—it was severe enough to have injured his arm and rule him out of the next game. While this was happening officials of the Otago RU were having a quiet dinner with Lillywhite and Shrewsbury, where a cheque for £518, being their share of the gate money from the two games, was handed over. The local RU, having to pay all the expenses, would be fortunate to have anything left once all the invoices were dispensed with. But what price could be put on the benefits the visit had brought to Dunedin and to the game of Rugby in Otago, as well as the personal honours and life-long recognition won by the players that met the Lions in battle?

"Thursday morning," continued Seddon, "saw us all at breakfast by 7 o'clock—quite an unusual time, 10.30 being more to our liking, but having to catch the 8 o'clock train for Christchurch, we were obliged to perform this difficult task. On getting into the train we were each presented with a free pass for trains running this month." And didn't that cause a little kerfuffle, pushed along by a few newspaper editors, including that of the *Star* in Christchurch. "Why have free passes over the New Zealand railways been granted to Lillywhite's team of footballers? It is true that they are not all professionals, though it seems doubtful whether the English Rugby Union does not think the professional element in the team suspiciously strong. But even if we agree to look upon them all as amateurs, they are none of them paying their own expenses. Nor are their expenses being paid by any football club or union, constituted simply and solely for carrying on the game of football, and winning nothing but honour and glory thereby. The team is travelling for the purpose of gaining money for Messrs. Lillywhite and Shrewsbury. The affair is a commercial speculation, nothing more and nothing less. The footballers have just as much right to free passes as an operatic company, a circus troupe, or the staff of the Canadian lady doctor."

The matter reached the colonial parliament, where the responsible minister back-tracked so fast he nearly tumbled over. He claimed if only he had known beforehand he wouldn't have granted the free passes. Upon getting this news the promoters and footballers were incensed—after all they were by their visits publicising the towns of New Zealand weren't they?

Dunedin to Christchurch was a 12-hour steam train journey, travelling northwards some 235 miles (360km). For most of the time this is an ever-changing panorama of sea and shore, pastoral lands and hilly slopes; one of the most picturesque sojourns one could ever take. At times it was frightening too; through Blueskin between the railway line cutting and a sheer drop of hundreds of feet to the beach below is less than from a man's elbow to his finger tips. The line follows the Pacific coast until it reaches, at about the midway point, the port city of Timaru, then flanks away across the Canterbury Plains and onto Christchurch. A carefully laid out city, Christchurch's chief natural beauty is the meandering Avon River, so picturesquely calm it is a favourite for dipping oars and watching swans.

The football writer for the *Star* reported that at the tourists arrival in the 'City of the Plains' the "crowd at the railway station last evening to welcome the English team was something immense, and as the express pulled up round after round of cheering went up". He also called upon all of the province to get to the game, as "the venture will cost the triumvirate a matter of £12,000, so we trust their energy and pluck in risking such a mammoth undertaking will be fully recognised and appreciated by the public of Canterbury".

The Canterbury RU also tried something novel, perhaps to get some extra coin to offset the promoters' cut, having each of the Lions play wearing different coloured strips of ribbon around their arm, and selling a game-day programme so the spectators could match name to ribbon.

For days beforehand the coming battle had been a general topic of conversation in Christchurch—not only in football circles but among many to whom the game was more or less a mystery. Few though held out hope of a Canterbury victory, particularly as the stronger Otago couldn't topple the visitors. They had noted the close result on Wednesday, but doubted their players would go in for the intricacies of the Britishers tactics, particularly screwing scrums. "Unfortunately some of our forwards have the bad habit of devoting too much attention to shoving in the scrimmages, sacrificing footwork in their endeavour to break through," wrote the *Star*. "We do not expect our representatives to make such a good show as the Otago men ... but they have our best wishes."

As in Otago both teams, stripped ready for battle, were gathered together in the city. Then via a procession of appropriately colour-theme decorated carriages and horses, they were delivered to the ground (Canterbury wore red-and-black hooped jerseys). The weather was again favourable to the event, drawing over 7000 people to Lancaster Park, the most to ever attend a football game in Christchurch. The tourists wearing coloured ribbon proved to be of little merit. The *Press* said "unfortunately the idea was better in theory than in practice. In the hurry and rush of the play it became impossible to distinguish the colours." Still, the ladies were apparently happy it worked well enough at half-time to be of some utility.

For the third time since their arrival in New Zealand captain Seddon lost the coin toss; for the third time the Lions were unable to score in the first half. Their play was very poor, not showing anything like the spark they displayed in the Dunedin matches, while their passing was wild and erratic. The home side's first points came from a smartly taken drop goal from half-back and veteran skipper George Helmore (he had made his Canterbury debut in 1880 and was a member of the New Zealand team that visited Sydney in 1884). "Tremendous cheering greeted this performance and Helmore was subjected to the usual process of patting and handshaking by his men," wrote *Press*. Unsurprisingly, the Lions' wayward passing was eventually punished by Canterbury, taking an intercept, which became a converted try for a 6-0 lead.

The "special reporter" for the *Otago Witness* wrote that at the break "the Canterbury men now thought they were certain to win, but there was not wanting a few who still pinned their faith on the well-known pluck and staying power of the Colours (Lions)". If that reporter is to be taken at his word, one of the British team, presumably not one of the day's XV, laid a bet at half-time, stating "one of the Englishmen was plucky enough even at this juncture to lay odds of 2-1 on his team". He must have been a trifle nervous when two Canterbury tries (that are now legal) were on appeal by Seddon disallowed. The first came when a Canterbury player chased a high kick, caught the ball on the full and crossed under the posts—both umpires had seen that he had not taken the ball with a clean catch, slightly knocking the ball forward—though the ball never touched the ground, the try was called back for the knock-on. The second instance came when two Canterbury forwards pursued the ball that had been kicked past the Lions full-back Paul; certain to score, the ball hit the upright, leaving it motionless on the ground, and an easy pick-up for the try—however, this too was ruled against, as a ball that has fully stopped moving is 'dead' and a scrum is required.

Finally, thanks to some long runs from Stoddart, the tide began to turn. Most of the play was now at the Canterbury end of the field. From a drop-out Paul took the ball on his own side of the half-way line but instead of following routine and kicking for touch (it was lawful to kick the ball out on the full from anywhere on the field), he instead launched an almighty 'pot shot' drop-kick at the goal and the ball fairly sailed over the cross-bar. Five minutes later Stoddart made a thrilling, evasive run, getting clean through and touched down beside the posts for a converted try that levelled the scores. Angus Stuart then broke clear near touch, dribbling the ball solo for half the field until Tommy Haslam picked the ball up close to the Canterbury goal line and crossed for a try near the corner post. Paul made a good but futile attempt at the conversion, leaving the Lions ahead 7-6. The home men from that moment seemed to lose all heart. A further three tries—two converted—to the visitors left the final score 14-6 in Britain's favour.

The *Otago Daily Times* gushed with praise at the comeback victory: "The game, especially the latter part of it, was an exposition of what sheer pluck and determination combined with skill can accomplish. No one who had not previously seen the Englishmen play would have thought at half-time that they could possibly have pulled the match out of the fire as they did, for a score of six points is a very heavy one to wipe out in one spell and yet within 30 minutes the Englishmen not only made that score but eight points more. It was quite a treat to witness their play in the last 20 minutes."

Speaking at the post-game 'smoke concert' dinner (suitably extravagant, overly indulgent, little actual dining) Helmore, Canterbury's captain, said: "Most of us would remember the old slow game we used to play, in which the scrimmages were likened to a lot of fellows trying to 'hatch out' a ball. Since then we have tried hard to improve our football and make it a fast game and there is now no 'hatching out' the ball in Christchurch. But we still have much to learn. Screwing the scrimmages—and breaking back through the scrimmages for instance—and the admirable passing and backing up of the English team, the like of which has never before been seen in Christchurch. We hope that our men will try and imitate the admirable way in which the Englishmen play this part of the game."

Seddon, after a long round of applause, stood at the same event to give a speech and took the opportunity to respond to "having heard strange tales told about their play" and the belief, albeit held by very few, that gambling and "playing dead" was part of their characteristic. "It might be thought curious the way the games had gone against us in the first spells and many have said that we might have done better had we liked in these earlier spells; but I must tell them that this is all nonsense" he declared. Dr. Brooks, quoted in the *Auckland Star*, added: "There has been a lot of talk about our playing dark in some of our matches. All I can say is that there was not the shadow of truth in any of the rumours." Coming from the respected doctor it conveyed the message this statement could be accepted as the gospel truth. The *Southland Daily Times* suggested there was no hood-winking going on, simply that "their superior training told" and "they made a much better stand than in the first" half as "many of their opponents, lacking training, did not display nearly the same amount of dash as during the first 45 minutes".

The next three days before they played Canterbury again were spent on long country drives, a shooting hunt on horseback, lunches and dinners, and, of course, time at the skating rink. The *Star* observed that Seddon, with his great liking for aquatic sports, slipped away from the team on numerous occasions to indulge in some rowing on the tranquil Avon. According to one source, Seddon was heavily involved in the Broughton Amateur Rowing Club on the River Irwell at home and could be considered "an oarsman of no mean distinction" who is "passionately fond of this sport".

A day was given over to work on Australian Rules under the tutelage of McShane and Lawlor, finished off with a 17-a-side game. The *Otago Daily Times* reported: "This morning the Englishmen had a punt-about at Lancaster Park. In the afternoon first practice at the Victorian game was held, a Canterbury team composed mainly of old Victorian players having been organised to meet the Englishmen. The latter soon picked up the main points of the game and succeeded in beating the Canterbury team by six goals to nothing. The Englishmen, however, notwithstanding their victory, felt inclined to ridicule the game; but of course it is premature to form an opinion till two first-class teams have been at work."

'Three-Quarter Back' of the *Otago Witness* viewed the game with interest but as with many bred on Rugby, found little to enthuse about, writing: "I cannot say that I was impressed with the beauties of the Victorian or Australian game—not Australasian, for it is not played by any club in New Zealand and it is impertinence to give it the bigger title. Making all allowance for the fact that most of the players were new to it, the game proved far from interesting. Its points were easily to be picked up but there was little to be found in them. The encouragement given to long and accurate kicking is to my mind about the only merit in the game—and that is a merit which the Rugby game, rightly played, possesses."

The return match against the Canterbury Rugby representatives was played on a Lancaster Park surface rendered slippery by a heavy fog which came in the night before, and continued most of the day. Being a workday and with the damper conditions prevailing, a crowd of 3000 was probably more than could have been reasonably hoped for. Seddon again lost the coin toss. The whole of the first half was of a give-and-take nature, each side having several narrow escapes. But there was no score until barely moments before half-time, Bumby and Nolan carried the ball into the Canterbury 25 and some hard work put in by the forwards on the goal line saw Alf Penketh touch down for the Lions near the posts. Paul missed the conversion. By some means Stoddart received a very nasty knock on the ankle while engaged in a heavy piece of work during the first half and was out of the contest for nearly 30 minutes. He finished the game but wouldn't play again until Sydney.

Despite their hard play in the second stanza, Canterbury could not prevent their opponents breaking through; at every opportunity the Lions forwards and halves hurled the ball to the backs and Nolan secured three unconverted tries. The wet made the ball heavy and greasy and along with the difficult angles Paul was presented with, it is not surprising none of his goal attempts were successes. Four unconverted tries meant a 4-0 victory.

With four games now complete—and no win by any of the home teams—Christchurch's *Press* argued that much was still to be gained in any match even if victory could not be achieved: "It is nothing that the colonial teams find themselves somewhat overmatched by their visitors. The same pluck and endurance which has made the name of Englishmen renowned throughout the world still enables them to fight a losing battle and to do their best in the struggle. There can be no doubt that the visit of the English team to the colonies will be of incalculable benefit to our football players, if they will only take advantage of the lessons to be learnt from the English players."

In the early Thursday afternoon "the friends and admirers of the team" mustered in great strength at the White Hart Hotel, where the footballers were housed during their visit to Christchurch. The Canterbury RU handed over to Shrewsbury and Lillywhite a cheque for £208. As each of the Lions came out he met a volley of warmhearted hand-shakes and farewells. For the players' part, they all expressed regret at leaving and hoped Christchurch would be on their itinerary when they return near the start of September. The team was then taken to the railway station, where more well-wishers were there to send them off. A special carriage was provided for the team for the short journey to the port town of Lyttelton; from there they would take a steamship to the colony's capital city, Wellington, across the often treacherous Cook Strait that separated the South and North Islands. As the train moved off, three cheers were given for the team, which were as enthusiastically returned and all joined in singing *Auld Lang Syne*. Arriving in Lyttelton, the tourists were told that heavy fog would make the crossing too perilous to attempt, so they would have to wait another 24 hours to sail. When they finally got on board, they found the ship had been overbooked. There were just five bunks for the 26 men in the group.

An account of the troubled Wellington visit has been given earlier. The first game, which included the accusations of rough bordering upon brutal play, intoxicated footballers and was played within hours of the team arriving in Wellington, ended in a draw (one try each). The second and far friendlier match, against 'Mr. Roberts' XV' was won by the Lions 4-1. In total the two games drew about 10,000 spectators, though the latter game was played in light rain and, of course, was marred by the Wellington RU's efforts to wreck the match coming off at all. In Wellington's *The Evening Post* it was revealed "Mr. Lillywhite informs us that he is satisfied with the receipts of the English team so far, although he expected that the takings at Christchurch would have been larger. His percentage of gate money at Dunedin, Christchurch, and Wellington amounted to a little over £1,100."

"The interest in the game is very much more noticeable [in New Zealand] than in England," Seddon said. "I was amused the other day to see an account in the papers of a lad who had been brought up for stealing and on getting his sentence of seven days wanted to make a bargain with the judge to let him out to see the [Lions] football match and in return he would tell the name of a friend who had stolen a watch valued £7 10s! Whether or not the proposal was accepted did not appear."

Leaving Wellington Harbour and sailing up the North Island's west coast, the team's schedule provided for a stop-over on the way to Auckland, allowing a few hours in New Plymouth to play the Taranaki RU's team. "We left at six o'clock in the evening and went on board the *Wanaka*, a small coasting steamer bound for Taranaki," said Anderton. Again, more than half the team couldn't get a cabin to sleep in. "There was a dense fog in the night, which we crawled through safely, thanks to the captain, and landed at Taranaki at 12.30pm."

"We had only just time to get lunch before we had to don the war paint," added Seddon. "It could easily be seen this was a great day in Taranaki: flags were flying, a brass band parading the streets and great crowds of people making their way to the ground (New Plymouth Racecourse). At quarter-past two, two waggonettes, with large flags flying, drove us to the field of battle, the brass band heading the procession, followed by conveyances of every description, and some 50 to 60 ladies and gentlemen on horseback. The result of this, our [supposedly] easiest match, was a great surprise to everybody. We had left out of our team four or five of the best men, giving them a rest for the Auckland match, and then had all the best of the game, but was very unfortunate in not having the referee's decision in our favour. There were four [Bayly] brothers on the home side—one the captain, another a player, another the umpire, and the other the referee; so between them we got out of the affair perhaps as well as we could expect, being declared beaten by 1-0." When the home side crossed for their try, 1000 people invaded the field to congratulate the try-scorer. "You can draw your own inference why we lost," said Anderton. "Candidly speaking, we got half-a-dozen tries that afternoon which were not allowed, Thomas alone getting two in as many minutes, and when there were about nine minutes still to play, Seddon objected to this continual disallowance of points when his side scored, whereupon the noble referee blew his whistle and declared the match over!"

The final disallowed try came after the Lions, as they had done in other games, surprised the opposition by taking a quick throw-in from touch near the amber-and-blacks' goal line. After the ball was bounced into the field of play, one of the tourists snavelled up the pigskin, and dived over for what they all knew was a legitimate try; then the Taranaki captain Alf Bayly appealed to umpire G. Bayly who looked to referee F. Bayly who blew his whistle and ruled no try. After Seddon remonstrated without success with the referee for 90 seconds, the latter called full-time, and the 3000 strong crowd rushed the ground. "Our very victorious opponents quickly skipped the field, and left us alone in our glory to saunter after them as we pleased!" said Anderton. Shrewsbury added: "It has given us a lesson, [henceforth] we are having a voice in the matter of refereeing [appointments]". Leaving the ground the continual cheering "Taranaki every time!" accompanied the Lions all the way back to the quay and could still be heard until they were safely away on the steamer, starting out on its passage to Auckland.

Meanwhile in Wellington, "for fully half-an-hour before the final result came to hand the pathway in front of the *Evening Post* publishing office was blocked by a crowd of between 200 and 300 persons all eager for the posting of the telegram [from New Plymouth]. When it arrived, about 5.15pm, it was read out to the crowd, and the news that the Taranaki team had beaten our redoubtable visitors was received with hearty cheering."

Too Much Whisky, Too Many Women

"If the first principles of sensible living are neglected, failure is bound to result. Excessive drinking, excessive eating, excessive smoking, late hours and other unnatural things tell against the footballer."
Arthur Conan Doyle, "The Moral Value of Football"

Three lusty cheers were given by all and the procession to the ground was on its way, leaving the meeting point of the Imperial Hotel in the Auckland commercial district, and onwards to Potter's Paddock [now Alexandra Park]. It is where the Lions would meet what was regarded for many decades before and after, the best Auckland representative team to have ever stepped onto a Rugby field.

"It could easily be seen our visit had long been looked forward to and much spoken of," Seddon said. "Auckland players had been in training for six weeks, having engaged two men for that purpose; being compelled to practice every day, and be in bed by 9 o'clock every evening, their supporters and they themselves were quite confident they would lower the Red, White, and Blue."

The public interest had been thoroughly roused, and a record crowd of over

12,000 had been expected. Unfortunately, the rain came, cutting the number in half. It was a tough blow for Shrewsbury and Lillywhite. A second game was to be played on the Queen's Birthday holiday five days later, so there was still hope for the promoters to make up the short fall. Many were also dismayed that Stoddart's injury would prevent his inclusion. "I am afraid Stoddart will still have to take a backseat," Shrewsbury explained. "There is a general disappointment felt in all places visited at his inability to take part in the game, as he has got a big name as *the* crack English three-quarter back."

The convoy was headed by a large brass band, with the two teams "in place of honour" immediately behind in four-horse carriages. Then came what seemed a thousand people in all modes of transport—in coaches, brakes, buses, on horseback, many on foot. Trams full to the brim with their human cargo continuously made runs to the gates at the front of the ground. As was both customary and necessary, the footballers had donned their playing gear at the hotel and ribbons, flags and streamers in the colours of both teams (Auckland played in blue and white hoops) adorned the vehicles and many buildings along the way.

"The greatest enthusiasm prevailed," wrote Shrewsbury. "The verandahs of the houses we passed being crowded with cheering people, the colours of the two sides being very prevalent. The Red, White and Blue were not absent, many flags of this colour having been specially made by English residents here and profusely displayed. One thing that struck us being very noticeable was a view on passing what was evidently an English resident's house; a very small girl waving a very large flag of our colours. You could scarcely see the little thing behind the flag!"

Just before the teams took the field, Seddon was handed a telegram.

To the Captain of the English Football Team,
England expects that every man this day will do his duty.
Yours,
GREAT BRITAIN

TOO MUCH WHISKY, TOO MANY WOMEN

The match was a very fast and good spirited battle, reckoned by the *Auckland Star* to be "the most exciting ever played here". The greasy and heavy ball negated the British hand-passing tactics, which was disappointing as much to the spectators as the team itself. The visitors took a 6-0 lead after two converted tries, the result of forwards following up kicks and seizing opportunities. The first came when Speakman took a pot shot at goal, the ball fell short but Seddon had pursued hard and picked up the rolling ball to cross for the try. The second was obtained in an equally simple manner, with Anderton following up fast from a drop goal attempt from Haslam which landed in the in-goal amidst the Auckland players' feet—here too the ball was still moving and Anderton dived among the forest of legs and scored a well-deserved try.

Auckland were hampered by injury to their captain, Bob Whiteside, who was generally regarded as the best footballer in the colony. An Auckland rep since 1882, he was a tall man standing over six foot high, dark-haired and sporting the obligatory Victorian-era moustache. Whiteside lacked the bulk though of the Britishers and late in the first half one of the opposing forwards charged at him just as he was taking a pass; he was seen to collapse to the ground, the result of a severe knock to the knee. Play was stopped for some minutes and he was examined by Dr. Smith (who was on the field in the role of Lions' umpire). It was found Whiteside had badly wrenched the ligament of his right knee. In spite of his injury which made him entirely ineffective, his teammates stood him back up and like any good toy soldier he held his place in the line. This immediately brought the home crowd to their feet in wild applause and cries of "Bravo Whiteside! Bravo!"

A few minutes later Auckland crossed for a try near the corner flag and Whiteside, seemingly desiring to either contribute in some manner or as a display of his stoicism, decided he would take on the role of placing the ball for his team's kicker. Despite the angle, the goal was a success and amidst the cheers even many of the Lions were seen to be clapping the effort. Now with a chance of drawing the game, Auckland lifted; the ball was passed to Whiteside. Looking up he saw he had a clear unchallenged run of 20 yards before him, so he set off but before gaining speed he fell face first to the ground, his leg completely giving way. Play was again stopped for a few minutes, many of the players of both sides pressing the Auckland skipper to "Give it away, man" (retire from the field), but he refused, and again they stood him on his feet and put him back in his place. Not long afterwards Whiteside could again to be seen in possession of the ball but being near the touch-line, one of the Lions instinctively threw him out of play—he fell straight on his injured knee. This time there was no more stubborn resistance, the hero gave up the struggle and as he was assisted to the grandstand, he was accompanied by another round of applause. A few days later he received the sad news that he would never play Rugby again.

The last few minutes of the game were consumed by "a fierce scrummage" that locked the ball up in the dark among the forwards, which for once suited the Lions fine, as it killed-off any hope Auckland had of gaining a late try. Thus it was a victory to Britain 6-3. "The game was played in the very best of spirit," said Shrewsbury. "The most perfect good temper existed between the players on both sides; this was a marked and striking contrast to our match with Wellington."

Once again a caravan of vehicles and supporters accompanied and carried the two teams of wet, tired and muddy footballers back to the Imperial. Along the way they once more saw the little girl with her enormous Union Jack coloured flag; Seddon had the carriages stop. The Lions all got out and standing in a line across the front of the yard, at the captain's call all in unison gave a salute. Just as quickly they jumped back into the wagons and were on their way.

The team had five days free before the return match, apart from one morning spent at a training session of Australian Rules on Potter's Paddock. Put together with the trial game in Christchurch, it hardly seemed the four weeks in New Zealand had amounted to much preparation for what was laying in wait in Victoria and South Australia.

TOO MUCH WHISKY, TOO MANY WOMEN

The men had become more discerning about what invitations they were prepared to accept by the time they arrived in Auckland. "Many drives having been refused owing to our men's lack of interest in anything so common as driving," explained Seddon. "We accepted a day's fishing [provided by Auckland RU officials and some players], going by steamer some 15 miles out, where we anchored [Rangitoto reef]. Before commencing to fish a sweepstake of 2s. 6d. each was got up, £1 to go for the first fish caught, and 27s. 6d. for the largest. An old hand at the game succeeded in catching the first ... but Harry Eagles caught one which he mistook for a whale, thus winning the prize of 27s. 6d. After the fishing we weighed anchor and then we weighed into the saloon, where a substantial lunch was spread, each one doing his best to put away as much as possible of the good things lying about. Songs followed, half-past six bringing to a close a very pleasant and enjoyable day. The evening, as usual, was spent at the skating rink."

"Thursday morning was beautifully fine," wrote Seddon. The weather and the tea-totaller Lions captain was fit and ready for match day but his team was not. Anderton revealed after the tour that in the time between the two games "we were so besieged with invitations for banquets and balls and all the other paraphernalia of a giddy round of pleasure, which I may say we as willingly accepted and thoroughly enjoyed, that when we turned out for the match there was scarcely a man among us who was not dead out of form".

The public rolled-up in enormous numbers, topping well over 12,000; some reports claimed 15,000. There was again a giant procession to take the teams out to the ground and all appeared a perfect setting for an epic dry weather Rugby contest. There was an early hint the visitors were not in a serious mood for Rugby. "The Auckland team took the field first and on our putting in an appearance, gave three hearty cheers for England which compliment we returned, finishing up with Buffalo Bill's war cry, which seemed to amuse the spectators greatly," said Seddon. "Auckland kicked-off, and it was pretty evident our men were dead out of form, for there was a lack of the great dash that was so prominent in Saturday's match."

"We concerted to play a defensive game," said Anderton. "We managed to keep them at bay for some time, but at last a lucky drop at goal did us."

Auckland also gained an unconverted try and, in the circumstances, only losing 4-0 was probably more than the Lions deserved. The Auckland XV, the crowd, and the newspapers were happy though, the victory proving very popular. Charlie Madigan, who played a terrific game for the home side even though he broke his collarbone early in the contest, was carried shoulder high from the field. The *Otago Witness* wrote "Auckland was decisive, for this the Englishmen have only themselves to blame, as many of them having indulged in a long bout of revelry were almost useless against the perfectly-trained men pitted against them". The *Auckland Star* volunteered to purchase a silver cup for each Auckland player, inscribed with their name and position, as a souvenir.

Shrewsbury was livid; the Taranaki loss was one thing, but this defeat had been self-inflicted. "We simply lost the second match through our players not taking care of themselves," he said. "Too much whisky and women." He reasoned when the team came back to New Zealand the Auckland RU would demand a higher percentage of the gate-takings than if they had been beaten by the Lions in both games. Lillywhite suggested the defeat was "not by Auckland playing better than on Saturday, but through half our men being settled through fast life. Half-a-dozen worked like Trojans, but that was no good. Most of the rest were 'stiff'uns.' They might have kept quiet till the match was over."

The result didn't stop the carousing. With five days at sea ahead of the team there was little value in locking them in their rooms for their last night on New Zealand soil. "In the evening we were invited to a dance at the Pier Hotel, where everybody seemed thoroughly to enjoy themselves, the oyster and refreshment rooms (all free) adding much to the success of the affair," recalled Seddon. "The fun was fast and furious, up to six in the morning, when as daylight dawned they dropped off one by one in time to get home with the milk. Friday evening found our men lamenting over the thought of having to leave the same evening for Sydney. Still all good things must have an end."

While packing his bags, Dr. Brooks gave an interview to the *Auckland Star* in which he spoke of how pleasing their tour through New Zealand had been. "Our welcome in Dunedin was unquestionably the greatest welcome we have had yet throughout the colony, but with the single exception of Wellington, we have been treated to unstinted hospitality and receptions," Dr. Brooks said. "Even in Wellington there were exceptions and we received a cordial welcome in certain quarters."

"Our trip has been so far most thoroughly enjoyable," Seddon added. "We have received on every side the most lavish hospitality and have been treated with every kindness. We are greatly taken with the scenery and climate of the country—particularly the climate—and our only regret is that our stay in each New Zealand city is necessarily so short. We shall leave the colony with regret and wherever we go we shall not forget the kindly manner in which we have been received by everyone we have come in contact with." In his own letter home though he added that the relentless cycle of travelling, banqueting and playing had taken its toll. "The team would not have suffered the two defeats, if it had not been for the too good treatment extended to us by the New Zealanders," he wrote.

The New Zealand correspondent for Melbourne's *The Age* wrote: "Their progress has been such a hurried one through the colony that the visitors have never yet been seen in their true form. They have been lionised everywhere, with the inevitable effects upon their condition, and except at Dunedin they have had little or no practice. Fit and well, they would run rings around any provincial team, but at the same time they would have all their work cut out with a carefully selected team representing the whole colony and careful efforts will be made to arrange such a match on their return from Australia."

Shrewsbury downplayed all talk of possibly playing a combined New Zealand team in this opening leg of the tour; he feared a loss would damage the team's reputation in Australia and thus impact gate-takings. However, he didn't mind the idea for when the Lions came back later, as a loss then would not matter, financially at least.

"Rugby football here, it is far better than we expected to see," one member of the team said in an interview with *Press*. "English footballers, as a whole, have no conception to what extent Rugby football has progressed in New Zealand. Indeed, there is nothing ever heard of football in New Zealand at all in England."

"There is no doubt that we, as Englishmen, coming out from Home, have been astonished at the great strides Rugby football has made in New Zealand," said Dr. Brooks. "All the forwards we have met here have been stronger than ours—of better physique than ourselves—but they have been lacking in combination. They have been very much superior to ourselves in breaking through the mauls and bursting-away on our backs. They have still got a lot of things to learn."

"Throughout New Zealand the men, individually, are quite equal to our own players, but they seem to play exactly as we did in England two or three years ago," Seddon said. "In England the game is cut so very fine that we have found out all the fine points and we utilised our knowledge in New Zealand and whilst the players here perhaps take a couple out of five chances, we score four out of five.

"The New Zealanders do not play a proper, concerted game. Sometimes a man got the ball and could have passed to someone in a good position to run in, but the man seemed to forget that there were 14 other men on his side and his sole idea was to score a try and everything else went out of his head except the plan of crossing the line. In our team the men play to each other and pass at the proper opportunities."

"New Zealanders have not got a good modern knowledge of the game—they want to study its finer points," said Brooks.

Speaking in the lead up to the arrival in the Dominion of Arthur Harding's 1908 Lions team, Harry Roberts—who had captained the hastily cobbled together XV against the visitors in Wellington—was in no doubt that "New Zealand football had been revolutionised by the visit of Seddon's team, whereas Bedell-Sivright's [1904 Lions] combination had taught us nothing in any department of the game". The *NZ Truth* agreed that Roberts' claim "was an absolutely true bill; Seddon's men taught us how to pass and the feinting tactics and the art of screwing the scrum, all of which were turned to such profitable account."

Dave Gallaher, captain of the illustrious 1905 All Blacks in Britain, who was 14 years old when the first Lions visited, wrote in *The Complete Rugby Footballer* (his famous book co-authored by fellow tourist Billy Stead) that "it was left to Stoddart's [sic] British team to show Maoriland the fine points of the game and the vast possibilities of combination. The exhibitions of passing they gave were most fascinating and impressive to the New Zealander, who was not slow to realise the advantages of these methods. One may safely say that, from that season, dates the era of high class Rugby in the colony".

Make the British Lion Bite the Dust

"The Britishers having met with two reverses in New Zealand will not appear quite as formidable as heretofore to our men — a fact which will tend to embolden them more in their endeavours to make the British Lion bite the dust."
The Australian Town and Country Journal, June 2, 1888

"On approaching Sydney Harbour our men were utterly dumbfounded at the magnificence of the scenery," recalled Seddon of the view from the *Zealandia* as she came within sight of the sheer rock cliff walls that run to the north and south of the entrance of Port Jackson. Then once inside, a turn to the south, then west, and the vista of the Harbour opened ahead. "It is certainly beyond description, and in our opinion, it maintains its reputation of being the finest harbour in the world."

The five-day trip from Auckland had not been a pleasant return to the sea for the tourists. "A very rough passage we had," Seddon said to the waiting newspaper reporters. "One of our men caused much laughter the other morning when being chaffed for his melancholy look, sorrowfully remarked,

'Let me put my foot on shore and you will never get me on the water again!"' The *Zealandia* had begun her journey in San Francisco (May 5), bringing to Sydney the American mail and the latest newspapers from the USA, the latter thoroughly devoured by the city's newspapers, who re-published, clipped, commented upon, and cabled the fresh content over the following days. The ship also contained a stowaway, a 21-year-old-man making an appearance when hunger got the better of him—the captain handed him to the Sydney Water Police and he soon had a choice between a £5 fine or two months gaol.

On the dock at Darling Harbour to welcome the Lions were dozens of footballers and NSWRU officials and others wanting to see the team. The enthusiasm for the tourists was no less in Sydney than it had been in New Zealand. Perhaps the team would eventually tire of the scale of the receptions they were meeting wherever they went, but to every city and town they arrived in, they were all exciting and new visitors. The tour party and their luggage were gathered up into carriages, driven up to the Oxford Hotel where they were to be housed and given a welcome function by the NSWRU (though it was still then going by its 1874 founding name of The Southern RFU—whether the Southern was the Southern Hemisphere, the Southern Cross, or the southern equivalent of England's RFU, no one has ever deciphered). Passing through the city, countless flags in sky blue ("Australian blue") were seen everywhere, part of a year long commemoration of Australasia's centenary of British settlement. The Oxford was Sydney's most prestigious hotel in the late 1880s but paled much when compared to the establishments of the gold rush cities of Dunedin and Melbourne.

No one knew it at the time, but the first British Lions team to Australia was officially welcomed by the man who would become the nation's first prime minister, Edmund Barton. A Rugby footballer of modest talents at Sydney University in the 1870s, Barton kept a keen interest in the game, being an official of the University's Rugby club and a vice-president of the NSWRU. Among the champagne toasts and musical accompaniments, the obligatory speeches were delivered. In proposing a toast to the health of the visitors Barton asked the hundred or so men gathered to consider "the fact that they are not only an English team but a British one, as some of the players are from Scotland, and the English and Scottish universities are also represented. This is the first occasion on which a football team has come here from the Old Country and we hope that the visit will lead to reciprocity on the part of Australians".

At a reception the following day held by the Sydney lord mayor at the town hall, Seddon expressed the same goal: "We hope that that we will leave behind a good impression of our prowess on the football field and I look forward at no distant date to seeing an Australian team in England". It took two more decades but in 1908 the Wallabies sailed to the UK; seven years after Australia became a federated nation—and Barton was elected prime minister.

Asked about the tour-opener against NSW at the SCG, Seddon replied: "We will probably be able to put our best team in the field for Saturday's match. Stoddart and Banks will likely don the jersey again, neither of them having played in the last five or six matches. We have been rather unfortunate in getting men disabled." Though all the tourists had got on the field in New Zealand, only Seddon and Eagles turned out in every match. For Stoddart a return to the SCG would mean achieving the unique feat of having played for the England XI in cricket and the British Lions XV in Rugby on the same ground within six months.

Confidence was very high among the tourists. "We think we shall win every match under Rugby rules," said Seddon. That the visitors had been defeated gave NSW supporters hope. *The Australian Town and Country Journal* (*Town & Country*) suggested: "The Britishers, having met with two reverses in New Zealand, will not appear quite as formidable as heretofore to our men—a fact which will tend to embolden them more in their endeavours to make the British Lion bite the dust." *The Australasian Sketcher* proffered a more balanced view: "As the New Zealanders can fairly claim superiority over any part of Australia at the Rugby game, these performances of the English team, quite as much as any reputation they may bring with them, prove them to be good players."

"There is not the slightest doubt that it will be a red-letter day in the football world, and that there will be a large attendance of the public," wrote 'Mark' in *Town & Country*. "In my peregrinations I find people who hardly ever saw a football match looking forward with much interest to the coming struggle and some of them even have gone in to study the rules and intricacies of the game, so that they may be able to appreciate it all the better."

That an important match was coming up in a few days had no bearing on limiting off-field matters. "Go where you would, the most cordial feeling prevailed; a picnic [and ferry cruise] down Sydney Harbour, and a banquet was given by the Rugby Union," one player wrote to a British paper.

Seddon added: "Since our arrival we have met with the most hearty welcome at every turn, free passes being given us by the managers of all the theatres in Sydney, the Alhambra being the favourite resort, where they are playing *Dorothy*, with a Manchester favourite (W. Elton) as the bailiff. By the invitation of the NSWRU we were taken by steamer to Manly Beach, where 100 sat down to dinner, after which we sailed round the harbour. The scenery is simply lovely and the Sydney people don't forget to tell you of it!"

Naturally, the skating rinks were sought out and Sydney had some large rinks to choose from, that often hosted crowds of up to 4000 patrons; while the highly anticipated opening of the Grand Crystal Palace rink in York Street would be just after the team left for Melbourne, there was also the Paragon, the Sydney Elite and the City Skating Rink.

The NSW team (or, as they called it outside of the city, "The pick of the Sydney clubs" team) had the rare distinction of having two players who in later life were knighted—Charles Wade and Henry Braddon. In another remarkable coincidence, both are today recognised as international representatives by other nations: Wade for England (1882-86) and Braddon for New Zealand (1884). In the "dark days" of the early 1920s, when Rugby Union in Australia was reduced to little more than eight Sydney first grade teams and the city's private schools, and newspapers were openly referring to the code being "crushed out of existence", NSWRU official Richard Arnold told a meeting: "So long as Sir Henry Braddon (NSWRU President) and Sir Charles Wade take such a keen interest in rugger, we can be sure that there is no fear that the Union will die."

One of Oxford's and England's greatest players of the early 1880s, Harry Vassall wrote in 1923's *RFU Annual* that Wade "was the best three-quarter we ever had in England. At Oxford they were slow to find him, but when at last they discovered he could play rugger, they soon learnt that he was an extraordinary man. At times it was practically impossible to stop him. Wade was the most robust runner of his time and perhaps of any time. He simply ploughed through his foes, throwing them off his hips by a sort of shift or shuffle. He ran very fast and straight and had a wonderful swerve when going at full pace, by which he foiled the tackler, who only received a nasty one from his iron thigh."

Braddon, born to English parents in India, spent his youth in Germany, France, and then England (attending the Rugby-playing Dulwich College in London) before finishing school in Launceston, Tasmania—his father had moved there, eventually becoming the colony's premier. In the early 1880s Braddon played Australian Rules for the Launceston FC, the Northern Tasmania combined team, and was the founding captain of the Latrobe FC. Working as a bank clerk, he accepted a higher paid position in Invercargill (New Zealand), where he played Rugby, appeared in the Otago team in 1883 and then came to Sydney with the first New Zealand side in 1884, remaining in the colony after the tour. Now against the Lions he was making his NSW debut, chosen at full-back, primarily for his deft tackling and accurate long kicking.

Seddon and the team's management committee acceded to the NSWRU's request to use local points scoring values for games (in NSW two unconverted tries were the equal of goal, whereas under the RFU in England and New Zealand it took three unconverted tries to equal a goal):

- 4 (not 3) points for a drop-kicked goal or a "field goal" during play
- 4 (not 3) points for a place-kicked or drop-kicked goal from a fair catch

- 3 (not 2) points for a place-kicked conversion
- 2 (not 1) point for a try

In another difference that evolved in NSW the position names of the backs, other than full-back, had come to be known as quarter-backs (instead of half-backs) and half-backs (instead of three-quarter-backs). As in New Zealand, 'scrimmage' was in far more in use than 'scrummage'.

The conditions for the match were perfect for watching and playing Rugby. The NSW governor general and many others filled the SCG's members pavilion, and the remainder of the 12,000-strong crowd stood or sat on the low embankment that encircled the picket fenced playing field. Among the throng Seddon spotted familiar faces of old from Rugby clubs in Lancashire: "We are not short of supporters out here. Herbert Fair, alias 'Buck,' the famous Swinton three-quarter back of some years ago, was trying his lungs in a most severe manner. Also I recognised sporting our colours Howard Mudie, an old Broughtonian; Cass Sadler and J. Holt, old Broughton Rangers past players."

When the 30 players came out in their coloured uniforms to complete the picture, a prettier setting is hard to imagine. The Lions of course in red, white and blue, with similar caps, while NSW, who "looked regular 'mashers,' wore dark maroon jerseys, and had upon their breasts a blue shield with the five stars of Australia's cross", blue socks, "their knickerbockers were pure white—caps set off the whole affair, being of maroon velvet with a gold band, and bearing upon the peaks the letters N.S.W. 1888". The NSWRU changed the jersey in 1892 to the colony's sky blue colour and waratah badge. Their first jersey in 1882 was olive green, sporting large stars cut out in white fabric, configured to the Southern Cross constellation.

"The visitors are all men of fine physique, the majority being of medium height, compactly built, and muscular," wrote a correspondent for *The Argus*. "The NSW team included some fairly heavy men but they contrasted unfavourably with their sturdy opponents." *Town & Country* referred to the hopes of the home supporters being dashed "when the burly forms of the Britishers filed out from the pavilion a change came over the spirit of their dreams—the difference in the two teams, physically speaking, was most marked—the visitors from the parent country having greatly the advantage in weight and height."

Almost from the outset the tourists proved to be too clever at passing and taking advantage of openings to cut through the opposition defence. While, yet again, a colonial pack had a slight advantage in its scrummaging, it didn't offer much help. The *Town & Country* lauded the example of the Lions' hand-passing: "The Britishers mastered our representatives in their admirable passing. No such passing was ever seen here like it. For timing, accuracy, and judgement it was simply grand. Very seldom indeed were the passes made by the visitors interfered with, until the ball had gone into the hands of four or five men; and the amount of ground covered during these pretty performances was always greatly to their advantage. Quite different was it with our men, who, with three or four exceptions, clung, as usual, tenaciously to the ball, until they were brought to Mother Earth; or when they attempted to pass they did it so badly and with such poor judgement that the ball very often found a resting place in the hands of some of the Britishers, who never neglected to make a better use of it." *The Referee,* using italics to emphasise to its Rugby-playing readers the crucial innovation, called the team work "utterly unselfish, *passing before being collared*".

The home side found dealing with the opposing forwards hard enough but when they somehow succeeded to find a way through, their 'reward' was to face just as powerful and certain defenders before them in the halves and three-quarters. The dazzling runs which were expected from the fast NSW backs did not take place at all, as they were not powerful enough to fend away or charge down the initial British tackling.

Once the Lions sized up their opponents by midway through the opening half, they put their passing game away, preferring instead to use raw power. Either mode would have achieved an easy victory. Implementing the latter option showed they had a ruthless streak to their character. "They are a weak team and our players just did as they liked with them," wrote Shrewsbury.

The Sydney Morning Herald noted that "passing and dribbling were not the main features of the game. Indeed, there was not a great deal of finessing, as the British players made most of their scores by downright hard running, assisted by fending or charging. Seddon, the British captain, however, got his touch (try) by a clever dribble close to the line. Stoddart's running and fending were the theme of general admiration."

Apart from the few heavy players NSW possessed, for the rest of the local men any attempt at fending-off the visitors was of no avail. Wade came nowhere near matching his reputation. Paul confronted NSW's Moulton, "caught him with one hand, without having to budge a step, and tumbled him over without being obliged to call his other hand into play at all". Whenever the British players got through the forwards, they found the NSW backs were lightweights and could not stop them. Stoddart fended off the lighter opponents time after time, and in securing one try, Bumby flung two would-be tacklers out of the way by charging them. His rushes carrying the ball were remarkably effective and his rapid and long-field runs were instrumental in securing three tries for the Lions.

Very quickly it turned into a rout. "From first to last the Englishmen ran through our players like water through the Nepean [River] supply pipes," wrote *The Referee* after the Lions' 18-2 victory, the visitors running in six tries to one. An account of the match in the *Otago Witness* concluded: "The Sydney men seem to be out-generalled at all points of the game, the Englishmen playing better together and showing an absence of selfishness which the losers might well have copied. The individual play of the English team was excellent. Stoddart surprised those who knew what he was capable of, and on one occasion, when an opponent stooped to collar (tackle) low, he sprang into the air, and clearing him with ease, gained an easy touch (try)." Another added that with the leap "he fairly electrified the people, who testified their approval of his cleverness with rounds of applause". It was also noted "Anderton and Haslam deserved special mention, as also does Seddon, the captain". Apparently of great Victorian-era mirth was when "one of the visitors had his shirt torn off his back, he was the object of much laughter as he ran into the pavilion".

The Sydney Morning Herald was pleased that at least the British dominance led to an open game, where the "scrimmages—the wearisome episode of Rugby football" were quickly over and infrequent. The newspaper was critical of "the British tackling [which] was in the main, very high, many of the players going for neck holds". A complaint that would dog the team all tour was that the Lions were incorrigible at playing the off-side game. Yet, the code's laws did not prohibit off-side play, merely regulated what could and couldn't be done. Eagles in particular had a penchant for loitering upfield waiting for play and the ball to come back to him. A defender waiting to take a catch could be harassed by an off-side player, provided he didn't touch his opponent until he had run five yards with the ball. Of course, should this close-up stalking cause him to muff the catch, the off-side player was now on-side. The off-side laws weren't so rigid that Rugby was ever akin to two standing armies facing and shooting volleys at each other. "Lots of fine points played by us have met with the disapproval of the spectators through their not understanding the game properly," said Seddon.

The Sydney Mail joined the chorus lamenting the lack of robust men among the city's clubs. "The physical contrast always proclaimed that pretty loudly. We do not get the right stamp of men here for international football. Our players show up very well in club matches but when it comes to hustling against nuggety-built men weighing 12st and 13st—and very fast to boot—they simply get left. It is necessary to take a turn among the miners, coal heavers, lumpers, masons, blacksmiths etc. before we can find the proper stamina for Rugby footballers. It will never be found at the desk or the counter."

The temperate weather conditions of Sydney meant cricket very early on established a "season" of some nine months long, starting in September and refusing to pull up stumps until the end of May. As that left football with a relative short period in the field—coupled with concerns about the risk of injury from Rugby—most of the city's cricketers opted for rest or some other sport. Whereas in Melbourne, where football often got underway in April and the local code was born as an intended means to keep cricketers fit and cricket fields manageable during winter, the cricketer-footballer was a far more common species.

Even more popular than cricket with Sydney's young men and boys at the time were rowing and sailing—the result of the happy coincidence of the city's climate and its abundance of waterways. "Cricket in England is much better than it is in Australia," Test cricketer Syd Gregory said in 1890, reasoning: "There [in England] every boy in the street knows cricket, as well as the Sydney boys do boating, or the Melbourne fellows football."

Unlike in many other cities in the Empire, Sydney's working class were not big participants in football, especially Rugby. And those that were rarely found themselves in representative teams. "We will never be able to put a team in the field composed for the most part, of toil-hardened citizens such as are the English and New Zealand players," declared *The Referee*. "It is a well known fact that most of the very best Rugbeians in England, and all the crack Association [soccer] players are working men. In Victoria, too, where they have brought their game under their own rules, to a height of popularity unknown in any part of the world, where the population is proportionate, all the pick of the players in the principal clubs are artisans."

"In New Zealand," continued *The Referee*, "they encourage working men to join the clubs and give them a show in inter-provincial matches. In NSW there is not one working man to be found playing in any important fixture." Looking at the selected NSW side that faced the Lions seven of the men were ex-Sydney University students and, as delicately put by that same journal, "the whole are young fellows who, for the most part, have never done any harder work than that required to propel a billiard cue with sufficient force to get an all round cannon".

While Rugby was the preferred football code of Sydney, it was far from being the most chosen sport to watch. Sydney and its surrounding suburbs had a population of about 300,000, some 50,000 less than Melbourne.

While the SCG was used for representative Rugby games, the Trustees, in the interest of fairness, also made it available for soccer and Australian Rules on many Saturdays.

"We are sorry to see how poorly the game of football [Rugby or that under any other rules] is supported by the public of NSW," wrote *The Sydney Sporting Life* that winter. "They won't patronise cricket, football, cycling, or even racing, as they do in Melbourne." A Sydney sporting man wrote to a friend in England, noting "Jim Lillywhite and Shrewsbury, who are immense favourites in Sydney, are with the [Lions] team, and everyone is glad they had a 'bumper house' on Saturday, for their cricket season, from climatic reasons, proved so unsatisfactory that everyone would rejoice to see them recoup their losses. Still the expenses of the team are estimated at no less an average than £400 a week, and *S. S. and L.* will require large gates to make the trip profitable. On leaving Sydney the team will go to Melbourne, where they will have to play according to Victorian rules. To one born and bred according to Rugby, the Victorian game cannot be appreciated."

Despite the "bumper house" Shrewsbury was not pleased, convinced the tour promoters had been short-changed. He had seen many cricket numbers posted for SCG days, so he had some experience of gauging the crowd sizes there. "We were done out of £100 if one penny!" he privately claimed. "I could have sworn there were 12,000 present yet the returns only show a little over 7000. They took over £200 in the grandstand. Will put some private persons on [the entry gates] to watch next Saturday."

Stoddart's leap found an impressionable following during the tour, soon horrifying mothers of young boys across the colonies, as their precious darlings tried to emulate the daring feat. Nowadays it against the IRB laws, being classed as "dangerous play". Among those who were regulars at the hurdling caper were two All Blacks either side of 1900: Albert Asher, the famous Maori, and Barney Armit. The latter sadly proved with fatal consequence how absurdly insane soaring above defenders was, when he was suddenly flipped over by a tackler, and came down to earth head and neck first. In England in the 1910s Billy Batten for Hunslet and Hull in the Northern Union (rugby league) was famous for the move (his son later too) and on the 1921 Springboks' visit to Sydney, winger and 1920 Olympic hurdler, Attie van Heerden, astounded all with his try-scoring leaps. The most lauded and spoken of, in Australia at least, came in 1907 at the SCG when thousands of supporters went delirious after NSW's home-bred star Dally Messenger scored a try by leaping over the backs of four All Black forwards about to bury him on their goal line. He was five years old when the Lions and Stoddart came to Sydney.

Whistle and Rifle

"Football, hunting, love, and war are the only Homeric things which our civilisation still retains."
William Henry Denham Rouse, *A History of Rugby School*, 1898

"Starting for Bathurst on Tuesday morning at 9.30am, the journey over the Blue Mountains by the Zig-Zag railway was the grandest sight imaginable," said Seddon. "One part we were 4000 feet above the sea level and looking through the clouds on the village below which, having the sun shining on the blue-coloured rocks, was a sight most of us will remember for some time. Getting to our destination by 5 o'clock, we were met by a large concourse of football officials and players."

Bathurst is approximately 200km to the west of Sydney, and was the site of Australia's first gold rush in early 1851. Today it is better known for the annual October V8s motor car endurance race at Mount Panorama. When the Lions came in 1888 the town had a population of 8000 and, indicative of what sort of place it was, during the mid-1890s economic downturn, it still managed to support 61 operating pubs.

For Shrewsbury and Lillywhite it was a welcome return visit, having played cricket in Bathurst with their England team in January 1887. There were many old acquaintances among the footballers and townspeople on the railway platform giving three loud "Hurrahs!" as the train with the Lions pulled to a stop. As usual, all then adjourned to the pub, on this occasion Shanahan's Family Hotel (still there today), where the team were formally welcomed over a bumper or two of champagne and toasts to "the Britishers" and "the Bathurst Rugby Union". The entertaining extended into the late of the evening.

The following afternoon the two teams were taken from the town in decorated horse-drawn carriages out to the Bathurst Cricket Ground for the match. A large crowd nearing 2000 were present, many obtaining a better view by sitting or standing on their dray wagons, others lined the picket fence and cycle track that circumvented the playing arena. The little grandstand was full, the staff of the new refreshment room were run off their feet and the local brass band provided entertaining musical interludes before and during the game. The presence of a good number of ladies in their colourful full-length dresses completed the picture.

Sometimes reporters, especially in home towns if the locals were beaten, begin with "the game was a hard-fought one through-out". This time though it was an accurate summation of the battle. It had been on first glance of the two teams "thought the superior physique, weight, and practice of the Britishers would give them an easy victory over the country men". But the home side proved unexpectedly strong in their forwards and quite held their own till the last half-hour, when fitness was beginning to tell and confusion over the flag-whistle system brought them undone.

Neither team seemed capable of landing a goal of any kind, so it became a game of unconverted try chasing unconverted try. The Lions got out to a 4-0 lead with two tries then Bathurst came back with one of their own, leaving the score 4-2 at half-time. As often happened in Rugby, both teams gathered in a circle to take refreshments while enjoying a friendly chat. The *Bathurst Free Press and Mining Journal* had observed that "the passing of the Britishers was greatly admired and after the game had proceeded for some time, it was evident that the local team were profiting by the lessons being taught".

The second half began with Eagles, always a resourceful man in a difficulty, on his knees and elbows crawling his way over the goal line under and between the legs of defenders to plant the ball for a try; this time Anderton got the conversion. But "the Bathurst boys were working like Trojans" and "never lost courage" which was soon rewarded when they crossed for their second try. They were doing better than NSW had done of making a game of it.

As happens with any flawed regulatory system, sooner or later it will come undone, and here the game swung on it. On half-way the Lions tried one of their quick throw-ins from touch, Eagles picked up the leather, but almost immediately the home umpire held up his flag for the throw not being straight. The flag of Lions' umpire Dr. Smith's went up in concurrence, and all the Bathurst team stood about while Eagles sauntered in for a try under the posts. However, inexplicably, the referee did not blow his whistle when both flags went up, even though under the laws the play unquestionably should have been whistled dead. Seddon wasn't satisfied the ball hadn't been thrown straight and perhaps with Taranaki in mind, pointed out that Bathurst RU alone chose the referee and therefore refused to relinquish the try. This caused some dissent among the crowd, "who groaned and hissed the visitors, demanding that the ball should be returned" to the half-way for a scrum. No heed was taken. Anderton missed the goal from in front and the game went on. As every footballer has known ever since, the unwritten rule is "always play to the whistle". Both teams got another try each, leaving the full-time score in favour of the Lions 13-6. Despite the local disquiet over the disputed line-out call, after the match both teams met loud cheers and applause heading to the stand.

The traditional post-match smoking concert was of a typical nature, mixing with "the Bathurst team and lovers of the game"—drinking, toasting, singing, smoking, reciting and laughing. It was revealed that as the day had been such a success on the field and off that negotiations had begun between the Bathurst RU and the Lions' promoters for the team to return for another match after they had been to Victoria and South Australia. Shrewsbury set a minimum guarantee of £80 and the committee was confident it could again raise that amount from generous local supporters. After the outing Seddon and some of his teammates enjoyed the next day, they made it very plain to Shrewsbury and Lillywhite they wanted to make a second visit to Bathurst.

"Thursday morning most of our players returned to Sydney, eight of us stopping to enjoy a day's kangaroo shooting, some 10 traps driving up to the hotel," told Seddon. For weeks after he was still giving vivid descriptions of the day, telling everyone and anyone this was "the best outing had during his trip". He wrote home:

> The drivers were instructed to drive us to the Rock Forest, some 11 miles away. The journey was very jolly, though perhaps dangerous. The way we were driven through the woods was not very comfortable, many times it seemed to us impassable, yet nothing troubled our horses and driver. Great trunks of trees were run over without a thought. Rocks and rivers were crossed as if they were driving along Market Street, while our men were firmly grasping the carriage side, expecting every moment to be sent down the mountain side. Kent remarking that were anyone at home to see us now they would think we had all gone mad. Anyway, we were all glad to once again stand on terra firma. And now commenced one of the most amusing parts of the outing. Hardly five minutes had passed before a large fire had been made and tea boiling. Two large trees were then cut down, so as to get long branches with forked ends; and soon each man was cooking his own steaks and chops. This being over, we were supplied with plenty of 'shot' [gunpowder muzzle-loaded into the rifle], and going in nine parties, four in each lot, we made for the North Jack Mountain. It was well worth the trip if only for the grand, wild, rocky scenery, but with this it was the jolliest day we have had since our arrival in the colonies. The return was made in darkness. We carried back a large number of hares, kangaroos, quails, pigeons, and parrots.

The Lions contingent that showed they could handle a rifle as well as a football returned to Sydney via the overnight train from Bathurst, walking through the doors of the Oxford Hotel just as the winter morning sun was emerging. Starting the following afternoon the team was to play three games in four days, with a second meeting with NSW first up. It wasn't an ideal preparation but no one was complaining.

The New Zealand team that came to Australia in 1897 had a similar first week but not with the expected ending. As with the Lions, barely days after getting off the boat, they too easily accounted for NSW (winning 13-8), and then set forth across the Blue Mountains, where they not only visited Bathurst, but went further west to Orange as well, to return again and meet NSW on the Saturday. Few doubted the black-jerseyed Kiwis would not win. How they were wrong. In a complete form reversal NSW flogged the visitors 22-8. The *New Zealand Times'* correspondent who accompanied the team wrote after the defeat: "They were a tattered lot of wrecks as they hobbled into the hotel on their return to Sydney from Bathurst and Orange."

The Bulletin, exhibiting its trademark unabashed candour, revealed that the New Zealanders had, in addition to playing football, "eaten, drunk, and knocked about considerably during the week. Such things, however, do not condone Maoriland's defeat, since to be a footballer is to play hard, drink hard, eat hard, sleep hard. When the [1888] English football team, for instance, was in Australia its drunks and disorderlies used to be stirred up by the policemen in the morning from door steps, bridges, footpaths, etc. used to have a bath, a rub down and feed—and then file out to the battle and win."

The weather was again fine for the game against NSW, perhaps on the warm side for football. Despite NSW's drubbing the previous Saturday, a crowd of around 7000 were present. The two future Rugby-playing knights were both out, Braddon injured and Wade overlooked. The play in the first half was all in favour of the home team—as happened in New Zealand a few times the Lions were down at the break, behind 6-2 thanks to a booming drop goal from Sydney University's Percy Colquhoun.

All the NSW resources seem to have been thrown into the first half effort; after the interval they did not score another point, whereas "Seddon and his merry men were soon on to the oval" no matter where it travelled. Through "better combination and generalship" they took control of the contest, notching up 16 unanswered points (five tries, two of which were converted) and an 18-6 win. Stoddart was again impressive, *Town & Country* writing that "Stoddart, among the Britishers, was a host in himself. Whenever he got hold of the ball [and it was very often] he made good use of it. His running was simply perfection, most of his opponents going over like nine pins before him. The struggle he had to go through before he secured his second try was a fine example of speed, strength, and endurance. No more deserving try than this was ever obtained on the ground." With Stoddart over injury and playing in every game, Anderton reflected upon his impact, saying "Stoddart, who was without doubt the finest three-quarter, if not actually the best player in the team, was simply grand at centre. His science of the code is something to be desired, and his effect on the rest of the men was very evident."

Sydney was a sabbath city in 1888—very little moved on Sundays. For the players, after church service for some, relaxing at the Oxford Hotel was the extent of the day's agenda. "All I want is a good cup of tea with hot or cold scones and butter," one of the tourists said. Time to write letters home perhaps. No doubt hours could be spent in the hotel's "handsomely furnished billiard room" or the "smoking room". The Oxford's two bars, as with every other public house in Sydney, were not permitted to be open on Sundays to the public. But being legitimate travellers staying at the hotel, the law allowed the "sale of liquors" to the visiting footballers. Others took a stroll through nearby Hyde Park to wander about, perhaps to escape on their own for a time (it wasn't infrequent that individual members left the team for days at a time, accepting invitations from relatives or newfound friends to stay and visit).

Advantage was also taken of the hotel's ample and continually replenished stack of British newspapers in its "well lighted reading room", the most recent additions a mere five weeks out of London. Everyone had a good laugh upon hearing one of the players read from a Bradford newspaper what had happened to Fred Bonsor, the England international who reneged on his tour agreement at the last moment, preferring the comforts of home life instead:

> Fred Bonsor, the noted half-back, is now enjoying the bitters of cycling. He was going down that bugbear of Yorkshire cyclists, Hollings Hill, when the brake of the tandem which he was riding failed, and he had to attempt the feat of knocking over an approaching horse and cart or smashing a wall. He chose to run into the wall. The result is that he is now suffering from a severely damaged shin bone.

A much sadder mood enveloped all when one of the team stumbled upon dire news from home in the *Manchester Times*. Seddon stated in a letter sent from Sydney to the *Manchester Courier*: "Much regret was expressed by all of our team on hearing the sad end of H.J. Fletcher, of the Manchester FC." Fletcher, his club and its home ground were very familiar to many members of the team.

> A sad accident occurred at a football match at Whalley Range on Saturday, which resulted in the death of one of the players. The match was a friendly game between past and present members of the Manchester Football Club, under Rugby rules, and one of the players was Mr. H.J. Fletcher, residing at Beancliffe, Eccles, 23 years of age, a buyer, in the employment of Messrs. A.P. Fletcher and co. In the course of the game he came into violent collision with another player and seriously injured his neck and spine. He was carried off the field and removed to the Royal Infirmary, where he died about nine o'clock on Sunday morning.

The risk of an injury from playing Rugby resulting in death was not high given the numbers that participated in it and how often they played; it certainly didn't belong in the perilous pastimes that involved waterways or guns. A contemporary wrote: "The sea and the river claim more victims in a year that football claims in a lifetime." However, as instanced by Fletcher's demise, given the robust nature of Rugby, and the limits of available medical treatment, fatalities were not unheard of. Today's Sydney club competition is for the 'Shute Memorial Shield', inaugurated in 1923 after the death of Sydney University prop forward Robert Shute, who suffered a cerebral hemorrhage after a heavy fall in a tackle on Manly Oval.

In the 1880s some employers in Britain and the colonies, issued instructions that any employee found playing football does so at the risk of instant dismissal if an injury occurred that meant time off work. In 1889 Monty Arnold, NSWRU secretary, caused newspaper controversy in the neighbouring colony when he suggested at a dinner in Sydney to support the visiting Victorian Rugby team that "in Melbourne if a young man took to Rugby football he was told by his employer that he need not come back to work again". Given Arnold had no connections to Melbourne he presumably was repeating something one of the Victorians had told him. The rumour had been heard before and it always rang true given the real and imagined risks appurtenant to Rugby football.

Town & Country wrote during 1888 that young men were attracted to playing Rugby *because* "it involves some element of personal danger; indeed, not a few people contend that involves rather too much of this element". Before the Lions sailed from England, Shaw organised insurance policies on behalf of each of the players but four of the team preferred instead to pocket the cost of the premium and wear the risk (Thomas, Haslam, Brooks and Seddon). As already instanced in the some of the Lions matches, the tour party carrying two Rugby-playing doctors has its advantages. Any Rugby footballer that happened upon the *Nelson Weekly News* that June would have nodded in agreement upon reading: "Doubtless it says a lot for the pluck of the young men of the day that they are willing to risk their heads, necks, arms, and legs in the *melee*—and if either of these parts of their bodies suffers fracture it is their own business and nobody else's."

The new week began with the Lions playing on consecutive days, in two matches that were more in keeping with traditions of Rugby in the 1870s, where teams were of mixed numbers, clubs played schools (usually on "past and present" lines) and thought of gate-takings were of no real interest. The first, again at the SCG, was listed as "Fifteen of England and Eighteen of NSW (Juniors)"; the Lions' opponents were allowed to take the field with three extra players to even up the odds. "Monday we had arranged to play 18 juniors," said Seddon. "I hardly know what qualifies a junior in Australia—certainly not his age, or yet weight; something after the style of a youth race at home, some pretty big youths turning out. Anyway, we had little difficulty in beating them pretty easily." To answer Seddon's query, the reference to 'juniors' was more to do with the status of the club, with the first grade clubs being called 'seniors'. There were many older players getting about the lower tier competitions. The match report shows the Lions had the game easily under control, with Stoddart getting many mentions from long runs and drop-kicks; despite having to deal with an opposition pack that often had a dozen forwards, the final result was a comfortable 11-0 win.

The next day the Lions travelled to the Parramatta Cricket Ground [now Old King's Oval] about 23km to the west of Sydney; boarding at Darling Harbour, it was a pleasant 30-minute steamer ride up the Parramatta River to the George Street wharf on the eastern fringe of the township. It turned out, said *Town & Country*, to be "The hardest battle the British team has yet fought … when it met King's School (past and present). Many people anticipated that the Britishers would walk over the School easily but they were very far out in their calculations, as the result proved. A more exciting game has not been played for some time." The King's School, now located at North Parramatta, is inexorably linked to the founding and development of Rugby in Australia, not least for being one of the pioneer clubs of the NSWRU in 1874 (Sydney University and Newington College holding equally revered positions).

King's School XV was comprised of eight 'old boys' including Wade, the England international, who would again face Stoddart, with the remaining seven places awarded to masters (teachers) and current students. Perusing the names of the school side suggests that at least six of the players were at one time or another NSW representatives: Bayliss, Hungerford, C. Wade, L. Wade, Bennett and Tange (the latter being the current NSW captain).

The surprisingly good attendance of 1200 for a workday afternoon were provided with an enthralling contest. "The first half of the game our men played wretchedly lazy," lamented Seddon. The Lions were—yet again—behind at the break (5-2 on this occasion). For the first time the captain seemed to despair at his men's attitude and effort.

He recovered his composure though when talking to another reporter later, offering instead that maybe the playing the day before had dulled the start: "I imagine that most of our fellows were sore and stiff in the first half." Whatever the cause, the Lions were in real trouble when the King's side were in for another converted try and now led 10-2. The Britishers finally rallied, and really did more than enough to have won. "This (being behind) put our men on their mettle, as eventually we scored five tries." That squared the game at 10-all. "With a few more minutes to play," *The Sydney Morning Herald* reported, "the Englishmen strained every nerve and at last succeeded in forcing the School (King's touching down the ball in their own in-goal) when time was called, the game resulting in a draw. Taking the play all through, the boys [sic] were certainly not behind their opponents. Their tackling was splendid and their passing and kicking was worthy of any team that could be picked to represent the colony."

"Our goal-kicking being wretched, the game ended in a draw," said a disappointed Seddon. "Three out of the five tries were behind the posts!" Poor place-kicking for conversions had been a largely unspoken blight all tour but until this game hadn't really impacted on any result. The team had been confident of winning every Rugby game in Australia. Now they would have to play semantics and go for the undefeated tag. Applying the RFU points values, the result was a victory for the King's School 6-5.

Clowes' Case Under Discussion

"The Houses of Lancaster and Tudor in vain tried to suppress football, and the efforts of the Rugby Union will be equally vain to suppress professionalism if it once begins to pay."
Montague Shearman, *Athletics and Football* (1887 edition)

Almost under the shadow of Westminster Abbey and the Houses of Parliament once stood one of London's most well-known landmark buildings, the Renaissance-style Westminster Palace Hotel. Eight stories high, it was an unusually angled building; presenting a very narrow end elevation opposite Broad Sanctuary, where its ever-converging side frontages (to Victoria Street and Tothill Street) didn't quite meet. The grand old building survived 'The Blitz' of World War II, but not the city's post-war redevelopment.

Built in 1859 the hotel's meeting rooms were host to noteworthy meetings—from political, business, military, social and sport. The site of the building still holds significance to Canadians, as in 1866 a conference of delegates met at the hotel, resulting in Queen Victoria assenting to the creation of the Dominion of Canada. The same meeting rooms were, in the last decades of the 1800s, the preferred location for the coming together of delegates from England's Rugby clubs at general and special meetings of the RFU. At one such meeting held at the end of April 1888, the Halifax club's delegate, their vice-president Captain Bell, sat quietly while the order of business was discussed; from the ongoing international dispute (establishing the IRB), putting in rules to that would stop squabbles over how players qualified for a County team and that "the intricacies of the rules" meant that their application on the field was sometimes difficult and "the poor referee was often placed in a very difficult situation". Finally, as the last matter before the meeting ended, he rose to his feet:

> Captain Bell (Halifax) drew attention to the case of J.P. Clowes (Halifax), at present forming one of Shaw and Shrewsbury's team for Australia, and wished to move a resolution to the effect that the Union reconsider their decision in the matter, but was ruled out of order. The meeting then terminated with the usual vote of thanks to the chair.

Bell was not to be dissuaded. He had the Halifax club put forward a notice seeking "to obtain a reversal or remission of the sentence" on J.P. Clowes, which resulted in a RFU meeting of all club delegates being called to London on 7 June. *The Athletic News*' account (and teasing commentary) of the meeting:

> A thoroughly representative meeting of the Rugby Union has spoken and that with no uncertain voice on this subject. There were doubtlessly many who, like myself, were inclined to blame the Halifax Club for calling a special general meeting with a view of bringing about the reinstatement of their member, J.P. Clowes, who has been declared a professional for receiving money from Shaw and Shrewsbury in connection with the visit of the English team to the antipodes and thus putting clubs and delegates to considerable inconvenience in order to be present at the meeting in London.

The action of the Halifax Club has done much good. It has shown the unanimity which exists among followers of the game in all parts of the country on this point. It has shown that clubs north, south, east and west are working hand in hand to keep the game out of the hands of the paid player and to preserve the amateur definition in the spirit as well as in the letter of the law.

It may be that this was the real object of the Halifax Club in appealing to "the country" on behalf of their absent fellow club man. It could not have been with the slightest hope of success. I am sure Captain Bell felt this during his long oration on Clowes' behalf. Although he spoke like a man who was playing a losing game for nearly an hour, he rambled on, reading extracts from this paper and that. The arguments all through were singularly lacking in force; indeed their gist may be contained in one short sentence: "Has not Clowes been already sufficiently punished?" Dark hints, too, were thrown out that other members of the Shaw and Shrewsbury team are far greater sinners. From the argumentative the venerable captain gradually descended to the pathetic and appealed pitifully to the meeting "to allow this young man when he returned to England to play for his old club. If he has erred he has erred in error, and surely he has by this time been sufficiently punished."

The speaker (Bell) then drew attention to the Halifax Club, pointing out its position, what it had done, for football, its loyalty, etc. etc. giving it a very cheap advertisement, in fact. I failed to see what this had to do with his question. The worthy gentleman built up a very pretty structure. More than once I felt inclined to weep and a sound like a distant blubbering reached my ear. It was a trying moment, but it did not last long. A very few plain unvarnished words from Mr. Mark Newsome (Dewsbury club), and down fell the pretty edifice erected by Captain Bell like a house of cards. All romance departed. The money Clowes had received he had spent in wearing apparel and not on a football outfit. He may have been a less sinner than some of the others, whose cases could not in fairness be heard while they were away. Clowes had been guilty of a flagrant act of professionalism, and must suffer if the laws of the Union are to be observed.

The revulsion of feeling produced was immense, while, when the Rev. F. Marshall followed on the same lines and went closely into the evidence as laid before the Yorkshire committee, which included a statement by Lockwood and Stadden, of Dewsbury, to the effect that both had been promised sums of money to join the team, it was apparent to the veriest tyro what the verdict would be.

Orator followed orator on the side of the committee but not one solitary delegate gave the slightest assistance to Clowes' cause. Even the member for Salford, who seconded the proposal, did nothing more. Poor Captain Bell, his reply was even more rambling than his opening speech. He rambled, hesitated and equivocated, and finally wound up with another pitiful appeal for the clemency which did not come. Out of a gathering which I roughly estimate at 120 (clubs can only send one delegate now), but six hands were held up in his favour.

Clowes though perhaps a less sinner than others—is a sinner, and to show him any leniency would be to offer inducements to other enterprising caterers to follow the lead of Shaw and Shrewsbury class on whom, if I am any judge, the Union means to put its foot firmly. But what about the other members of the antipodean team you will ask, what is to be done with them? Well, we must wait and see but it strikes me pretty forcibly that those who do return to this country will find, at least as far as football is concerned, their occupation is gone. They may certainly go into the Association [soccer] ranks, but very significant remarks were made as to the course Mr. Hill and his committee intend to pursue on the subject.

> At present there is no getting away from the fact that there is professionalism in Rugby football. At the same time it is equally certain that the authorities are determined to leave no stone unturned to grapple with it in the bud. Whether they will prove successful time alone will tell. They certainly are going about their work in a most business-like manner, and it will not be their fault if they fail.

With that result, there was nowhere else for Halifax to turn. Even if they could compose a new argument, they were not going to get another hearing. The cabled news that the RFU had rejected Clowes' appeal began to appear in Australian and New Zealand newspapers on 9 June, the day of second meeting between the Lions and NSW. *The Bathurst Free Press and Mining Journal* spoke for many when it plainly stated: "The English Rugby Union is, I should imagine, for the benefit of the game, but such acts as that will not, by any means, promote football. The action of the home Union is very arbitrary and all footballers must feel sorry for Clowes and the uncomfortable position he is placed in."

Indeed it was very arbitrary. The RFU did not pursue the Halifax club's complaint against Lockwood, even though he had signed a tour agreement with Turner and, just like Clowes, received £15. Lockwood continued to be chosen for England teams over the following seasons and in 1894 was twice awarded the captaincy.

The fact that none of the Lions players or the promoters were prepared to ignore the RFU edict about Clowes, even for the Australian Rules games, shows the power and influence the RFU had. The threat of disqualification upon returning home was to them very real.

What is remarkable is that upon a close reading of the RFU's laws against professionalism, it states: "It is illegal for any player to receive from his club, or any member of it, any money consideration whatever, actual or prospective." Yet, there was never any assertion made or evidence given to the RFU to suggest anyone from or for the Halifax club paid Clowes the £15 payment that was at the centre of the case. In fact it was openly admitted by Turner [and accepted by the RFU] that he paid Clowes the £15 in respect of expenses relating to a football tour to Australasia. Clowes had breached no RFU laws at all.

Upon learning that Clowes would not be reinstated Shrewsbury wrote to Shaw claiming that the defence mounted by Captain Bell (wholly or partly at Turner's agitation) was flawed and "he made a great mistake" in strategy:

> What he ought to have done was to ask whether the Rugby Union [RFU] could exercise any jurisdiction or control over the Rugby players out here whilst playing the Victorian game. For my own part, and also the majority of our players, are strongly of the opinion that the English Union has nothing whatever to do with them whilst playing the Victorian game. In fact there is no similarity between the two games anyway. The Victorian Union would in no way recognise the Rugby Union, neither would the English Union recognise them. Stoddart also thinks the English Union has no control over our players under the circumstances mentioned. If you had stated this to the Rugby Union, perhaps Clowes would then have been able to play with the proviso that the Victorian Association did not object. However, Clowes won't play at all, and I should make no bother or application to the Union at home about the matter. Of course if you could get to know unofficially, without making any formal application, or the affair getting into the papers, you can do so and let me know.

It never came, and unless Clowes took the field in some country town having temporarily assumed the identity of one of his teammates, he never played a game during the tour. The only consolation he took was that Halifax had defeated Dewsbury in the replayed Yorkshire Cup match and then went on to beat Wakefield Trinity in the final. Newsome had made his complaint but gained nothing.

What became even more galling to the promoters and each of the players was the news that the RFU had given its assent to the visit of Joe Warbrick's

'New Zealand Natives' football team to England. "I see by the papers here that English RFU have sanctioned the Maori Football Team's visit to England," said Seddon. "This is very strange considering that only a short time ago one of their own players—Jack Clowes of Halifax—was dubbed a professional for receiving expenses only."

"Talk about a speculation," laughed Shrewsbury, "that is one with a vengeance, and for the Union at home to give their support to it, after refusing us, this is the clincher! These men are professionals hundred to one more than Clowes, and all of them I believe have arranged as to the terms to be paid to them." He was sorry they hadn't contacted Warbrick as they became aware of his plans and become joint promoters—but then, after a moment's pause, thought better: "We should have had to keep in the background, as I am afraid the Union (RFU) would not have granted us their patronage, as they would Warbrick."

The Unprosperous Trinity

"It may be strange, but it is no less true, that there is almost as great a difference between the fiscal laws and governments of the various Australian colonies as between those of foreign states in Europe."
Ernest Giles, *Australia Twice Traversed*, 1890

Sydney has never really given Australian Rules a particularly friendly welcome. In September 1877, Victorian football-cricketer George Coulthard—"one of the finest players who ever wore Carlton colours"—was in a small boat on Sydney Harbour with newly-made friends, doing some fishing. He was the first in a long list of Melburnians sent to Sydney on a proselytising mission for Australian Rules; taken on instructing and coaching of players at the city's Waratah FC that was contemplating a code switch from Rugby. With the boat sitting low in the water, bobbing about on the waves, according to *The Argus*, Coulthard "suddenly disappeared over the stern. His coat, trailing in the water, had attracted a shark, which took a mouthful of it. Fortunately, the coat gave way and Coulthard was rescued but after that experience he was never happy in Sydney, and soon returned to Melbourne."

When it came to devotion to football, Sydney, as with many cities and towns in NSW and Queensland, were similar to those to be found in Great Britain, where different codes existed side by side—some evenly divided, some favouring one over the other to varying levels. In Britain this rivalry was between soccer and Rugby but in the two northern colonies of Australia's eastern seaboard, it was not only soccer and Rugby but Australian Rules as well. Rugby dominated many areas but soccer was popular among the mining communities in the Hunter and the Illawarra. In the southern border regions of the colony such as Albury, which are closer to Melbourne than Sydney, the greater interest was for Australian Rules. Sydney University briefly had an Australian Rules club (1887-89), and the game was played at Sydney's St Ignatius' College (until 1892).

Sydney was the key battle ground—where its loyalties lay would decide whether Australian Rules would be the one national game for all Australia, maybe Australasia. "Those of the Victorian faith term themselves the liberals, while the Rugby followers are considered out and out conservatives," wrote Sydney's *The Referee*. "The former, by virtue of their name of 'Australian Rules,' are perhaps quite justified in supposing that all other creeds should be annihilated or suppressed, so that their game may be the only Australian football played. On the other hand, the Rugbyites are quite as just when they refuse to be converted to the other side, giving as their reason that their game is the game of the NSW footballer and while the Victorians are content to patronise their own game they do not wish to thrust Rugby rules upon them and therefore mean to resent any such invasion on the part of those of the Australian faith and the NSW public has given them their sanction and support most emphatically."

The Maitland Mercury said of Australian Rules: "This is the game Victorians rave about. More people assemble to see a first-class club match in marvellous Melbourne than congregate at Randwick to witness the Sydney Cup. The seven-year-old youngsters in that city can give you an opinion on any point of the game with less hesitation than they display when you

THE STEAMSHIP KAIKOURA IN PORT: Powered by coal-burning and sails, the New Zealand Shipping Co.'s *Kaikoura* brought the 1888 Lions tour party to Australasia and took them home again; a journey of six weeks each way. Built in 1884 in Glasgow, Scotland, she carried passengers, mail and cargo between England and the colonies until 1899.

'OUR LONG JOURNEY HAD COMMENCED': From *The London Illustrated News* a sketch of the team on board the *Kaikoura* on March 8, 1888, as she readied to leave Gravesend and head south to South Africa, then east across the Indian Ocean. The majority of the players are wearing their red, white and blue tour caps, presented to them the day before in Nottingham by co-promoter of the venture, Alfred Shaw.

CAPTAINS OF DISTINCTION: Robert (Bob) Seddon (left) was elected captain of the first British Lions by the team shortly after they sailed from England in March 1888. The previous season Seddon had won selection for England against Wales, Ireland and Scotland in the Home Nations series. Andrew Stoddart (right) represented England 10 times between 1885 and 1893, and holds the unique triple honour of having captained England's cricket and rugby teams, as well as the British Lions.

AN ALL-ROUND SPORTSMAN:
Arthur Paul, born in Belfast (Ireland), captained the Lions in one tour match; not only a versatile rugby player, he was a top-class cricketer with Lancashire throughout the 1890s, and in 1899 he was goalkeeper for the Blackburn Rovers football (soccer) team.

PATIENCE AND COOLNESS:
Arthur Shrewsbury, a rival to the great W.G. Grace as the best Test batsman of the 1880-90s, was a cricketer and sports promoter with a cool head and steady hand. Along with fellow English cricketer James Lillywhite, he organised the Lions' tour matches, and then as team manager accompanied the footballers throughout their long campaign.

RUGBY—THE 'GENTLE' GAME: The extent of violence meted out by footballers in rugby games was often more imagined than real. This cartoon of the Lions' tour-opener against Otago at Dunedin's Caledonian Ground appeared in *The New Zealand Punch* on April 28, 1888.

OPENING ENCOUNTERS: The Lions in Dunedin just before taking the field against the Otago representative team in their second match of the tour, on May 2, 1888.

Back row (left to right): Fred McShane (Australian rules trainer), Jack Clowes, Jack Anderton, Tommy Haslam, Willie Thomas, Alf Penketh, Jack Lawlor (Australian rules trainer), Arthur Paul, Alex Laing, Willie Burnett, Dr. John Smith. **Middle row:** Tom Kent, Andrew Stoddart, Robbie Burnett, Bob Seddon, Tom Banks, Harry Speakman, Angus Stuart, Charlie Mathers. **Front row:** Harry Eagles, Walter Bumby, Johnny Nolan, Sam Williams. **Absent:** Dr. Herbert Brooks

A HISTORIC CONTEST: A wood-engraving of the action during the Lions' opening tour game in Australia, played on June 2, 1888 at the Sydney Cricket Ground. A NSW player makes a desperate lunge for a try, but the British defenders remain resolute. An umpire armed with a flag closely watches on.

FAMOUS OLD GROUND: With nine forwards in each pack, a scrum sets down at the Sydney Cricket Ground in one of the Lions' three games against the maroon-jerseyed NSW team (now Waratahs). Umpires (each with a flag) stand either side of the scrum, while the referee has taken up position behind the home side's forwards.

TAKING ON AUSTRALIAN RULES: After opening their Australian Rules tour against Carlton, the Lions' daunting challenge continued when they faced South Melbourne (now the Sydney Swans) on June 23, 1888. Both sides gather for a group photo in front of a packed grandstand at South Melbourne Cricket Ground before kick-off.

THE FIRST LIONS: "Their proportions remind one of the famous British lion; all the men are sturdily built, not even excepting two or three unusually tall men," wrote the *South Australian Register* on July 9, 1888, when the team arrived in Adelaide to continue its Australian Rules leg of the tour.

RESPLENDENT QUEENSLANDERS: The Queensland team, wearing black armbands, which played the Lions at the Brisbane Exhibition Ground on August 18, 1888.

Back row: A.R. Pierson, T. Hughes, P. Small, R. Stronge.
Middle row: F. Baynes, T.P. Carr, J. Campbell, R.J. Wilson (c), F Belbridge, J. Scott, P. Real.
On ground: J. Atkinson, J. Orr, J. Exton, W. Eason.

HONOURING A COMRADE: About to play Queensland in Brisbane on August 18, 1888, first game after the tragic loss of the Lions skipper. Stoddart has stepped into role of captain, but a place has been left for Seddon, the ball resting before his ghostly feet. All are wearing black armbands.

Back row: Kent, Banks (suit), Paul, Smith, Thomas, R. Burnett, Anderton.
Middle row: Speakman, Williams, Stoddart, [Seddon], Nolan, Eagles, Stuart.
On ground: W. Burnett, Haslam, Laing.

THE WAR HORSE: Salford forward Harry Eagles proved to be an unyielding force, turning out in all 54 games of the Lions' arduous tour. As if to restate the point, he out-lived all his teammates, enjoying life in the English seaside town of Cleveleys in the late 1940s.

MR. STODDART PASSING THE BALL: A tribute to Andrew Stoddart published in England in 1895 in a series on 'Portraits of Famous Footballers'. During the Lions' 35 rugby games on tour he appeared 28 times, never played in a losing side, and amassed 73 points (including 20 tries)—an astonishing tally given the low-scoring of that era.

STAYED BEHIND: Runcorn's Harry Speakman never returned to Britain, spending the rest of his life in Queensland. He played for the colony against NSW from 1889-91.

FEINT PRAISE: One of the most prominent backs of the team, Batley's Tommy Haslam, is credited with introducing the 'dummy pass' into Australian and New Zealand rugby.

TRIPLE CROWN: Forward Tom Kent spent much of the Lions' tour on the injured list, but went on to gain selection for England, including the 1892 team that won the Home Nations without defeat.

HOMEWARD BOUND: *Illustrated Sporting and Dramatic News* (November 24, 1888) published sketches of the Lions on their voyage home on board the *Kaikoura*. From New Zealand the steamer travelled eastward across the Pacific Ocean, rounding Cape Horn at the southern tip of South America, stopping over at Rio de Janeiro in Brazil, then crossing the Atlantic as they headed northeast to Plymouth.

ask whether there are 24 or 26 letters in the alphabet. In sleepy Tasmania everyone from the chief justice down to the just liberated drunk, supports the game. Adelaide, the city of religion and embezzlement, throws aside its orthodoxy on Saturday afternoon and all those who are not going to don football togs turn out to barrack for their favourite club ... in our colony (NSW), in the northern districts (Newcastle and Maitland) it is the popular game; in the southern districts it is almost the only football game played; and in the metropolis (Sydney) it is gaining in popularity."

The British government engendered a spirit of economic competition between the colonies, believing this was the best [and no doubt cheapest and easiest for the Colonial Office and Exchequer back in London] means to encourage development. All were loyal to the parent nation, spoke the same language, and cheered the 'Australian XI' playing England at cricket. After that, common ground wasn't a given. A rail trip from Sydney to Melbourne was interrupted in Albury by needing to change trains as each colony developed different gauge (track) sizes. Also at the border crossing were customs officials for inspections of goods and imposing tariffs, in much the same way that you would see in Europe between countries. NSW had a free trade policy, the Victorians taxed everything imported across its borders. The Tasmanians and South Australians followed Victoria along the protectionist path. Queensland was a bit of both. Indeed each colony had its own armed military force. No wonder a federation to create the Commonwealth of Australia seemed to be a good idea.

Should we be surprised then that there was no national football game? *The Referee* at the start of the 1887 football season in Sydney discussed this issue:

> The prospects of the Rugbeians are as rosy as of old, while I am happy to say those of the Australasian disciples are no less blooming. In fact, the football mania in NSW seems to me to be a most prolific soil, that propagates and nourishes at one and the same time no less than three distinct breeds of leather-worriers; but, sorrowful to relate, each and every

one of the happy, unprosperous trinity are immeasurably inferior to those of the colonies where the votaries to the king of winter games are undivided in their affects and allegiance to either Rugby or other rules. For instance: New Zealand will always stand superior in Rugby to us, while Victorian football and players are as much our superior as the heavens are high above this terrestrial globe. The followers of the Australian game in Victoria have the most numerous and enthusiastic football society in the world and can command funds almost enough to liquidate the Dibbs deficit (NSW government debt over £1million) by reason of the monster crowds who turn out to see their matches, which have a complete monopoly from want of an opposition game. The game has grown with them almost, and it is quite within reason to suppose that had Rugby rules been properly planted in Victorian soil the public would have patronised them as they do the present game.

It was an ever-upward path for the Victorians—the cricket clubs in Melbourne that owned the grounds gained valuable income from football gate-takings, which led to better facilities for players and spectators, which generated more gate-takings. And so it went on, to the stage that the game switched from having a rectangular flagged pitch as in other football codes, to one that extended to almost the fences of the cricket ground, bringing the game to the spectators. Sydney-based correspondent for *Town & Country* wrote:

When reading over the reports and balance sheets presented to the [annual football club] meetings which are now being held in Victoria, one cannot help remarking the striking evidence of the prosperity of the game in the neighbouring colony. The senior [football] clubs have for years been a source of wealth to the leading cricket clubs. All their matches are played in enclosed cricket grounds to which a charge is always made and the public are content to pay. So willing indeed are they to support the game that each match of importance is

witnessed by thousands, while in Sydney the spectators, except
on very special occasions, rarely exceed a hundred ... the
figures must make the teeth water of some of our treasurers
who have to struggle hard to make ends meet.

In Sydney all three codes jostled for access to the SCG, but most Saturdays their regular club games were held side by side on the adjacent open fields of Moore Park (still today parkland, but doubles as an overflow carpark for major events at the Sydney Football Stadium or SCG). Gate-takings were impossible as there were no stands, and the ground was riddled with small stones, pot holes, divots and even broken glass. *The Referee* elaborated:

Should the footballers of NSW by any means become
possessed of a good ground for football matches, I am certain
that the public will not be slow to support them handsomely
as in Victoria. Leave it to the public to say whether this or that
game is the better. Be sure that though slowly yet surely will
the only remedy come; for no organisation can afford to go on
year after year losing money and in want of funds. The Rugby
game owes its present flourishing condition to the public
of NSW alone, who patronised it more than any other game,
and on that head it is the game of the colony.

The arrival of the Lions gave fresh impetus to the debate. A letter writer calling himself 'Australian' said in *The Sydney Morning Herald* that "on the one hand we have the old bullocking Rugby game, in which a man must either be as big as a house or else be 'slung about like a rat' and, on the other hand, the modern scientific Australasian game, in which a little man— provided pluck and stamina are there—has quite an equal show with a big one".

After Dr. Brooks told reporters he thought Australian Rules was a "tricky and mongrel" game, a supporter fired back by writing: "Rugby is rough and brutal, tending more towards brute force than anything else—in fact, like a lot of hungry dogs after a bone."

During their fortnight in Sydney the tourists stepped up their training sessions in Australian Rules, though it was far from daily. Seemingly at the behest of the local Australian Rules community, attempts were made to have the Lions play a game on the SCG against the visiting Fitzroy FC, one of the premier clubs from Melbourne. It didn't eventuate. In all likelihood Shrewsbury and Lillywhite were worried that a flogging in Sydney was hardly positive advance advertising for the coming show. Instead, according to Seddon, the Lions met "15 of the Fitzroy team, [who] opposed us in a practice match, playing the Victorian rules. From what I can gather from this afternoon's play, I am afraid our success will not be under the above rules."

An unattributed clipping stated of the trial game: "They (Fitzroy players) were not favourably impressed with the form of the Englishmen, who did not mark well at long distances or show any proficiency in drop-kicking. The Rugby habit of throwing the ball directly [as] they were 'collared' (held or tackled) also clung to them. Fitzroy expect that the Englishmen will be severely 'drubbed' when they play in Victoria."

The Sydney Mail added: "Judging by their present form the game they play in Melbourne will be little better than muff matches; and as the big money for football is to be made in Melbourne, the Britishers are acting against their own interests in not getting ready to make a better fight. Stoddart and one or two others can bounce the ball going at half-speed."

The Referee reported the Lions "say that when ahead of the kicker they can't feel safe in taking the ball, dreading the 'off-side' cry. Then, when they have got it, they feel inclined to tuck the leather under their arms, and go as hard as they can for the goal line". And "how will it be when they come to play Rugby again? They will be everlastingly grabbing the ball off-side and will be constantly in hot water". An Australian Rules supporter told the press "the Britishers are not partial to the Australian game so far as they know it, but when they see two good teams at it in Melbourne, they will likely alter their opinion".

The day after the drawn Rugby game against the King's School, a trial 18-a-side Australian Rules game was played in the morning (the team left for Melbourne by train that afternoon). Seddon was a bit more positive. "It could be seen what knowledge we lacked in the game was equalised by the determination and condition of our men, the game ending in a win for our team by three goals to one." Lillywhite was not convinced the team was ready. "I fear we shall not be able to play the Victorian game well enough to cause any excitement over it at least, in the first few matches," he said. "After that our men might improve."

Though Lillywhite and Shrewsbury were not happy with the terms agreed to in every case, a full schedule of more than a dozen matches over six weeks had been arranged for their visit to Victoria and South Australia.

"Wednesday afternoon, 5.30pm saw us on our way to Melbourne, 600 miles from Sydney, many friends and footballers wishing us a successful journey," wrote Seddon. "By 10 o'clock most of us were in bed, having engaged a sleeping saloon." When the train arrived at Albury at 5am, those sleeping had to be woken up—still well before dawn, drawn out in the bitter winter dark and cold; here everyone and everything had to be unloaded from the NSW train and put on a Victorian train, the consequence of, as author Mark Twain put it after he went through it in 1895, "the paralysis of intellect that gave that idea birth".

As the train was nearing the Victorian high country town of Benalla, the team was having breakfast in the dining carriage. There was some excitement when it was pointed out that Benalla was hometown to Ned Kelly, the notorious bushranger that had been captured and hung after a series of sensational events that ended just eight years earlier. The story of the "Kelly Gang's Last Stand" against the Victorian police troopers at Glenrowan had been read with great interest around the English-speaking world. Most of the Lions players were then in their early teens when they heard the wondrous reports of an iron-clad bushranger taking on the constabulary in a fight to the death in the Australian bush. Indeed it was from Benalla railway station that Superintendent Hare with his officers, ammunition, and some 17 horses left on a special train to Glenrowan to capture [or kill] Ned Kelly and his gang.

At Benalla two newspaper reporters sought out the Lions' skipper. The first was trying to get everyone's name who was a Melbourne-bound passenger—across the colonies it was the quaint but nevertheless useful custom to publish ahead the names of who was travelling on trains or ships about to arrive or who had recently checked-in at one of the city' hotels, so that friends, relatives or business associates could meet them. Seddon was faimiliar with the routine, but in a playful mood, gave out "the names of R. Churchill, Oliver Gaggs, Bianco M'Quinty" and another good dozen of other fictional inventions. A reporter from Melbourne's *Herald* found the two Australian Rules footballers, McShane and Lawlor, and through them gained an introduction to Seddon. As the train resumed its journey and headed southwards towards the Victorian capital, the two chatted away about football. "Mr. Seddon, who is a stalwart specimen of humanity and jolly at that then unburdened himself," wrote the reporter. "Of course the conversation turned upon what show the Englishmen would have with the Victorians in the Australasian game."

> Mr. Seddon, who is a capital conversationalist, said: "At first when our fellows heard or read of the Australian game we certainly did not favour it in the least, as it is quite a different game to ours. Under Victorian rules knocking the ball forward and off-side play is allowed, but not so under our rules. Naturally the impulse is in seeing that style of play for the first time to say: 'That is wrong.' But after the practice we had in Sydney yesterday, our fellows seemed to rather like the game and in fact, some of the men said they liked it better than Rugby. But for myself, I would rather wait and play in a few matches before I give an authoritative opinion. However, I have not the least doubt that after we have played a few matches we will acquire such a knowledge of the various tactics that we will be able to give a good account of ourselves, against the best teams in Melbourne."
>
> Reporter: "How many practices have you had?"
> Seddon: "Just about four. Now, in reference to the bouncing

of the ball, my opinion is that it is hardly necessary to do so. Very prominent features of your game are the long kicks to each other and the awarding of free kicks for breaches of the rules. I do not see why a man should risk a run with the trouble of bouncing the ball when with a long kick he could send it to any player at another part of the field and probably do more good. I admit that with your larger playing space if a man carried the ball as in Rugby he would perhaps be able to run the entire length of the field and doubtless the rule requiring the ball to be bounced at intervals forms a good check against any such form of play. Should a man do a run of 50 yards and lose his kick, would it not be just as well to have kicked in the first instance. Had we picked a team to play the Australian Rules we should have picked different men back. We thought in England we had quite enough back players who could kick and dodge and run. Our forwards are not expected to kick in the least, their great characteristics being the ability to dribble and tackle, and they must be of good fitamina. However, after a few practices our back men ought to play as well as yours. Personally, in the two or three practices I had in New Zealand in your game, I kicked more than I had done in England for the past five years."

'Mark' in *Town & Country* wrote on the prospects of the Lions playing Australian Rules:

It behoves them to buckle to as soon as possible, and get themselves into thoroughly good fettle for the challenge ahead is a big one.

Unless they are able to master the intricacies of 'little-marking' and bouncing the ball, etc., very quickly, all the leading Victorian clubs will smite them hip and thigh in every match. The two fine footballers engaged by Lillywhite to teach the Englishmen the Australian Rules are good and tried men;

and I am certain that they will leave no stone unturned to bring the visitors as near perfection as possible.

Unlike the Rugby game, the native rules cannot be picked up in a week or two; but they require arduous study and practice. Never in the annals of Victorian football has there been a player known to jump into the very first ranks of the 'cracks' (stars) without some years' knowledge of and practice at the game. On the other hand, I have known those who had no previous knowledge of the Rugby rules play for the first time in a match under those rules and establish themselves favourites from the beginning.

It is not because the game of Rugby is more simple— for nothing can be clearer than the Australian Rules. Nearly every child in Victoria who knows what a football is thoroughly understands the game. But it is simply because a player requires far more practice and training to attain the proficiency necessary for a first-class exponent of the game. And this I do not think our visitors will be able to have with only a couple of 'coaches'.

If Lillywhite's team can only manage to win its first match in Victoria, its success in that colony will be assured. For, if there are any people under the sun who like to see their own men beaten by others who have not graduated in the rules of their game, it is the Victorians.

Melbourne's *The Argus* had a bigger objective in mind, of one day a team of Australian Rules playing footballers from Britain coming to Melbourne:

What the Victorians claim is that their game is not a crude inherited tradition but a game philosophically developed and perfected by much reflection, following much experience. It is less brutal and risky than the Rugby game—which was made for boys, not men—and is therefore better suited for manly sport. It takes more learning, requires more teaching, training, self-restraint, and watchfulness and therefore is better both physically and mentally. It is a man's game, in fact, as distinguished from a boy's game. All these things are alleged by those whose business it is to know, and it is to be desired that the Englishmen will inquire diligently into them, and discover if they are really true. Then, being convinced, they should go home and change their old game for the new and having learned it thoroughly come out again.

London's *Pastime* came to a succinct and unambiguous conclusion: "The most conceited of English patriots can expect nothing but a series of miserable defeats or what the Americans term 'hippodrome exhibitions'."

Shrewsbury wasn't confident of the team's prospects at all. Writing to Shaw in England, he said "we are certain to get a lot of lickings in Melbourne".

Brave the Lion in His Own Den

"A good football match in Melbourne is one of the sights of the world."
Richard Twopeny, *Town Life in Australia*, 1883

With hundreds of hither and thither trams, cabs and carriages, Flinders Street was packed, and even the surrounds beyond were fairly filled as thousands upon thousands of people were making their way to the Melbourne Cricket Ground (MCG). "Waggonette drivers were pushing desperately and hansoms were flying in and out at rates and fares which were by no means in accord with town hall regulations," wrote *The Argus*. The sky was pale blue all over, the air crisp, the breeze fresh; an early winter afternoon made for football. It had the feeling of anticipation of Melbourne Cup day at Flemington. As people hurried along the streets or stepped out of the doors of nearby pubs, all heavy coats and covered heads, many could be seen disporting the colours of their favoured team in ribbons or crape on their lapel or hat—"the dark blues of Carlton" or "the Union Jack men". Similarly, all the waiting and scurrying vehicles were adorned to show their driver's allegiance. "A large and fashionable crowd," Seddon described them as.

As the time of the kick-off drew ever closer, there could not have been less than 26,000 within the enclosure. "Every part of the ground was packed with spectators," continued *The Argus*. "In the grandstand there was not a spare seat and the lawn in front of it, looked at from the south, suggested some strange pavement of human faces, while the slope round the ground presented very much the same appearance. The reserves have not for a long time past looked so bright nor so well packed, an unusual number of ladies being among the spectators." On one hand Shrewsbury and Lillywhite must have been most pleased. On the other, they would have been despondent that most of the gate would end in the bank accounts of their cricket rivals, the MCC.

The Lions had arrived in Melbourne just two days before. Primarily as a result of the profits from gold mining boom in country Victoria, that began in the 1850s, the colony's capital had surpassed Sydney for number of people, the height and scale of buildings and just about all else, aside from the Yarra River being no Port Jackson. "We had the greatest reception we have met with throughout the tour," said Seddon of the greeting. *The Argus* reckoned the Lions "were accorded the most cordial welcome ever extended in this way to a body of English visitors. Several hundred spectators assembled at Spencer Street station, and as the express came in three cheers were given for the visitors. When the VFA decided to take no action in the direction of formally welcoming the team, the more manly among the lovers and followers of the game resented the spirit thus exhibited, and instead of the mere formalities observed by a reception committee, the reception took something of the form of a generous demonstration."

Despite the VFA's stance its secretary, Theo Marshall, who had declared earlier "An English team would have no chance against a Victorian 20", went out to heartily shake the hands of the Britishers in his capacity as a Carlton FC vice-president.

Leaving the station, the team was driven in a convoy of horse-drawn drags to the Melbourne Town Hall and by the time they reached their destination a crowd of several hundred surrounded them, hoping to get a glimpse or a quick word with any of the team members. Hurried inside, the Lions were led to a balcony to witness a musical performance in the main hall, "a special programme concluding by way of compliment to the visitors with a selection of English airs," wrote *The Argus*. "The organist played *Home, Sweet Home*, very feelingly, and it seemed to touch our lads very keen," Seddon said. The players were then, along with a large number of local gentlemen accompanying them, led to the mayor's private rooms for champagne at the generous price of a few speeches.

In returning thanks to the mayor, Seddon said: "So far we have been so absorbed in our Rugby matches that we had only a few opportunities of practicing the Australian game. But the more we saw of the game, the better we liked it! Some of our players have gone so far as to say already that they like it better than their own game, while others do not care to express any definite opinion until they have seen a few matches. We are certain that Victorians will be much pleased if, on a closer acquaintance, the members of our team take kindly to the Australian Rules and introduce the game into England upon our return so that in a few years we might expect to see an Australian team of footballers meeting the best teams of England, as the cricketers are now doing!"

The afternoon was spent at another formal welcoming function in South Melbourne and afterwards at the local cricket ground where an Australian Rules match was being played. Ever eager, Speakman dived into some football togs and was into the game. In buoyant news for the promoters, the South Melbourne club (today the Sydney Swans) had resolved to not keep any of the gate-money, leaving all of their share to the visitors. It was hoped this would set the other metropolitan football clubs a generous example, though the real brigands, said the *Morwell Advertiser*, were the Melbourne and South Melbourne cricket clubs, who continued to "insist upon the exorbitant charge of one-third of the gate receipts for the use of their respective grounds".

BRAVE THE LION IN HIS OWN DEN

An unattributed clipping said, "Shylock, in the *Merchant of Venice,* would have his pound of flesh, and by all accounts so will the MCC. The Victorian Government when granting the land [which became the MCG] to the MCC never intended that the same should be the means of extorting money from visitors and strangers."

For the team the daily and evening "grind" of being entertained by one and all continued at full pace. The only discernible difference was that many of the team, including Seddon and the promoters, were dipping out on many of the football club concerts and civic receptions—"Mr. so-and-so sends his apologies"—opting instead to accept private invitations to dinners and parties, catch up with friends, pursue business opportunities or to simply escape.

The day that the tour had been leading up to since the venture was first mooted had finally arrived. The Britishers and the Victorians, in the form of Carlton, were to meet in battle on the MCG under Australian Rules. Despite modern hearsay, none of the Lions games were played under concessionary rules or a merged code.

The British players were under no illusion as to this contest's importance: "Upon the merit of the game will depend very largely the success of their Victorian campaign," wrote *The Argus*. A poor and inept showing would ruin the appeal of further matches whereas a victory, though exceedingly unlikely, would make Victorians sit up and take notice. Shrewsbury's local recruits, Scarborough and Chapman, the two Englishmen who had migrated to Melbourne, were welcomed into the touring party, though their names will never appear in the list of British Lions representatives. Playing as a "20" meant almost every member of the touring party would be needed and with Kent and Penketh still injured and Clowes *persona no grata*, the two new men (both backs) came straight into the starting team. The only one to miss out was forward Robbie Burnett.

When the Lions appeared from the pavilion, they were met with rousing cheers and applause which was renewed again when the two sides drew up near each other, raised their caps and cheered one another. One immediately saw that many of the Victorians, who had over time and tradition adopted the gladiatorial practice of wearing sleeveless guernseys (linen or dungaree front lace-up vests, chamois shoulders) presumably to hinder opponents grabbing at the arm in contests, contrasted distinctively with the Lions in their triple-colour hooped baggy woollen jerseys, buttoned and collared at the neck, fully sleeved to the cuff. In Rugby territory, especially if ladies are wanted to watch the contests, it was considered "anything but good taste" to take to the field in an "exhibition" of bare arms or not fully covered legs.

Today Australian Rules games commence with the teams having already taken up their positions and the umpire bouncing down or tossing up the ball in centre-field. In 1888 it wasn't so—the match began with one of the last of the easily recognised remnants of Rugby still to be found in Australian Rules—the on-side place-kick kick-off. The captain that won the coin toss chose which way his team would run and the losing skipper's team got to kick-off. While each side's defenders dropped back to take up position, the rest of the players were corralled in their own half of the field until the kick-off had been taken. This obviously redundant but still insisted upon (by the laws) routine was also repeated after each goal. With the game underway, the forwards immediately took off towards the far goal posts, to square up with their opposing back—essentially there were five players from each side always 'on the ball' (followers), and another 15 pairs of opponents each stationed in their allocated part of the field.

As with soccer, the score was simply a tally of goals, and while 'behinds' (kicking the ball between the outside of either goal post and the smaller post 10 yards away marking the limit of the goal line) were recorded, unlike today they had no relevance to the game's result. There was no cross-bar between the goal posts to worry about, and goals could be kicked via a punt, drop, place or 'soccering'. A player taking a 'mark' (catching the ball on the full from a kick, from either friend or foe), was rewarded with a free kick.

Carlton opened up the game very quickly, having three shots on the Lions' goal; though all went wide of the posts, it became evident that the concerted play of the home side would altogether puzzle the visitors. The British backs though—particularly Haslam, Eagles, Stoddart, and Chapman—made a gallant defence, repeatedly turning away the forays of the Carlton forwards. The spectators realised the Lions were not giving in despite the difficulties they were facing trying to come to grips with the new code—every bit of good play was warmly cheered. Their followers too were playing a sound game, but said *The Argus*, "perhaps were a bit too conscientious in striving to follow our rules" instead of trying to bring a bit of Rugby's "lusty vigour" to the contest.

Scarborough secured the first behind for the Red-White-and-Blues, however, by then the Blues already had a few behinds of their own plus a goal. "The visitors were most puzzled by the marking of the Carlton men and the style in which they played (kicked) to each other," wrote *The Argus*. The Lions were soon failing to "stay on their man", leaving the home men free "to give a very pretty exposition of those two most attractive points in the Australian game". The 'little-marking' between the Carlton players completely perplexed the tourists—the laws of the game awarded a mark provided the kicker and catcher were at least two yards apart and any team of modestly competent Australian Rules footballers could exploit that opportunity at will. The speed, manner and dexterity with which it was done was often incomprehensible to the Britishers.

After Carlton obtained their second goal, "the English captain, Seddon, fairly got the best of a tussle with Moloney, and the latter pushing him from behind gave the English side their first free kick. The great fault in their play, however, was that the forward men to a greater extent than the backs, were nonplussed by the requirements of the new game."

The Lions were playing their Rugby forwards in the forward positions here too; yet these men were the not the best kickers of the ball (apart from dribbling and in some cases place-kicking). The team individually and collectively had no concept of working the ball between each other by kicking and catching to position themselves and their forwards to within range of

175

the goal. Passing the ball backwards with the hands they understood but passing with the feet in any direction was another matter entirely.

Dr. Brooks and Paul ("the spectators got a fair idea of what a dangerous forward his straight place-kicks must make him at any point within 60 yards of the enemy's posts") were the only two of the forwards to regularly threaten Carlton's defence and goal. Scarborough and Seddon obtained their share of cheers but overall "the disheartening thing to the team was the weakness of their forwards". At half-time the score read 7.7 (7 goals, 7 behinds) to 0.1 (0 goals, 1 behind) in favour of Carlton.

After the long break the visitors seemed a different outfit, coming back with three successive goals (though one must suspect Carlton lightened their own effort) with first Thomas, then Dr. Smith, followed by Banks scoring. Among all this happening, a kick by Bumby hit the post and a long distance place-kick from Mathers just went wide. Each goal received an almighty roar from the crowd "who were much pleased with the way in which the team were fighting against their heavy handicap". The rally faded. The team could out-last any Rugby side, but they were soon out of condition compared with Carlton and in the last quarter their effort died away altogether. The crowd cheered both teams off the ground, thus bringing to a close the first international game of Australian Rules football.

"Our first match under the Victorian rules has been played and lost," was Seddon's entire summation of the game for the readers at home. Carlton won 14.17 to 3.8. Even by today's high scoring game, that would still be a belting; in 1888 it was as a big a hiding as one could hand out between equally capable footballers. By way of comparison, on that same afternoon Richmond beat North Melbourne five goals to four, Port Melbourne downed Essendon 3-1, Williamstown rolled St. Kilda 3-1 and South Melbourne and Fitzroy drew 2-all. But the post-game consensus, perhaps being generous to the colony's guests and wanting to encourage them, was that the Lions did better than many expected. *The Argus* offered an ultimately positive review of the tourists' first outing:

Their opponents had them at their mercy all through the last half-hour, and left a record on the board which disclosed about as thorough a beating as one team ever administered to another. And, therefore, what? Hurrah for Australia or for Carlton or the Victorian game of football as against the Rugby?

There are not wanting those who say that the Englishmen would at their own game give their late opponents just as decisive a beating, and there are others who say that the Englishmen were inferior in all essentials of footballing under any rules They could not kick so surely, nor catch so well, nor dodge so smartly. Be this as it may, they are all good men and the Victorian is a good game, the Rugby also, doubtless. The visitors played the Australian game better than their most sanguine friends anticipated, for the fact may as well be admitted that on going into the field on Saturday, all that they knew of it practically had been picked up in two muff practice matches. In face of this, the task they were asked to perform in going into the field against such a team as Carlton was an impossible one and it becomes a matter for wonder how they managed to play as well as they did.

At least half the team gave evidence of being naturally fitted to play our game, and it would surprise none of those who saw them play yesterday if by the close of their tour they are able to hold their own with the best of our seniors. At present they lack perfection in drop-kicking, and made no attempt at marking from long kicks, in which Carlton were so successful. Neither was there any of that roughness in their play which might have been expected from players so long accustomed to Rugby rules. The game was played in a fine spirit by both sides and in this respect also the Englishmen, after their experiences in some of the New Zealand towns, will be in a position to make comparisons not unfavourable to our game and those who play it.

> During the week the English team will play matches at Sandhurst and Castlemaine and on Saturday next they will meet another formidable 20 in the South Melbourne team.

The *Bendigo Advertiser* reported that Seddon "expresses admiration of the way in which the Carlton team play, and their sustained energy. As to the game, he considers that it is full of tactics, and that it is the study and introduction of these that makes the success of a team. He fancies that if the tables had been turned and Carlton had been playing Rugby, the result would also have been reversed. The captain of the Carlton team (Leydin) thought the Englishmen would have done much better. 'But we mustn't expect too much' (he says). 'They are under terrible disadvantages in playing our rules. They have more actually to unlearn than they have to learn. From my observations to-day, I think that the unlearning part of the business will be found by them to be the more difficult. I suppose they will improve as they go on, but I am afraid they will make slow progress at it. They are a fine set of men and play a gentlemanly game. Not a sign of roughness.'"

Melbourne correspondent for *Sporting Life* told football enthusiasts in England: "In my opinion, if they continued playing for a year, they would have no more chance of winning a match against these men than they would have racing the 'Flying Scotchman' (Edinburgh-London train)."

The next game was at Sandhurst—though all preferred to call it Bendigo and the name was officially changed in 1891. Just under three hours steam train ride north-west of Melbourne, the town grew rapidly when gold was discovered thereabouts in late 1851. The Lions game against Bendigo FC was played at the Back Creek Cricket Ground. There was also a Sandhurst FC (who would be played later in the tour) and among the city's many smaller, workplace and junior teams could be found wonderfully lyrical names such 'The Sailors Gully Stars', 'Dark Town', 'Union Jack', 'Moonlight Stars', 'Ironbark Stars' and 'Snobs' Hill'. The tally of young men and teenage boys forming teams in just the Sandhurst area, let alone the whole of Victoria, was more than ample to reduce any NSWRU official back in Sydney to tears in astonishment and envy.

The weather in Sandhurst had been bleak and cold with heavy rain for days leading up to the match and on the day itself. In a measure of the interest in the Lions at this part of their tour, despite the dreadful conditions to be outside standing in rain, near on 5000 people ringed the oval to witness the encounter. With the new players Chapman and Scarborough being among the tricolours best against Carlton, the decision was made to add Lawlor (24 years old) and McShane (30)—the team's two Australian Rules coaches—to the side for games outside of Melbourne, and ignore any claims they weren't Britons (Lawlor countered this by pointing out he was born in Kerry County, Ireland). Apparently Seddon also now carried a clearance from VFA allowing the two Victorians to play due to the number of injuries the British had (though it seems a little odd that the VFA would provide such a letter given they refused to sanction the tour).

It was very quickly seen by the tourists that the Bendigo team couldn't keep their feet in the heavy going and had all sorts of difficulty attempting to pick up the ball in their hands. Seddon recognised opportunity and commanded his players to "adopt the dribbling game", making use of their skills as Rugby forwards. The Britishers were also noticeably bringing more robust and forceful play into marking contests. At times they caused roars of laughter from the crowd due to the boorish and clumsy way they threw themselves into the ruck, but it succeeded in disconcerting the home men, disrupting their ability to move the ball in a chain-link upfield.

The *Bendigo Advertiser* praised the visitors' efforts to master the new game: "Though the Englishmen were favoured by the condition of the ground, there can be no question that they are a much finer team than Bendigo and when once they become familiar with the rules of the Victorian game, the metropolitan teams will find them very difficult to beat. They are continually on the ball and their speed and dash enable them to carry all before them in their rallies." By full-time the Lions had notched up their first victory under Australian Rules, defeating Bendigo 5.16 to 1.14.

The Bulletin, in its own uninhibited style—and with a little Sydney preconception—wrote that "the English footballers are developing far more aptitude for the Victorian game than was anticipated after the strong Carlton team had made such a 'holy show' of them. But, given more practice and less cakes and ale, it may yet be possible for the burly Britons to beat a premier Victorian team at their own game. And if such an event did come to pass it would bring lamentation and woe to an army of critics who honestly believe that their particular kind of football surpasseth all outside understanding. The Carlton captain, for example, expressed a scientific opinion that the Englishmen couldn't play 'our game' properly if they practiced for 20 years. Yet those same novices defeated Bendigo in their very next match. If they are intelligent young men and avoid banquets, they will certainly knock the stuffing out of many foolish notions peculiar to Victorian footballers."

The two teams gathered for the post-match dinner at the Beehive Exchange, one of the many hotels in Sandhurst, before all the footballers went to the skating rink for a series of match races against each other. In the morning all of the Lions were taken down a gold mine to see how that strenuous industry operates. "By 12 o'clock we were in the train again on our way to Castlemaine, some 50 miles away, where we had to play Castlemaine and district," said Seddon.

In this game the weather was again bad and the field and ball slippery. The Red-and-Blacks scored the match's first goal—which brought forth many loud cheers from the locals—but the Lions responded shortly after when Nolan dribbled the ball between the uprights. The final result was a tie, Castlemaine 1.4 drawing with Britain 1.2. "England had the honour on this occasion of the 'best man of the 40' in the person of Stoddart, who played brilliantly," declared the *Melbourne Sportsman*. The *Bendigo Advertiser* said of the visitors: "The general opinion is that they are a jolly lot of good fellows who, when they learn Victorian game, will make it warm for any Victorian team."

The team boarded the late evening train and headed back to Melbourne. "Saturday's match against South Melbourne is, perhaps, the best match we have to play," said Seddon. "Although we cannot expect to win, I hope we shall show some improvement on last Saturday's play."

A Complete Transformation

"The game of football in Victoria is most popular with the public and very properly so. From start to finish the excitement among the onlookers is kept at fever heat. I witnessed only one match, but saw sufficient to convince me that the Rugby game can never prosper near it."
Otago Witness, New Zealand, March 28, 1889

"If the South Melbourne men were inclined to hold the Englishmen in small esteem," wrote *The Argus*, "they were soon awakened to the necessity of doing their best, for the visitors showed at that early stage of the game a marked improvement in their play and a better acquaintance with the tricks which enabled the Carlton team to gain so decided a victory over them." For the first part of the contest the Lions were showing they were starting to come to grips with the game and more creditable it was as they were without McShane and Lawlor on the field. The crowd was much less than against Carlton, dropping down to 7000; not entirely due to their playing form, but the grey skies and drizzling rain that hung over the city that afternoon. The barneying over how to divide the South Melbourne Cricket Ground's gate receipts had in the end not mattered too much after all.

"Seddon and Williams, who were particularly conspicuous for their smartness, out-did three South Melbourne players and Williams especially showed great proficiency in running and bouncing the ball," wrote *The Argus*. Anderton said of the new game: "It is peculiar at first but I've no doubt that it is a rattling fast game. Its rules and mode are so diametrically opposite to the Rugby that, try as we would, we could not grasp its intricacies in the short time we [so far have had] an opportunity of showing ourselves. Sam Williams seemed to be the only one among us who could play the game equal to the Australians. It requires speed and splendid kicking abilities."

Paul secured a mark close to the South Melbourne posts and a great cheer arose as the ball went through the posts, making the first goal for Britain. Unfortunately for the tourists, as the game went on, such moments were increasingly rare. "Any advantage now gained by an individual player of the English team was nullified by the others leaving their places in the field. They seemed imbued with the idea that if three of them could be present to resist one opponent, considerable advantage was gained and they gave no thought to the danger to which they exposed their goal in leaving other opponents unattended." All agreed the visitors made a good fight of it against the Red-and-Whites—"the Englishmen played a much better game than they did with Carlton". Seddon was satisfied enough to say "our performance was a great surprise to the many spectators who had watched our play against Carlton; South Melbourne are this year considered the best team in Australia, and to be beaten seven goals to three is a most decided improvement, which is some encouragement for future success under the Victorian rules".

"Tuesday morning saw us going by train to play against Maryborough, some 150 miles up country," said Seddon. Yet another gold rush town, Princes Park is one of the oldest sporting ovals in Victoria, first used as a cricket ground in 1857. Still a picturesque setting today and though the grandstand appears very old, it was yet to be built when the British team came. The match drew a crowd of 6000, almost rivaling that at South Melbourne a few days earlier. The spectators were cheering loudly in the final quarter, after a very spirited

A COMPLETE TRANSFORMATION

game was locked at three goals each; all afternoon the home side edged in front, and then the Lions would come again to level the game. Nearing the final bell, Maryborough took a mark within range of the posts, and cooly kicked what turned out to be the winning goal. To say the locals were decidedly happy would be an understatement. A news correspondent wired to Melbourne that "the Englishmen, wanting in a thorough acquaintance with the niceties of the Victorian game, lost many advantages".

"After a banquet many of us were shown through the Chinese encampment," revealed Seddon. "The miserable way in which these people exist is pitiable. We walked through most of the houses. In England this interference in their domestic life would not be tolerated. Here not a word was spoken, as we walked round the houses as if they were our own." The Chinese were one of the largest groups on the gold fields. In many towns the locals treated where the Chinese had gathered to live as some sort of a promenade to stroll upon and take in the happenings, both interesting and appalling.

The Lions were now confronted with games on consecutive days, with a 110km rail journey in-between. The first was against the South Ballarat club in 'The City of Gold' and then against Fitzroy (now the Brisbane Lions) back in Melbourne. The continuous cycle of travelling, banqueting and playing was starting to take its toll, on the field and off. "Bumby, some of his Swinton friends will hardly know, as he has put on over a stone in weight!" laughed Seddon.

For once the team let the relentless meet and greet get the better of their behaviour. Arriving at Ballarat railway station the players could see and hear outside their saloon carriage a large contingent of excited and cheering locals, all eager and ready to commence the entertainment and sightseeing they had been planning and organising for weeks. "Yet the reception committee had to keep cool and wait at the station till their highnesses had finished a game of cards begun in the train," reported the local press.

After the round of receptions and drives, the Lions made ready to take on South Ballarat—one of three clubs from Ballarat that competed in the

16-team VFA premiership centred upon Melbourne. "Three o'clock saw us walking on the football ground amidst loud cheers from some 6000 to 7000 spectators," said Seddon. McShane and Lawlor were still playing every match outside Melbourne and it is not difficult to deduce how their presence greatly benefited the team; even so, in the first half the Lions failed to obtain a single goal, while the home team had four. "The match needs little description," said a Ballarat reporter in *The Horsham Times*. "The visitors were painfully not up to the game and got beaten by seven goals to three. The South should have kicked as many more but their forwards were off-colour or merciful. They (Souths) looked like schoolboys beside their big opponents, who were splendid runners, but all abroad at marking and dodging. It was the old comparison of the unwieldy Spanish galleons of the Armada and the light English vessels. Time after time would the small South players calmly dodge around their bulky opponents, unable to turn quickly and often falling in the attempt. Looking at their size and fleshiness, it seemed impossible for them (Lions) to last through a match, but they did, and played better in the last quarter than at any other time. Their pluck and determination at a new game deserve the highest praise."

"The kicking and catching of our men being far behind what they have shown in the last two or three matches," said Seddon of the contest. "It is hard to forget the rules played by most of us since children, consequently having to forfeit many a good chance by keeping the ball too long or running with the ball over the stated distance (seven yards). We are severely handicapped in all our matches, having some men in the team who could never play the Australian game."

Shrewsbury agreed: "I can play better than some of our players. They don't shape up and never will. The elder Burnett (Robbie) and Laing don't appear to have the slightest idea how to play. All the players in the Victorian game are good kickers while Rugby forwards are not supposed to kick. Hence some of our best players at Rugby are the worst at the Victorian game." Seddon added: "Yes, our forwards are the weakest part of the team. Had we known that kicking is such an essential feature in the game we would have brought out men who could kick. There are plenty at home but a good kicker is regarded as a poor forward in the Rugby game, in which the forwards have only to dribble."

It was evident that while in the country centres the Lions were proving to be a popular draw, with Melburnians the interest was waning very fast with barely 5000 "partisans of the maroon and blue" of Fitzroy FC in attendance at the Fitzroy Cricket Ground. "The game had not commenced long before it could plainly be seen that our men were 'stale,' which did not wear off until close on the finish of the game," said Seddon.

Again, reported *The Argus*: "the Englishmen had too many players in the ruck and consequently got in each other's way occasionally but the chief fault of these tactics was that some of their opponents were left unguarded and it was these men that nullified the efforts of the Englishmen to carry the play into Fitzroy's territory. When the bell rang [for the end of first quarter] Fitzroy had five goals and five behinds recorded in their favour, while their adversaries had nothing on the scoring board. A good deal of merriment was caused by the eccentric dribbling [of the ball] of the visitors."

One interesting moment was when one of the Fitzroy men and Dr. Smith were running for the ball and the latter, who stood head and shoulders over almost all the players, legitimately shouldered his opponent out of the way, causing him to fall heavily on the ground. When he rose from the grass it was immediately apparent that his left arm had been injured "and Dr. Smith at once examined the limb and pronounced the collar-bone to be broken".

Fitzroy continued to maintain mastery over the Britons, chiefly by use of little-marks, at which the visitors were still at a loss to defend or carry out themselves. One highlight was "the lengthy kicks of (Willie) Burnett, who kicked-off for the Englishmen whenever the ball went behind". At full-time time the locals departed well satisfied, the scoreboard showing a Fitzroy victory 12.20 to 3.4. "The visitors took their defeat in good part but it was evident that their want of success was largely due to their lack of an intimate knowledge of the Victorian game, their energies being frequently misspent in consequence," concluded *The Argus*.

After the game Seddon confirmed he had some difficulties with the umpire over little-marking. "We learnt the rules quick enough but that is of little use; you want to learn what custom allows to be done," he said. "The rule distinctly says that the ball must be kicked at least two yards but we found that the majority of so-called little-marks were not kicked half a yard. Nine out of 10 of the Victorians' little-marks against us were not more than a foot away, many never left the toe of the kicker before the marker had it. Custom allows them to be taken right off the toe of one man by the hands of the other. I remonstrated with the umpire but he said it was all right so long as there was daylight between the men. We do our best to study the rules and also to play according to them but are placed at a disadvantage when they are not strictly carried into effect. Rule says one thing must be done, custom allows another and we had to pay for our lesson in this respect by defeat. The sooner the rules are altered or players [are] compelled to stick to the rules, the better, as any new team will be at sea while the rules they read are not adhered to."

In Rugby, the two umpires and referee, who often wore no special sporting clothing, rarely moved any faster during a game than a slow trot and the notion of paying them never entered anyone's head. In Australian Rules an umpire stood behind each goal, but the field, as large as it is, and in a game where long kicks of the ball to and fro are commonplace, was patrolled by just one man (until 1976). As Anderton explained to those back at home: "The referee (field umpire) in this game (the VFA competition) is generally a professional, whose first claim for the position is that he is a speedy runner. He is a jerseyed individual and has to do more flying about than any of the players. So arduous is the nature of his duties that these men are well and generously paid for holding the position."

Seddon didn't put in an appearance at the post-match dinner hosted by the Fitzroy club. Dr. Brooks, acting his stead, said in a thank you speech: "I and my comrades fully appreciate the uniform kindness and hospitality

A COMPLETE TRANSFORMATION

with which we have been received throughout the colonies; we have not yet had time to master the game but hope to make a good show before we go away again [to the Rugby colonies]. We hope before leaving Melbourne we will play a Rugby Union game; you will then see what we can do at our own game. The hospitality shown to us in Fitzroy will ever be remembered by us."

Shrewsbury and Lillywhite must surely have felt ill as kick-off time drew near against Port Melbourne at the East Melbourne Cricket Ground. Admittedly it was a workday Tuesday, but even by those limitations, a gate of less than 1000 was an unexpected disaster. With the visit to Adelaide to come (four matches), plus another six games in Victoria after that, Shrewsbury admitted he would rather have cut his financial losses and moved back to NSW, Queensland or more desirably, New Zealand.

The Lions came with a fresh approach for this game. First move was to make Lawlor and McShane full members of the team. Seddon and his men had also reflected long and hard upon what had gone on during the Fitzroy match. "We have learnt lessons," said the captain. "We began with the idea that we could introduce some features of the Rugby game, especially dribbling the ball, but soon found our mistake. Having seen how the opposing teams played little-marks and at last recognising how necessary they are, we began our match against Port Melbourne with one idea, and that was to play little-marks, win or lose. We found they paid and consequently came out of the game very well. We had quite as much of the game as the Ports. Therefore we intend to stick to the little-marks. Indeed, we would not have lost had it not been for a bad decision by the umpire."

It was a particularly tight game and greatly impressed its few onlookers, as Port Melbourne were a strong team in the VFA competition. Though sharing in common two of Britain's team colours, the home club's guernsey was primarily all blue, with a red vertical trim stripe running down the sides. The Lions began brilliantly, gaining the first two goals. As half-time neared 'the Boroughs' had drawn level, but then Penketh kicked the ball to a waiting Seddon sitting wide of the home team's goal; the skipper took the mark and with a place-kick sent the leather sailing through the posts. Moments later Penketh came at the goal again and evading defenders, put the ball through for another goal for the Lions and a 4-2 lead at the break.

The game continued to ebb and flow but at the final bell 'the Ports' were the side in front, taking the victory 7.15 to 6.11. The winning goal was hotly disputed, for seemingly everyone but the umpire recognised his mistake. Seddon went so far as to assert it was intentional: "At Port Melbourne the umpire deliberately broke the rules and won the match for the Ports. It was thus: A man got a mark opposite goal and the rule says he should have kicked at goal or in a straight line for it. Instead, he kicked across to a man he thought better placed for a better kick position. This breach of rules ought to have been punished with a 'free' to us or a bounce by the umpire. Instead, he recalled the ball and gave the man another kick and he scored a goal and won the match." Indeed, just weeks earlier the VFA had issued a "ruling that under such circumstances a second kick is not allowed and a free kick should be given to the opposite side".

Despite the defeat the men took great encouragement from how they had performed. "They have met with varying fortune," a local football columnist stated. "Although they have not yet beaten a leading team, they have shown great improvement and in the last match on Tuesday against Port Melbourne, performed creditably. Opinions vary considerably as to whether or not they will become really proficient in our game. There is a good deal against them and under the circumstances they have done remarkably well."

The increasingly positive reviews and their own acceptance that they were making progress greatly lifted spirits, as did the change of setting, with the Lions now moving to the South Australia colony.

"Four o'clock saw us in the train on our way to Adelaide, a distance of some 500 miles," said Seddon. Scarborough stood down due to work commitments, while Clowes was left behind among the farewell party on the station after Shrewsbury found him alternative quarters rather than providing another free trip and accommodation. "Arriving at 10.30am,

A COMPLETE TRANSFORMATION

we were met by representatives of the different football clubs, who gave us a hearty welcome. Considering we had been travelling over 18 hours, we might easily be forgiven for being glad when it was over and we could get to the hotel."

An Adelaide newspaper heralded their arrival: "They come to us with the reputation of being very hard to beat, of being able to play an uphill game with pluck, temper and perseverance. We are not wholly sure that their contest with local players on Saturday and during next week will prove that 'soft thing' which some people imagine. They seem to have grasped the main points of the Australian game, with its intricacies, which are so different from those of the Rugby game."

After their first look at the touring party the *South Australian Register* concluded that in comparison to local footballers: "The Englishmen are in every respect different, in fact their proportions remind one of the famous British lion. All the men are sturdily built, not even excepting two or three unusually tall men."

"Friday morning we received a public reception in the Town Hall," said Seddon. "After introducing our team to the mayor, he welcomed us to Adelaide in very flattering words, and commented on the very fine body of men before him, and especially on the picture of health that could be seen in every face. We adjourned to the mayor's parlour, where wine and cakes were provided. This pleasant part of the reception being over, a few more speeches were made." One of which belonged to Seddon, where he again spoke of how his players had to take a moment to think what to do in any given situation and then "they found that their chance which was within their grasp was gone". He also continued his complaint that the rules say one thing but were interpreted differently: "We are now becoming gradually accustomed to the game and hope to make a better display. We hope that one result of our visit will be that the game will be introduced into the public schools in the old country, and that there will be visits by footballers as there are now by cricketers."

After a little consternation—though nothing like the VFA—the South Australian Football Association (SAFA) had granted its sanction to the tourists playing in Adelaide with its clubs. They cautioned though they would not look so kindly upon any future football tours organised by private speculators. With Adelaide and South Australia possessing a much smaller population than Victoria, the SAFA was not on the scale or influence of the VFA. The *South Australian Register* stated: "It is not necessary here to discuss the principle of sending English footballers to the colonies [on money making ventures]. Here the players are and it would be unseemly to cavil at their mission. All that need be said is that the visits of English athletes to Australia is at least as defensible as that visits of Australian athletes [and cricket teams] to England. We can at least count upon a good and honest exhibition. No ill results need be feared with two medical men in the English team and we can assure the visitors that their victories as against our players will be if not highly popular, at all events taken in good part, even as it is certain from their past record that their defeats, should they happen to lose, will be accepted by them philosophically and in the spirit of genuine British sportsmen."

The colony's capital city was named in 1836 in honour of the Empire's Queen Adelaide. Most of the Lions knew the oft-told story that in 1839 she visited Rugby School, and after inspecting various buildings and the chapel, went to 'The Close' to watch a game of football between School House (75 players) *v.* Rest of the School (225). To mark the occasion the House boys were each presented with a velvet cap of dark red with gold tassels and this gave birth to a tradition of clubs and representative teams in Rugby awarding 'caps' to players.

The Lions' first outing on Adelaide Oval was remarkable for how unexpectedly poorly they all played; to the disappointment of the 6000 strong crowd little of the recent improvement seen in the matches in Melbourne was evident at all. The final score was 8.9 to 5.9 in favour of South Adelaide FC, with two late goals from the visitors masking the scale of the beating. Perhaps it was the after affects of the long train journey followed by the Adelaidians' generous hosting.

A COMPLETE TRANSFORMATION

The *South Australian Weekly Chronicle* wrote after the game: "What may be considered a new era in the history of football was the match on the Adelaide Oval on Saturday, when a team from England entered the lists to do battle with our local men, the South Adelaides having the honour of being the first to engage them. After receiving several severe drubbings in Victoria the Englishmen were not expected to do very much against the Souths, who were the favourites, fairly long odds being laid on them. The match proved that the visitors had a great deal to learn before they could hope to beat our teams. Mr. Seddon, the captain of the Englishmen, stated after the match that they had showed worse form than in any match in which they had played under the Australasian rules. Their marking was wretched, while they had little or no idea of running with the ball, one of the most difficult points, perhaps, to learn."

"Another mistake they made," the writer continued, "was that they waited to question the decision of the umpire, and in the meanwhile their opponents had made off with the ball. Mr. Blackman had a difficult task in umpiring but was generally applauded for his discretion, though several of the visitors rather questioned his decisions with regard to little-marks."

"To my mind the umpire has too much power," Seddon replied. "No umpire should be able to frame his own rules, for he can do this or that as he pleases. On the ground there is a license allowed the umpire as to stopping the game or proceeding. This is absurd, as players remain in doubt as to whether they should go on or not." In Rugby they made their appeal to their own umpire and kept on playing unless the referee's whistle blew. In Australian Rules, where the desire was to keep the game moving and the field umpire was an advocate for neither side, the player making a failed or ignored appeal quickly found the ball and the play moved on without him. As the Rugby men were about to find out in their own code, the football official with the whistle was policeman, ringmaster and sentencer.

The same newspaper wrote: "The very great difference between the Rugby and the Australian games made the task of playing the latter well by men who had practiced the former all their lives an almost impossible one. The visitors could scarcely have hoped to hold their own against the best twenties of the colonies in a game which is peculiarly their own, being the only national sport evolved by the people of these lands, but still they have done as well as could be expected. It is less than a month since they first took the field to do battle under the Australian Rules and they have still many opportunities before them of practising the game."

The game against Port Adelaide FC (today an AFL club) loomed as an especially difficult challenge; they were in second place on the premiership ladder, fighting with the mighty Norwoods for the pole position. Two years later the 'Ports' would become the "champions of Australia" by defeating South Melbourne, that season's Victorian premiers. Against the Lions they brought their full strength team. Commenting on the game *The South Australian Advertiser* wrote: "Those who had seen the match with the South Adelaides were not favorably impressed with the Englishmen's style of game and many predicted that they would not win a match while in the colony. The odds were all in favour of the local men and in some cases as many as three and four goals were given in. A surprise, however, was in store for them." Referring to the tourists, the writer continued: "A complete change came over them, and at times no better football has been witnessed on the oval for a long while. Though they showed but slight improvement in the little-marking department of the game, they kicked with greater judgement, kept to their men, and showed all round that they had profited by experience."

At the start of the match the weather was very bad, a sharp shower of rain falling. The attendance was just 2000, and though it was a workday Wednesday, many more were expected. After early play saw both teams kick wide of the posts and register a few behinds, Britain were the first to make a more formidable charge, *The South Australian Advertiser* recorded: "With a rush the Red-White-and-Blues carried all before them, and then some pretty marking was witnessed, Bumby, Stoddart, and Thomas each catching the ball in turn. Thomas proved reliable [kicking], and amidst cheering the first goal of the day was credited to the tricolours."

A COMPLETE TRANSFORMATION

By quarter-time Mathers had kicked another goal for the visitors, and early in the second stanza Eagles kicked to Paul who marked "and loud cheering announced that he had kicked the visitors' third goal". The 'Magentas' (for their purple-hued guernseys) were somewhat stunned but responded immediately. They "rushed the ball into their opponents' ground and Miers marked to Phillips who proved reliable—first goal for the Saltwaters. The Englishmen once more acted on the aggressive." Soon "Paul marked and passed it on to Mathers, who in turn put Stoddart in possession He also failed to score, the ball landing in front [of the goal]. Kent then gave to Stoddart, who followed up his kick, a mark and this time he kicked a grand goal." The Lions were playing very well and astoundingly were ahead by four goals to one within sight of half-time.

However, the home side suddenly came alive; potting three goals in quick succession, leaving the scores level at the long break. On this evidence, the Lions were now in trouble: "Many of the spectators thought that the local team had been taking things very easily and they confidently expected them to easily master their opponents during the last half." Three more goals to 'the Ports' in the third quarter left the Britishers looking at a now surely unassailable deficit. Deep into the final quarter the visitors, playing much better in combination and showing a lot of pride in their effort, were pleased to have at least prevented Port Adelaide from adding to their lead. The final minutes, as described by *The South Australian Advertiser*, produced a most remarkable thing: "The Englishmen with some fine long kicking and marking transferred the scene of action to the other end and Mathers, marking in a scrimmage, kicked another goal. From the kick-off Stoddart collared the ball and with a run and a long kick landed it in front of the Ports' uprights, where Kent was in waiting. He eluded a couple of Portonians and kicked the sixth goal [Ports 7-6]. Another behind was kicked by Mathers before Stoddart marked and made the pegging level [7-7]. From the kick-off the Englishmen showed about the best form in either match, the ball travelling into their opponents' ground with wonderful rapidity. Stoddart then kicked the winning goal of the day [Lions 8-7]."

"A complete transformation came over their play," wrote *The South Australian Register*, "while in the last 25 minutes their play was as brilliant as anything Adelaideans have ever seen at the finish of a game." The *South Australian Weekly Chronicle* added: "Among the public who did not witness the match there were many who expressed their belief that the Ports allowed the visitors to win, but they worked too hard for that, and during the last quarter they were simply romped over and were quite unable to prevent the Englishmen from scoring. The idea, I consider, will not hold water for a moment, and it is only fair to the Englishmen to say so. They surprised even themselves, I believe, by the manner in which they had developed. Running with the ball was one of their most marked points and Stoddart was especially strong in it and the way in which he and several others eluded the Ports called forth rounds of applause. They also marked well in a crowd, and if they could not obtain the ball themselves they generally spoilt their opponents' marks. Their rapid advance will make the remaining matches more interesting and on Saturday they should make a good fight with the Norwoods. The match should prove interesting not only as a novelty but also as a contest."

At the post-match dinner the team was as pleased as they could be. Shrewsbury and Lillywhite had hoped for more when it came to attracting crowds and gate-money but for the Lions themselves, they had finally toppled one of the front rank of football clubs in the colonies at their own game.

Seddon wrote home that night from the team's hotel: "It is now four months since we boarded the steamer *Kaikoura* at Gravesend for New Zealand and I can safely say there is not a single one in the whole crowd that at any time regrets coming out. You have only to be in their company a very short time to see how every man is thoroughly enjoying himself and to look at their faces to see the great good it has done most of our team."

Southern Cross or Union Jack

"Wonders will never cease! The idea of a team of Rugby footballers coming from the birthplace of the Australian game would not have been entertained a year or two ago, even by the most enthusiastic Rugbyites."
The Australian Town and Country Journal, July 20, 1889

———

During the team's visit to Ballarat, Arthur Paul made a remark in conversation that fairly startled the locals. It seems in December 1854 his father was at the vanguard of the British forces that forcibly ended with muzzle-loaded muskets and fixed bayonets Australia's one and only rebellion. Now that might not cause much affront today in what were Victoria's goldfield towns, but in 1888 many of the rebellious miners directly involved and others that were witness to the times and events were still about. And judging by the letters to various newspapers right up to 1904 at the commemoration of the 50-year anniversary, there was little forgiveness for how the British strong hand put down the dissenters that summer morning.

The scene of conflict was Bakery Hill on the east side of Ballarat, and came to be known as 'The Battle of the Eureka Stockade'. Generations of

Australians have regarded the event as the birth of Australian democracy and nationhood. The uprising was caused by the Victorian colonial government tripling the fee for gold digging licences on crown land and then followed the infamous "digger hunts" by police troopers, empowered to seek out those mining without a licence and imprison them (or worse). Incensed at their treatment, and with all their peaceable protests being ignored, the 'diggers' built a rough fortress, those that had them burned their licenses and they raised their own flag, comprised of the Southern Cross stars in white on a blue background and no Union Jack.

Though thousands of miners were active in the movement and 1500 had been engaged in military drills in preparation for a battle should it come, when the surprise attack from a 275-strong force of British soldiers (of the 12th and 40th Regiments) and Victorian police commenced, the encampment had only 150 men to defend it. Barely two years out of Eton College, Lieutenant William Paul led 65 rank-and-file of the 12th Regiment (The Suffolk Regiment) in the attack advancing on the Stockade. The official report of the battle states Paul "received a severe wound (shot in the hip) but continued to do his duty in the ranks". The British forces crushed the rebels in no more than 20 minutes; 22 miners and five of the military were killed, with many on both sides wounded. The flag was torn down and now resides on display at the Art Gallery of Ballarat.

In calmer times, the British military that came to be stationed in Australasia, sometimes played football among themselves on barrack grounds and open fields—the earliest documented in 1829 at the George's Square Barracks in Sydney, the last remnant of which is now Wynyard Park in York Street. By the 1860s visiting British "redcoats" (army) and "bluejackets" (navy) were meeting civilian teams and clubs in friendly battle on the football field.

The first known instance of a British football team of soldiers meeting an outside opponent came in September 1855, when the now fit and well Lt. Paul was back on duty in the Victorian gold fields. Though the path to fully addressing the miners' demands was already by then well underway, Paul organised a football game to further help heal and restore a peaceable feeling between the Eureka protagonists. The match was recorded in *Castlemaine Mail*:

> On Saturday last a match at football came off on the camp reserve between Lieut. Paul, Mr. Naylor and 12 soldiers of the 12th and 40th Regiments and an equal number of diggers. Owing to the extremely wet state of the ground, the running was very precarious and no end of upsets ensued, some of them of rather a forcible nature. After kicking some two hours with no advantage on either side the ball burst and so the match terminated. The return 'kick' comes off on the same ground tomorrow and we cannot refrain from expressing our gratification at the good feeling evidently subsisting on this gold field between two parties lately so antagonistic on others. During the whole afternoon we did not hear one hasty or angry word on either side and a parting glass 'all round' testified the continuation of the evidently predominating feeling.

The game was some sort of a Rugby hacking-style rough-and-tumble football, if how the two groups played in the 1860s can be used as a guide. Henry Colden Harrison, who chaired the first VFA meeting that refused to sanction the Lions tour, said of his football playing days in Melbourne: "We had many matches with the military, especially with the 14th and 40th Regiments" and these men "played a most vigorous and daredevil game and my shins are still black and blue with the effects of it. But they did not have much science." Another Melbourne footballer of that time remembered the military teams, and added it "reminds me of the games played against the miners of Ballarat, which for wild rough, lawless play could not be excelled. Most of the miners were Cumberland wrestlers and the game was more an exhibition of wrestling than football and the idea seemed to be to fell each player, regardless of reason and rule."

The football team of the 14th Regiment (a predominantly West Yorkshire-raised unit) was, as reported in *Empire* in 1867, "under the command of

Captain Noyes, an old Rugbeian, if we mistake not, and a capital player, as most from that noted public school in England are".

They left a litany of broken and bloodied footballers behind as they slowly withdrew from Australasia at the end of the 1860s. In what were intended as games played to Australian Rules, the 14th simply did as they pleased. This was generally to use any means available to trip, throw, charge or hack an opponent over, dispossess him of the ball, indulge in long and rough Rugby School type scrummages and then run off to the goal without ever bouncing the ball. The "redcoats" entered the field of play by marching onto the ground, and their football kit was merely "their undress toggery". Harrison recalled: "They played with their trousers tucked into their heavy boots, and with coloured handkerchiefs tied around their heads. They were mostly big, heavy men, and their appearance was pretty awe-inspiring! They had a playful way too, of kicking an opponent in the shins to make him drop the ball."

It is perhaps singular to note that every city they played in—Melbourne, Hobart, Adelaide and Perth—tradition has handed down the belief that Rugby (which many subsequent generations never saw a game of) was a brutal game that possessed dangers and violence that were too much for anyone of sound mind to countenance as a sport to be played or watched. It is also thought that the words "barrack" and "barrackers"—given to describe the one-eyed spectator aligned to one flag only, which first began to appear across the southern colonies in the early 1880s—owe their origin to the uniform-wearing regimental soldiers who urged their football-playing comrades on with a display of partiality as forceful as that which they played the game.

The impending arrival of the Lions in 1888 ignited interest in the English football code in Victoria, leading to the founding of the Melbourne RFC. Organised by Charles Chapman—the England international who had been playing with the Lions in their Australian Rules games—within weeks of its formation the city's first Rugby club boasted it had (though perhaps unlikely) more than 100 members. Most were emigrants to Melbourne from Britain, but others too had come from New Zealand, NSW and Queensland.

Having "long been debarred from indulging in their favourite game", many were keen to get involved.

Shrewsbury and Lillywhite had at the outset given an undertaking to the VFA for the tourists not to play any Rugby games in Victoria but obviously what the VFA desired was no longer a concern. The approach by the Melbourne Rugby supporters to the promoters was very spirited—it seemed they could in fact put together quite a competent 'Victorian XV' team.

The Argus, like many, was not averse to a Rugby exhibition taking place, but seemed ignorant of the quality of Rugby players laying dormant in its midst. The journal instead suggested the best Australian Rules footballers should follow the Lions lead and swap codes for an afternoon:

> There is no reason why it (a Rugby team) should not be done; but it is certainly advisable that, if done at all, it should be well done. An appeal has been made to old Rugby players to combine for the purpose but a team of derelict footballers taking the field as representatives of Victoria under Rugby rules would be a sad spectacle indeed. If the Rugby men want their game, why not induce a score of our leading footballers to practice the rules, for with their capacity for lasting out a hard game, it maybe assumed that very little tuition would be required to enable them to beat their instructors. And to play a good match with the Englishmen under their own rules would certainly be something of a triumph, while not doing the Australian game the slightest injury. Messrs. McShane and Lawlor are teaching the Englishmen what they know of the Australian game, our players might ... arrange a little surprise party upon Rugby lines. There is, however, nothing to hope for from the muster of old Rugby players unless we take them in the capacity of instructors [for a Rugby team of Australian Rules footballers].

Meanwhile in Adelaide letters to newspapers appeared along the lines of "There are many native South Australians like myself who have never seen a Rugby game, and probably never will" unless the tourists play their own code. The *South Australian Register* wrote: "The Englishmen are all first class Rugby players, and as soon as they arrived in Adelaide many Rugbeians who had not forgotten the old game, and who preferred it to the Australasian, conceived the idea that the game played by such skilled opponents as the Britishers would commend itself to Adelaideans. The Englishmen were willing to play, Captain Seddon especially anxious to introduce the 'beauties' of the game to the notice of the colonials."

The first call for players in Adelaide saw 30 'Rugbyites' come forward, almost all of whom had gained their Rugby knowledge in the UK. The most prominent Rugby School 'old boy' was colonial politician and journalist Henry Allerdale Grainger. Possessing a towering and solid frame, it was presumed that he would be the ideal man to lead the team. However, at 40 years of age, he thought the game, particularly on the hard surface of Adelaide Oval, was beyond his physical capabilities and declined to take make himself available. He did though greatly assist in preparing the team. Seddon also gave his services, refereeing a trial game, along the way helping the players update their knowledge of Rugby laws and tactics. Unfortunately Seddon and Grainger were to be sadly disappointed at the end result.

"On Monday, July 16, our 15 played 20 of South Australia, under the Rugby Union rules," said Seddon. "Quite a treat it was to get back once more to our good old game Rugby. A large number of spectators assembled to witness the play, perhaps more out of curiosity than their love of our game." Played in the centre of Adelaide Oval, Grainger could be seen through the afternoon, prowling the touch-line, shouting out words of encouragement and direction. However, despite facing an opposition with five extra players, the British ran in seven tries and kicked seven goals to win 28-3—the home side's only points were from a smartly kicked drop goal in open play. "It is unfortunate the game was so one-sided, taking away all the interest and excitement of a really good close game," said Seddon. "We had no difficulty whatever in scoring whenever we chose."

The Lions skipper thought winning the Melbourne game would be a tougher proposition. "Considering the many trial games our opponents have had for this match, our task will be no light one," he said. The contest was played on the East Melbourne Cricket Ground, alongside the MCG. "Owing to a great match under the Victorian rules being played on the next ground between the two best clubs in Melbourne," explained Seddon, "the number of spectators was not so large as was expected; some 5000 people gathered around the ropes." Convention had it that when a visiting team from outside a colony played a match, all other top level games in the city or town, irrespective of the code, were called off to leave the field clear. The MCC had negotiated to have an out of competition game between Melbourne and Carlton on the MCG, citing they "were prompted to hold the match by the unusual interest which was shown in the first meeting and the absence of any powerful counter attraction". The Melbourne football correspondent for *The Referee* called it an "unsportsmanlike and selfish" act and nothing but a "gate match".

The Rugby game proved competitive, though not spectacular. "The score at the finish stood: England three goals, Melbourne one goal," wrote Seddon. "For the Melbourne team Scarborough (member of the Lions for their first fortnight of games in Victoria), Halifax and Martin, centre three-quarter, showed grand form and Cowan, the Cheshire county forward, played a rattling good forward game. Most of the team were players from England or New Zealand." In a cruel twist Chapman, who had begun the movement to form a Melbourne Rugby team to play the visitors, injured his arm so severely in an Australian Rules game for the Lions in Adelaide that he could not take his place.

"The ground being wet, the play was confined mostly to the forwards, passing being a great uncertainty," said Seddon. "The scrummages seem to be a great source of amusement to them (spectators), but the match was not a good exhibition of the Rugby game." *The Argus* wrote: "The damp state of the ground prevented very much open play and confined the struggle to scrimmages, which awakened little enthusiasm on the part of the spectators. All the forward players place their heads together over the ball, and by a trial of strength, the exact reverse of what is known as a tug-of-war, the heaviest team force their opponents away from the ball and leave it to their own three quarter-back players to score."

In Adelaide one spectator said: "The conclusion that I came to after seeing the game played is that to be a good Rugby player you must be efficient in three things: (1) To see how heavily you can bring your man to grass, (2) when you have succeeded in doing so, to see how many players yon can pile on top of him, and (3) to see how neatly you can deprive him of his guernsey."

Of the Melbourne exhibition *The Referee* suggested that the crowd was "unable to rouse up an excitement over the interminable scrummages, kicking out of bounds, working along the boundary line and throwing the ball from one to the other. In the Rugby game half the time is wasted by the scrimmaging—which is neither skilful nor graceful—but sheer bulldogism and the working the ball up the boundary lines by deliberately kicking it out of play seems an absurdity, whilst the ludicrous attitude assumed by the player placing the ball for a shot at goal must be witnessed to be appreciated. No arrangements appear to exist by which any punishment is inflicted for players wilfully knocking each other about, consequently accidents are numerous, and catch-as-catch-can contests constitute an element in the game which is one hardly likely to gain favour in this community."

The Argus continued on the theme of roughness:

> Though the game lacks much of the life and rapid change of that played in Victoria, it is much rougher, and more liable to lead to accident. Two medical gentlemen [Drs. Wilmott and Smith] had been selected as umpires yesterday and the selection certainly seemed most fitting. On more than one occasion players were stretched out limp and breathless on the turf, owing to the heavy falls which were given them without any breach of the rules. Fortunately, however, they recovered and were able after a short time to resume the game. No really serious accident occurred.

> The spectators were not roused to excitement during any part of the game. This of course is largely to be attributed to the fact that they did not understand the points, the game being in all its essential aspects entirely distinct from that which they are accustomed to witness. But it is certainly lacking in the opportunity for brilliant individual display afforded by the Victorian game.
>
> On the other hand it is claimed for it by its supporters that it leaves fewer idle men in the field, the whole of the team being constantly called into requisition during the frequent scrimmages. There is little reason to suppose from the exhibition afforded yesterday that the game will prove a rival in public favour with that which is already so popular here.

After the game Seddon stood in the grandstand and addressed both teams and supporters. Pleased to be in front of a Rugby audience he told them (as reported by *The Argus*): "He had been surprised at the excellent game played by the Victorian men that day. They had proved themselves a first class team. The game had also been played in a very pleasant manner. The Rugby players took the knocking about which they got in the game more pleasantly than the Victorian [Rules] men. If a Victorian was knocked down he was very apt to get up and put up his hands and state that the Englishmen were playing roughly; but the Rugby players took it like men, knowing that they were not knocked down on purpose. He hoped that the Rugby game would get a fair show in Melbourne and felt sure that if it did, the great majority of people would like it."

Before the visit of the Lions in 1888 there were no Rugby clubs in Melbourne but from that beginning the game fought ever onwards and, while it fell into darkness and rose again a number of times, permanency finally came in the late 1920s. In the 1930s Victoria contributed 13 players to the Australian Wallabies, including the highly revered Weary Dunlop.

How Do You Like Our Game?

"The Australian [Rules] footballer is following only a natural and healthy impulse when he looks round on all the developments of his sport that the world possesses, and feels that there is none like his own."
Alexander Sutherland in *Athletics and Football* by Montague Shearman (1894 edition)

———

On his way to a late breakfast, Lillywhite pulled back the window curtain in the private lounge room at the front of 'The South' (Adelaide's most luxurious lodgings, the three-storey South Australian Hotel) and looking across the wide expanse of the Terrace towards Parliament House, he saw no let-up in the rain that had been falling all night. It did not bode well for a large crowd at that afternoon's game. Turning around to head to the dining room he came upon Shrewsbury, who simply shrugged his shoulders at being told of the conditions outside. The attendances at the Lions' two games so far in Adelaide were comparable to what the team had attracted in some Victorian country towns but been bettered by those in New Zealand; the latter colony being where Shrewsbury increasingly wished the team now was playing and reaping gate-money.

The mid to late 1880s were a low ebb for interest in Australian Rules in the

South Australian colony, with the Adelaide premiership down to just four senior clubs. Indeed the colony had only adopted the code from Victoria in 1876, prior to that playing a locally devised game of its own using a round ball and the novel feature of Rugby goal posts with a second crossbar higher up creating a square through which the ball had to be kicked through for a goal. The Britishers next opponents, the Adelaide FC, had won the premiership in 1886 but was a club with a rocky history of mergers, disbanding and reforming, and finally, in 1893 going into extinction.

Once the teams arrived at the ground for a 3pm kick-off, Old Sol finally began to break through the clouds and though there was still a stiff cold breeze blowing, a few late arrivals saw the crowd finally settle around 3000. 'The Adelaides' had their best team on the field, while the Lions had to leave Chapman out—the England international had impressed many as an Australian Rules player but in the win over Port Adelaide, badly injured his arm.

Seddon launched the kick-off straight into the teeth of the wind and the Red-and-Blacks had the Britishers under pressure immediately, as they "notched a goal half a minute from the start". The attacks kept coming and after four long strikes from Adelaide that each produced a behind, they again put the ball through the uprights for their second goal. With a quick dash running with the ball into open space, McShane finally got the Lions on the move; Haslam then repeated the dose, and kicked on to Paul, who forwarded it "to the ever reliable Stoddart, and he kicked a beautiful goal from an acute angle". Minutes later Stoddart took another shot, but it hit the post. McShane dispossessed the Adelaide team of the ball in their own half, and gave a little-mark to Thomas, which he turned into maximum value by kicking a goal. Nearing half-time Stoddart emerged out of a scrimmage with the ball and sloted through another goal. The bell rang with Britain ahead 3-2. The visitors had fewer chances but their accuracy (one behind to nine) was proving the difference. After the break though Adelaide were not to be denied. They booted four unanswered goals and carried too many guns for the British to handle. In general play the Lions "gave a genuine hard game" and were at least the equal of their opponents, but their shots at the goal in the second half were all astray.

The tourists now faced Norwood FC in their final game in South Australia. Similar to Port Melbourne, the Norwoods had a navy blue guernsey with a red trim down the sides. Their red socks led to the club being nicknamed 'the Redlegs'. Long-time skipper of Norwood, Alfred 'Topsy' Waldron, missed the game, but the home team did include future Australian Rules Hall-of-Famer, rover John 'Bunny' Daly. Norwood were not only undoubtedly the power force in local Adelaide football but just a few weeks after facing Britain, they conquered South Melbourne in a three-game series to determine champions of Australia.

The meeting of Norwood v. England attracted "one of the largest attendances witnessed on the [Adelaide] oval this season, there being about 8000 spectators in the pavilion and around the chains". The final result did not favour the visitors, "defeat again dogging our footsteps" a frustrated Seddon said after the 5-3 loss. The side had notched the first two goals of the game and it was three goals apiece at the start of the final quarter. *The South Australian Advertiser* wrote: "The Englishmen played really well and at times the spectators could hardly believe that it was only a few weeks since they had played their first game under conditions to which they were almost perfect strangers and they deserve every praise for the perseverance they displayed. No matter how badly things were faring with them they played their hardest, and never accepted defeat until all was over. The game was somewhat rough at times and several of the players were hurt but fortunately not seriously. The Norwoods, profiting by the experience of 'the Ports,' did not trifle with their opponents but played a hard game throughout."

"Sunday morning two coaches, drawn by five horses in each, drew up to the hotel," said Seddon. "Some 15 minutes later about 65 of us started for a drive of 18 miles into the Adelaide Hills, the scenery being almost indescribable." The following evening the South Australian component of the tour was brought to a close with a bang and not a whimper. "We were entertained by the mayor of Adelaide at his house, where a grand banquet was prepared in honour of the Englishmen's visit to Adelaide," Seddon put in his notes. One of the team wrote home: "A banquet at his private residence the eve of departure left nothing to be desired from the good people of South Australia." Among "a most enjoyable evening," Dr. Smith proved he had potential as a diplomat, telling the gathering, he "had played under three rules, namely, Rugby, British Association, and the Australian, the last of which I consider contained many advantages which the first two did not have".

"Tuesday July 17 at 3.30pm, saw us gathered together on the Adelaide Station," Seddon wrote. "After a vast amount of hand-shaking and good wishes from 150 friends who had come to see us off, we started on our way to Horsham [in western Victoria]. Unfortunately, we had to leave Chapman … behind, having damaged his arm. Since, I hear he has been taken to a private hospital."

The plan of campaign for the next 11 days was to traverse country Victoria before finishing up in the capital to play Essendon at the East Melbourne ground. The initial itinerary included a game on the intervening Saturday with the Melbourne FC at the MCG, but, as Anderton politely put it, the "little soreness between the MCC and Shrewsbury on account of the cricket team" was now beyond all reconciliation. The MCC again wanted terms too steep for the promoters' liking and that game was abandoned. Another contest in Ballarat was instead organised. Discussing the issue, the Melbourne correspondent for *The Colac Herald* concluded: "It is rather a humiliating confession to make, but it is true that we Melbournites never lose sight of the main chance in whatever we occupy ourselves with. Melbourne and *Mammon* go hand in hand."

"Arriving at Horsham, soon after midnight, we were driven to a hotel and in a very short time were in the land of dreams," wrote Seddon. "Next day saw us on the ground, and after usual three cheers for England and the English cheers for Horsham we kicked-off with the wind. Amidst the cries of 'Go it, John Bull' and 'Well played English beef', it was soon seen that English beef was too good for Australian mutton, for in a short time we scored two goals, and when time was called the score stood—England six goals [to] Horsham's nil. The early part of the evening was spent at a dance. Very soon we took our leave and met the members of Horsham at a 'smoking concert' given for our benefit. Leaving Horsham at 12 o'clock on Thursday we arrived at Ballarat late in the evening, being met by many officials of the [local football] association."

Making their second visit to Ballarat, the Lions were to play two VFA premiership clubs on consecutive days—Friday against Ballarat Imperial FC and then Saturday against Ballarat FC. Here the men from Britain finally got a real taste of some home weather. The conditions for the opening game on Saxon Paddock (now City Oval, including the historic grandstand opened in 1887) were so absurdly bad that the game became a football burlesque and was treated so by many of the players, particularly on the British side. A very brief account telegraphed to *The Argus* stated the match was "owing to the cold and wet, witnessed by only a limited number of spectators. The ground was very slushy from the snow and the game was played under very unfavourable weather conditions." The 'Imperials' won 4.15 to 1.2. Seddon noted: "The ground is certainly the worst I ever saw either here or at home— large pools of water every few yards. It was great fun to the spectators to see the ball floating in one of these pools and a man make a rush to kick it out, waiting the result. As often as not the ball would have the best of the encounter, for the man could be seen spluttering about full length in the water, amidst the laughter of a thousand people, while the ball was still floating on the water, a yard or two from where it was so rashly attacked. The farce ended in a victory for the 'Imps.'"

"The following day we had again to play on the same ground, which had improved greatly, the water having disappeared," said Seddon. At first this game was played in relatively dry and fast conditions. The Lions were to the fore at the start, moving the ball well and securing the opening goal then the Red-and-Whites of Ballarat replied with two goals of their own. *The Sportsman* said at this point: "The Britishers seemed to be all astray now; it looked as if they were in for a big drubbing." More so as the home 20 sent the leather twice more through the uprights for goals. "The Englishmen were playing as if the game was altogether strange and the blunders they made caused roars of laughter." It wasn't yet the end of the first quarter.

Then, it was if someone turned on a switch, activating their Adelaide form; compared to what the Lions had shown the day before, and on their first visit to Ballarat, it was if novices had been instantly replaced by masters. *The Sportsman* told readers: "There were no more little funny movements of the pig jumping order as they rose for the ball and no standing in surprise if opponents bested them. Theirs was now a hard, desperate game, characterised by brilliant dribbling and good kicking and marking. Where before it was their custom generally to keep their hands from opponents, they now demonstrated their strength by sending men flying in all directions."

Two goals came in quick succession for the Lions. The first when Robbie Burnett, who was never going to score a goal via conventional methods, was given a clear run to the sticks by his teammates shepherding and bowling over all the defenders around them on their way. Soon after the "Britishers massed again, bore down on the opposition and with those dreaded dribbles, were now down to the goal. The Ballarat backs closed upon the dribblers, but 'ere they could reach the ball a Britisher had booted it through for England's fourth goal, amidst the greatest excitement. England and Ballarat were on a par now." Whenever any of the Ballarats got near the visitors' goal, they were met by "smashing dashes of the Old Country boys", which turned attack after attack away.

A heavy snow storm came upon the oval at half-time. "Snow fell continuously and the scene was a very pretty one" continued the reporter. "Not a supporter of the game moved as the flakes fell thickly on them. All round the ground there were umbrellas and overcoats snow-covered, while the players, defying the elements, stuck to their posts, though it was terribly cold. Blinded at times by the falling flakes, the players again and again ran wide of the mark in their dash for the ball, while with hands frozen, some of the place men had work indeed to hold the slippery leather." As one player put it there were frozen hearts as well as frozen hands among the wearers of the red-and-white; and this was very evident at times when, with a thundering devil-may-care rush, a burly Briton went for an opponent. The tourists were now playing with such pace and dash that their opponents hadn't a chance to score." By a "constant succession of brilliant dribbles and irresistible dashes" from the visitors the ball was forced through between the posts, giving the Lions a well-earned five goals to four triumph.

The captain was asked afterwards: "Will the game ever be popular in England in your opinion Mr. Seddon?" His reply was in the negative. "I do not think so. There are too many men standing idle who would be perished by the cold in our climate like that of the Old Country, as you colonials call us. In the game that is played here one half of the men do little or no work and for quite half the time they are absolutely idle, so that your game is really carried on with 10 or a dozen men. In Rugby such a thing as this is impossible, for out of the 15 men engaged on each side nine are forwards—players almost the same as your followers and the remaining six are so disposed in the field that they are continually engaged."

"The main feature of the game, the marking, is a thing no Rugbeian would ever like, because of the waiting, off-side, and man playing for man; that is," continued Seddon. "Instead of looking after the ball, the men, all but five a-side (the followers) are looking after one another [in pairs]. If in Rugby a man pushed you on your back while you were waiting for the ball to drop into your hands, you would feel inclined to reach for him with your right [fist]. And that is just what we felt like till we got used to it."

He added: "Your players are soft. That is the tendency of your game. If they get knocked down they resent it and ask angrily whether it was done on purpose. If we get knocked down we simply get up again and go on playing and perhaps, if we are inclined in that way, look out for a chance to treat the man who tumbled us over in the same way. Yes, of course, Rugby is rougher; that is just what I say, and perhaps it requires heavier men, although I fail to see it myself, for with scarcely any exception the best players you have are the tallest and the heaviest."

Some features of Australian Rules greatly impressed the Lions though. "There are some brilliant men in their own particular rules among the clubs," Seddon declared. "Their marking and kicking are something wonderful; indeed I never saw better kicking!" Anderton added: "Why I should think that nearly 40 goals were registered against us by drops taken at least 50 yards from the goal posts. The Victorians are really grand and accurate drop-kickers. They had a tremendous laugh at us when, in ye good old English fashion, we placed the ball for a kick, a proceeding they never dream of doing, so skilful are they at drop-kicks."

"Tuesday saw us once more on the way to Sandhurst, where we arrived about 8.30pm," said Seddon. "After dinner the rink was visited. Driving down to the ground the following day large numbers of the crowd sported the 'red, white, and blue,' ladies especially being to the fore. Out of every six of the fair sex, five were sporting our colours." Returning to the Back Creek Cricket Ground, where the Lions had defeated Bendigo FC for their first win in the Australian Rules code, the Sandhurst FC were hoping to succeed where their cross-town rivals had failed.

"The match was a very exciting one and fast," Seddon recounted. "At half-time we were unfortunate in losing Stuart, who had two ribs broken, and later on Eagles had to retire with a disabled shoulder. This handicapped us severely. Still we just managed to win by three goals to two. In the evening we were entertained by the gentlemen of Sandhurst at a large banquet. We had to refuse a day's shooting, which had been arranged for us, noon seeing us on our way to Kyneton minus Dr. Smith, Banks, Nolan, Stuart, Chapman, and Lawlor, all of whom are on the injured list."

"Getting into Kyneton station, it was evident our visit had caused much excitement," said Seddon. "Though the weekly holiday was only the day before, the mayor had declared this as a holiday in honour of the English visitors. The match was very keen and fast throughout, travelling from one end of the field to the other in rapid succession. Up to the finish it was very doubtful which side would win, however 'no side' (full-time) brought us another victory by two goals to one." The game was played on the Kyneton Racecourse and drew a crowd of 2000, an impressive number for a small town. "A banquet at which 130 sat down was given by the Kyneton [football] association, after which some of us left by the 9 o'clock train for Melbourne, the majority staying for a day's rabbit shooting," said Seddon.

The British were still to play another match under Australian Rules in NSW (at Maitland), but their final game in the code's strongholds was a meeting with Essendon, the eighth club from the VFA competition the Lions faced. To the tourists' credit, in the six other games they played in Victoria, they were defeated just once (Maryborough). Among the top tier VFA clubs they didn't meet were Geelong, Richmond, North Melbourne, St Kilda, Melbourne and Footscray (Collingwood and Hawthorn were not yet senior clubs).

"After performing so well up in the country a very close game (*v.* Essendon) was looked forward to, which would have been realised had our team been in anything like the condition they have shown in previous matches," Seddon explained. The captain was alluding to three men in particular—Drs. Smith and Brooks, and Anderton. According to Mathers in his diary, all three had come onto the field drunk. All were members of the team's management and selection committee while Dr. Brooks was also vice-captain. Clearly, a much better example was expected of men acting in these positions. In the days that followed they were all replaced on the committee by Stoddart, Eagles and Mathers (joining Seddon and Williams). Stoddart became the team's vice-captain.

The opening day against Carlton and the 26,000 were now a memory. *The Argus* noted "the attendance was meagre" at the East Melbourne Cricket Ground for the clash with Essendon. At half-time the home side was ahead 6.9 to a dismal 1.1. The second half was more of a contest, beginning with

Stoddart place-kicking two goals. Nearing three-quarter time the Lions "maintained their attack on the goal of the home team and while one of them, who had secured a mark well up in front of the Essendon citadel, was setting the ball, the time-bell rang, and robbed the Englishmen of what looked like an almost certain goal". Seddon was livid over the umpire enforcing such a pedantic rule: "When a man gets a mark under the Rugby rules he must have his kick before the bell can ring to stop play. Now, in our match with Essendon, on two occasions we got marks right in front of the goal and within easy shooting distance but both times the bell rang just as the man was placing the ball and we consequently lost two goals." In the final quarter the Lions also unluckily missed out on another goal when the ball was touched by a defender just as it was bouncing between the Essendon posts. The final score of 7.16 to 3.5 in favour of Essendon didn't indicate how well the tourists had played in the second half.

"Thursday, August 2 at 5pm, we bid goodbye to a large number at the station, Tom Scarborough, of Halifax, and his brother, along with Chapman, being among the crowd. A few minutes later, amidst cheers, the engine steamed out of Melbourne on its way to Sydney."

Melbourne's *Daily Telegraph* reviewed the tour: "The team has met the crack clubs of Victoria, as well as those of South Australia, and though it does not terminate exactly covered with a crown of victory, still the defeats it has suffered do not disgrace it, for it must be remembered that the 20s it has met in contest have been made up of men who have studied the intricacies of the rules from childhood and who now play the game intuitively. They came here to do their best against very serious odds and the results of struggle do them credit."

"I do not know whether the chance is likely to occur or not," said Seddon before leaving Melbourne, "but I should dearly like the opportunity of picking 20 men (suited to playing Australian Rules) in England just to give you an idea of what Britons are at football".

"A much better record than we expected," boasted Dr. Brooks, again pointing out that the team was "picked entirely with a view to the Rugby game, and in undertaking the Victorian contests, we never dreamt of so nearly bearding the lion in his own den as we have done."

Though he had played in every one of the Australian Rules games, Eagles later told *The Athletic News* (Manchester) he "does not care a small lemonade for the Victorian game and says there was a lot more like him. It was this half heartedness that must account for the defeats."

Seddon told Sydney's *The Referee*: "I imagine that none of our men like the Victorian game, and that Haslam's words pretty well sum up the case. 'How do you like our game?' asked a Victorian. 'I like it just as well as I do lawn tennis' replied the crack back player, and we all know he hates lawn tennis." Seddon then added, "Mind this: We may be prejudiced by having been brought on from childhood to the Rugby rules. But one thing is certain. The most prejudiced Rugbeian cannot be as one-sided as the Victorians. They are married to their game, and think there is no other game in the world but their own."

"After all the games we have played, I must confess to liking the Australian system much better than I anticipated when we came to Victoria," Seddon admitted. "But I am of the opinion now that we have finished our tour so far as Victoria is concerned, that the Rugby game is still far and away the best. There are many good points about the game and many bad ones."

It is clear from the number of times he raised them that three relatively small areas of the game greatly impacted his players' opinions and enjoyment of the Australian game: little-marks generally, and the two instances that may have cost them victories (preventing kicks from marks if the bell has sounded, and not kicking at goal after taking a mark). "Such things as these cannot impress a footballer with the game," was Seddon's view. "Either you should mend your rules to bring them in accord with the game you play or else insist on them being properly interpreted by the umpires."

Melbourne's *Daily Telegraph* wrote: "Mr. Seddon is a famous footballer of Great Britain and his club, Swinton, is said to be the best in the North of England. He is one of those, too, who has shown some ability in playing the Australian game; therefore, his condemnation of it deserves a little consideration." Tellingly, at that year's annual conference of inter-colonial football delegates in Melbourne in November, the rules of the game were altered—no longer would the ringing of the bell for time prevent a man from taking his attempt at goal from a mark, and the player taking a kick from a mark could now kick in any direction. The Britishers' remaining bug bear, little-marks, were soon out of the game too, abolished in 1897, when the minimum distance for a mark was increased from two yards to 10.

Though he had spoken plainly, Seddon had not wanted to leave Victoria on bad terms, adding "I do not wish to be thought boastful, harsh, or ungrateful but I honestly believe that the Rugby game is far superior to the one played here. The liking for it is purely local." In saying farewell, all sorts of promises were made about the Lions playing a game of Australian Rules in England, but nothing eventuated along that path. The VFA later in the year considered and rejected the idea of examining the feasibility of taking a team to the UK.

Seddon's claim that the "liking for it was purely local" was a view that had been expressed by *The Argus* when it said: "There is something doubtless to be said for football [in Victoria] though an outsider may find a difficulty in discovering it, but there would not be much interest left if party (club) feeling were taken out of it."

The nature of the game and the fervent crowd support fed off and nurtured each other. Australian Rules was and is intricately and inexorably intertwined with the clubs and their supporters that have built it and lived with it. Attempts to take the game to new areas couldn't take the local enthusiasm and rivalry that made it what it was in Melbourne with it, other than to the smaller neighbouring colonies that became dependent upon the Victorian capital socially and economically—Tasmania, South and Western Australia. Whereas Rugby—in the eyes of many people—was at its most attractive without club factions, at the representative and international games.

The Argus concluded as long ago as 1894 that "in making a comparison between Rugby and Australian [Rules] football it would be pure waste of time to do so on the assumption that Rugby is ever likely to displace the

Australian game in Melbourne or that our game has any chance of taking the leading place in Sydney. On this particular sport, at any rate, the two colonies have agreed to differ and anything approaching compromise is out of the question. The game played in the schools of a colony will be the game of that colony and merit has really very little to do with the case. In one sense it is a pity that all Australia is not playing the same game—not, as has been suggested, that we might send teams Home, for such an undertaking is, I fancy, a bit too big to pay its way—but merely that Victoria and NSW, established rivals in so many things, might also meet in football."

Bare the Marks of War

"Once more the British footballers are in our midst to show our men how to play the Rugby game as it should be played."
The *Australian Town and Country Journal*, Sydney, August 11, 1888

The thud of a footballer's boot on the ball. All eyes looked upwards, into a clear bright Sydney afternoon winter sky, that brown leather football seemed to hang there forever before soaring away between the familiar tall white posts; there was no escape, their yells were deafening—the joy of the barracking undergraduates, who were out on force for this unique contest, knew no bounds. You could still hear their roar half-way to Circular Quay. "University four points, British players two."

The Lions were playing their final match in Sydney, facing the city's premier team for the past two seasons, the Sydney University XV (past and present). "The University is the strongest club in Sydney," explained Shrewsbury. "The representative team (NSW) is practically chosen from its ranks."

For the first time in the tour the Lions were pitted against a team of Rugby footballers that played together each Saturday and thus possessed the instinctive reaction that one-off combined sides, though having perhaps better individuals, lacked in unity. In front of 2000 spectators at the Sydney Showground, one of the biggest crowds to yet see a football match at that oval, the British prepared for the Students. The ground is still there today, sitting quietly, forgotten, just to the south of its more famous neighbour, the SCG. For over a century it was home to Sydney's Royal Easter Show. Most of the audience was varsity students, current and former, as well as boys from the city's private schools. Because of the status of the tourists, who included representatives of Cambridge and Edinburgh Universities, the University Chancellor, professors and others of rank had too deigned this football match worthy of their presence.

For one of the rare times on the tour so far, Dr. Smith was included in the Rugby team, chosen in the forwards; he unintentionally provided comedy relief for the crowd in the role of the absent-minded footballer, insisting upon playing a doddering form of solo soccer in the middle of a Rugby game. He loitered outside the scrums, and whenever a loose ball appeared, he was on it in a flash with his boot, dribbling goalwards until one of the Blue-and-Golds of the University team arrived to dispossess him of the ball and get on with the Rugby game.

The real contest was particularly serious business, *Town & Country* stating: "No game the visitors have yet contested in this colony gave them half as much trouble as the one they played on Saturday. The play all through was very rough; some of the Unis being responsible for a good deal of it."

Seddon was playing a great game in the forwards. At one point he was seen running with the ball back through the thick of a dissolving scrum then bursting away upfield; unfortunately he had his thumb twisted in the process and was kept out of the fray for a short while. He soon found cause to dispute a decision with the University umpire and the referee, which brought the game to a complete stop and gained the skipper a few more minutes recovery time.

The Lions tactics that had given them an advantage throughout the tour were not working here. Whatever they did seemed to be of no surprise to their opponents. The Students were indeed quick learners. Exhibiting really smart and fine hand-passing of the ball, it was they that were often stunning the

Britishers with the methods they had learned from watching them. The visitors' little tricks weren't succeeding either. British three-quarter Haslam made a great try-saving tackle near the corner flag, relieved his prey of the ball and then ran across the front of the goal posts, preferring to feint a pass instead of taking the customary kick into touch and safety. It was a move he had been duping colonials with since the tour opener in Dunedin. However, the University defenders did not fall for his 'dummy' and brought him crashing to ground in a dangerous position for the Lions. In a scramble for the ball, University grabbed hold of it and in a flash passed the leather to a waiting back—in this case, a familiar foe, Percy Colquhoun. He seized the opportunity, took a quick look at the posts and the result was the drop goal that sent the University supporters into raptures of delight and left the Union Jack brigade two points adrift.

The game resumed with even more vigour and as the intensity of the on-field battle grew, the crowd became more vociferous in equal measure—more so as time began to run out and victory seemed a genuine possibility for the University men. However, while the home side had their gun man in Colquhoun, the Lions had Stoddart. The play was on the half-way line, when suddenly the ball was in Stoddart's hands, then it wasn't—his cannon-like boot had landed a mighty drop goal to put the Lions in front by 6-4. At this the contest, especially from the Varsity players, became very rough and the crowd turned very heated. The British then crossed for an unconverted try and won 8-4. What the chancellor had witnessed did not reflect well upon the University.

"Their excitement worked up to such a pitch that it was hard to have victory so cruelly snatched from them when they fancied how secure they had it within their grasp," said Seddon. "The spectators also took the defeat with very bad grace."

"They are a very good team," explained Dr. Brooks. "They were, however, very rough—in fact they almost equalled Wellington for roughness. The spectators, they were terrible. I never saw such conduct at any other time throughout our tour. Talk of barrackers, they were all at it."

One newspaper account noted the crowd "hooted and yelled at the visitors but bestowed most unbounded applause on the University team". There is nothing shocking about that behaviour today but it was then. Football in Sydney was used to spectators who applauded good play from either side and not the one-eyed style of barrackers that had first emerged in the Australian Rules colonies. Some account should always be given for a little local feeling in cheering for the home side but *The Referee* said of the University game that those "howling and boo-hooing at the visiting players" should "crawl away under someone's house and die. What a very paltry and ignorant spirit they showed and what scant courtesy they displayed toward 16 men (team and their umpire) who had travelled all those thousands of miles to play *friendly* games of football with their colonial brother kickists."

"I should be sorry to think that the crowd who barracked and howled at the visitors in such a one-sided, brutal manner were University students but at all events the 'Varsities have no reason to be proud of their followers, for a worse exhibition of bad taste I never heard of," added another commentator. "One minute Jack Shaw could not be beat for a referee and the next he was hooted for deciding fairly against the locals. The crowd looked respectable but they acted like blackguards and while such conduct obtains at a football match, it is little wonder respectable people stay away and leave the patronage of football in Sydney to a miserable thousand of low barrackers."

The University's followers were mostly annoyed about the apparent off-side play of the visitors; forgetting that the officials' roles were not to detect and pull up the game to punish at every breach they happen to see, but only after an appeal. The University players later said they were disgusted with the crowd's ardour and the claims of biased officials were absurd.

The tourists had arrived back from Melbourne just over a week before the University game. At the station *The Referee* noted: "They all look in blossoming health, though Banks' ankle is still far from well and he limps with a stick to assist his progress, having had fresh injury to it recently. Others of the team bare the marks of war pretty freely distributed over their frontispiece (face), like the true warriors they are."

With no rest or a training run behind them, the next day the Lions met NSW for their third and final time. No doubt the Britishers were decidedly rusty early but NSW put in a much better game than in the first two encounters; still, by full-time they were again on the wrong end of the result, beaten 16-2. "Our lads showed up as well as the visitors," wrote *The Referee*, "and yet did not score while the others did. This is easy of explanation. When the English got near the local line their thorough combination, great weight and experience told." Only when close to the goal line—and then only the bulkier men—did they run headlong into the defenders; the rest of the time the Lions did as they had done all tour, passing to teammates to keep the ball alive and moving in search of a gap. Even when they didn't score a try, their efforts gained significant territory.

As in the University game—and for most of the tour—the Lions use of the off-side laws continued to perplex many. "I really must say that the English players do play off-side a lot," said *The Referee*. The failure to appreciate that it wasn't an automatic offence at the mere appearance of player between the ball and his opponent's goal line, robbed local teams of valuable scoring opportunities. Haslam made a kick he intended to come down near the NSW goal, however, it skewed towards the corner—but immediately seeing an "off-side" Eagles near the ball, Haslam raced upfield in a straight line to put his teammate on-side, arriving over the goal line in time for Eagles to lawfully drop on the rolling ball for a try. Reporters suggested NSW missed three easy tries of their own if the kicker had merely followed Haslam's example instead of standing about gawking at their kick.

Town & Country was in awe of the Lions, particularly Stoddart, writing: "Those who played on Saturday played if anything better than we saw them do before. Stoddart was simply immense; his performance eclipsing anything we have yet seen here under the Rugby rules. The way he gets through his opponents is wonderful. He appears to hang fire for a second or so, whenever a man is approaching him; and before his would-be collarer is aware of it, a sudden turn of the body gets him clear of the intended grasp;

and off he bounds once more at a great pace, either to score or improve the position of his team on the field. In nearly all the runs he made on Saturday he generally passed three or four men in the manner alluded to above before he was overcome by [force of] numbers."

Two days later, again at the SCG, the Lions met Sydney Grammar School (past and present). "Having Bumby, Banks, Penketh, Haslam and another on the injured list, our team was not a very rosy one," said Seddon. "Owing to the very fine weather they have had here for many months the grounds are like playing on the roads and all our men more or less are cut and bruised all over the body and legs. If this kind of thing goes on much longer we shall have some difficulty in getting a team together of any kind. Today we had every man available playing and a little bad luck will place us in a very lamentable position."

Before kick-off there was a bit of quandary when the school found, due to some misunderstanding, they had 16 players arrive dressed in their black-and-gold jerseys ready to take on the British and understandably none wanted to forsake the experience and honour. Seddon gentlemanly resolved the dilemma. "One of the 'old boys' having travelled some miles expecting he was on their team, was allowed to play, not wishing to disappoint him making their side," he explained, "16 men to our 15." It would be no easy game, with *The Sydney Morning Herald* revealing "of the school players about one-half ordinarily play for the colony".

Another Grammar 'old boy' who had a keen interest in Sydney sports and may have been there that afternoon was 24-year-old 'Banjo' Paterson, at that time still a city solicitor. While the tourists had been working their way through Australia's rural towns, meeting the people, seeing the mountains and the vast bushlands between, Paterson was crafting his bush ballads—just over a year later his run of now famous poems about episodes in Australian life first appeared, beginning with *Clancy of the Overflow, The Man From Snowy River*, and in 1895 *Waltzing Matilda*. He also contributed a Rugby poem to *The Bulletin* during the 1899 Lions tour, paying tribute to the team's captain, Reverend Mullineux.

The hotly contested game against Grammar ended in a 2-all draw, both sides crossing for an unconverted try. The Lions try that squared the result had come from a colossal solo run by Stoddart that began near the 25-yard flag at his team's own end of the field. However, he wasn't infallible, missing the conversion from a relatively simple position that would have given victory. The school and its supporters greatly rejoiced at the final result.

The following day the team was on the road before 8.30am. "A most unusual hour for us to be abroad," said Seddon, "we drove to the station, catching the 9 o'clock train for Bathurst. We arrived close upon 6 o'clock, amidst the cheers of some hundred people who had assembled to welcome us. Being driven to the hotel, the mayor welcomed us, with the usual flattering speech and toast to the English football team."

The Lions were still a depleted outfit, some remaining behind in Sydney. Meanwhile, Bathurst had retained most of the players from the last meeting and having kept training sessions up, fancied their chances of conquering the tourists. After Haslam at full-back missed picking up a kick, the locals gathered the loose ball up and crossed for the opening try. They converted it too, which sent the home crowd into loud and prolonged cheers. By half-time though the British were in front 7-5, with Williams and Kent gaining tries (one beautifully converted by Stoddart from near touch). In a repeat of the game's opening, Haslam again muffed a kick, giving Bathurst another converted try and 10-7 lead. From one of the Lions' favourite moves—the quick throw-in from touch near the opponent's goal line—Kent went over for a converted try. "This seemed to be the last straw for the home team," said Seddon. "Their exertion in the first half began to tell upon them and we had pretty much our own way from this point to the finish, tries being secured by Dr. Brooks, Stoddart, Eagles and Anderton. Eventually we won by 20 points to 10."

"Speakman, for his first time a half-back, played a good game, Stoddart and Dr. Brooks being the best at three-quarter back, the forwards, especially in the second half, playing a very fast game," said Seddon. "The passing of our team is undoubtedly our success, for the ball goes through some 10 or 12 hands before a try is secured."

Seddon noted that "all the players are enjoying themselves immensely" but for once the post-match evening in an Australian country town finished early; the much anticipated kangaroo hunt being on at dawn. Much bigger than their previous outing, this was a party that comprised over 100 people.

Seddon wrote:

> Six o'clock next morning saw about 15 waggonettes at the hotel ready to convey us to the field of slaughter. Half an hour later we were on our way, each being supplied with guns and shot. After two hours' drive we arrived at the forest (bush), and very soon all was bustle and commotion. In a very short time fires were lit, tea brewing in 'billies' and each man cooking his own steak at the end of a long stick. It would have surprised a careful housewife at home to see the vast quantity of steaks so quickly disappear, besides fowls, tinned beef, cheese, etc.
>
> Soon after we started for the forest. The 'beaters', 20 in number, all mounted, formed a half-circle, the shooters forming another. The beaters drove the kangaroos, hares, etc., which we shot down. The first 'beat' was pretty successful, somewhere about 35 kangaroos and hares falling to our guns. After this we moved on to the mountains, where we were again successful.
>
> The day's outing was one of the most enjoyable we have had. Getting the spoil together we found that our day's sport resulted in bagging about 120 kangaroos and hares. Many of these we skinned, some of us carrying home the skins as trophies.

Seddon had a moment that gave him pause though:

> The scenery here was simply wonderful. I was so lost in my admiration that I had almost forgotten the shooting and rambled down the rocks but was brought up short by hearing a gun shot and feeling a few pellets on my back. In very short time I had forgotten the scenery and rushed for safety!

After a long afternoon of entertainment and fun-making that extended deep into the evening, Seddon and the other tourists boarded the train back to the city. With the victory over Sydney University, the Lions' final fixture in the colony's capital, some summations were made as the team prepared to head north for games in Queensland.

"We had some very good games in Sydney," Shrewsbury told reporters, "and a lot of people attended the matches. The NSW men played a very good game but there is no doubt they are behind New Zealand in football. They appeared to have no show of winning with our team. They are very fond of the Rugby game and there is every reason to believe considerable improvements will be made in the next few years. Our visit has given the game in NSW a great fillip. The Rugby Union (NSWRU) does all it can to encourage the game. I do not believe it made a penny out of our visit but did all it could to make the matches popular. There was a large attendance at the first match in Sydney, but the public would have liked to see the games more equal to induce them to turn out better."

"NSW players are certainly not up to the New Zealand standard," agreed Seddon. "Generally they are much too small for Rugby. They are thus placed at a disadvantage. They have some smart players but I think a good big one is better than a good little one. They are three or four years behind the time."

"The fact that NSW football is considerably ... behind real football as she is played has been pretty considerably proved by the visit of the English players," *The Referee* lamented. "Having the plenitude of good material at our disposal that we undoubtedly have, it behoves us to try and make the best of it ... I should like to see, and I have said before, the working-man element introduced into our clubs."

During the time the Lions were in Sydney the interest and attendances at Rugby, for once, rivalled that of sculling and cricket. *Town & Country* urged Rugby in "NSW to do as some great countries of old—namely, to learn from defeat how to gain victory. Then football will remain popular even after the British team shall have left us. Consequently, if the players of football in

NSW will only learn to play so as to make their performances interesting to the people, they may be certain that the popularity into which the game leaped on Saturday will not be permitted to lesson as far as the public goes. But the NSW players must make up their minds to do this. As far as football or any other manly game is concerned, NSW has as good material to go upon as has Britain. All she wants to do is to learn to use it. Let her do as she did in cricket. At first Britain walked over Australia in that. Now there is at the least not much to choose between the two. This is what must be done in football."

As many had hoped—and many in the VFA warned—the Lions tour gave Rugby a vital boost. By the mid-1890s Australian Rules was no longer played in NSW except along its southern border towns (though under a post-Federation nationalism it began again in Sydney in 1903). In less than 20 years after the visit of Seddon's team, Sydney had gone on to establish the record for the top two largest attendances for any football games in Australasia and for Rugby anywhere in the world (NSW *v.* All Blacks, 52,000; Australia *v.* All Blacks, 48,000—both were at the SCG, winter 1907). Rugby had been embraced right across all walks of life in Sydney. *The Referee* wrote at the start of 1908:

> The Sydney public has been educated to Rugby and every year the game is being played in improved style with greater skill. The international and New Zealand matches bring into Rugby an element that nothing in the Australian game [in Melbourne], however brilliant big club games may appear to the local eye can compare. In order that Melburnians may not be deluded, it is well for them to know that the Rugby internationals and those against New Zealand in Sydney draw far bigger crowds and excite deeper interest for the time, than Test matches at cricket. When Messrs. Harrison and T.W. Wills and others broke away from Rugby football and founded the Australian game, one great point was lost sight of—others beside themselves were capable of thinking out improvements in football. And today, Rugby, played well,

is a grand game. When played badly, it is probably not worse than the Australian game played badly.

Ironically, or regrettably, or however you wish to frame it, that staggering success (and the resulting build up of gate-taking money) caused deep divisions, envy, opportunism and questions of equity and fairness that brought forth a rebellion within Rugby in Sydney, culminating in the arrival of Rugby League.

Noble Guests of Football Fame

"Football, as played under Rugby rules tended to give players and onlookers savage, barbarous feelings … a person might as well look at a prize fight."
Reverend Canon Tyrell, President, Northumberland FC,
The Maitland Mercury, July 19, 1883

"The sail was a most beautiful sight, which will long be remembered by most of our players," wrote Seddon in a letter home. The captain was describing the team's journey north from Sydney to the inland city of West Maitland. With no railway bridge yet constructed, traversing the Hawkesbury River necessitated leaving one train at Kangaroo Point (near Brooklyn), taking an eastward ride on an American-style paddle-steamer up to Gosford, where another train was waiting. "Sailing up the river, a bright moon was out and creeks and tall mountains covered with trees on each side of us, while we were smoking and singing as if we had not a care in the whole wide world."

For the tourists their great adventure still had two more stages—first Queensland, then a return visit through New Zealand. On their way to

Brisbane, the Lions would stop at Maitland, playing a game of Australian Rules, then move across to the coast again for a Rugby match at Newcastle. Penketh and Bumby, still on the injured list, had remained behind in Sydney, while "the passenger" Clowes was "absent in Yarrunga," a small village near the spectacular Fitzroy Falls in the Southern Highlands to the south-west of Sydney.

"From Newcastle," explained Seddon, "we have two days and nights' journey by train to Brisbane, where we play some three or four matches in the districts. Mr. Lillywhite has had a very pressing letter asking us to visit Rockhampton, some 400 miles further, and play two matches, but our time being so fully occupied I hardly think it probable we shall visit them."

Maitland is located 30km upstream from Newcastle on the Hunter River and developed as a major inland commercial centre, the result of being the furthest point cargo carrying boats could reach. This was enhanced when the rail came through and by the 1880s, as with much of the Hunter region, coal mining became a major industry and job provider.

Arriving in the town after midnight, Mrs. Hodgson, the landlady of the Royal Hotel, had ensured all was in readiness for "the noble guests of football fame" from Britain. Still there today (246 High Street), though no longer a pub and with its ornate front verandahs long gone, the three-storey Georgian building had first class dining, ample bars and billiards rooms. A few of the players were housed at the Excelsior Hotel as well.

Maitland and the region had its adherents to Rugby but the preferred game was Australian Rules. The Northern District representative team the Lions were to meet was a mix of players from Wallsend, Newcastle, Summerhill, Northumberland (West Maitland) and Our Boys' clubs. Any VFA clubs from Melbourne that came to Sydney to play invariably made their way to Maitland as well, Fitzroy and South Melbourne among them.

Being a working Tuesday, drawing a big crowd was made more difficult when the local mayor declined to declare a "half-holiday" afternoon, as had been customary nearly everywhere else the British team visited for mid-week contests. A start just after 3pm meant bank and office workers could get there, but not anyone from the local stores or other workshops. Special trains were laid on from Wallsend and Newcastle.

Arrangements had been made for the visitors to be given a tour of the "the picturesque country about Maitland, but by special request they were allowed to pass the morning roaming at their own sweet will, as they expressed themselves as tired and sadly in need of a rest". The afternoon was perfect for football. "The weather throughout our tour has been very summerlike," said Seddon (who must have driven the Ballarat snow game from his memory). "When we hear the colonials complaining of it being cold, it brings a smile to our faces. Our match was played in 78 degrees (25 celsius) of heat; this is the winter weather we are enjoying out here."

The Lions had long-tired of hiding their desire not to play any further Australian Rules games; compounded when barely 700 people turned up to watch them. Seddon and his old friend, the "war horse" Harry Eagles, were the only men left that had played in every game of the tour. The kick-off was delayed as the visitors couldn't muster 20 fit and willing men, "as two of the team were a bit off colour" come game time. P. Kennedy and R. Norman from the Northumberland club took their places in the British team. "Our men didn't seem to enter into this game with any spirit whatever," said Seddon with disappointment.

"Seddon fought bravely for old England," recorded *The Maitland Mercury* but it seemed a lone hand. Even their star kickist had an inexplicably off-day. "Stoddart missed three or four very easy goals, an unusual occurrence," wrote a somewhat puzzled Seddon. The result showed it too: "English football team defeated at Maitland (Northern Districts) by nine goals (19 behinds) to four goals (five behinds)".

The Maitland Mercury, who before the game described the home team as "a weedy looking lot" compared to the Lions, decided afterwards the tourists "are just a bit too heavy and too slow to be champions of the Australian game". *The Newcastle Morning Herald* added: "The team is an unusually heavy one and the game calls forth not weight, which is essential in Rugby, but the activity and dexterity which the solid looking Britons seem to lack—in other words, 'They're not built that way'." All the promoters could do was lament what the tour earnings might have been with a team more suited to Australian Rules. "If they had, they would have taken a ton of Victorian gold back to England with them," *The Maitland Mercury* suggested.

The footballers, still in uniforms, returned by horse-drawn carriages to where they had prepared for the battle; for the Lions it was back to the Royal Hotel. After a bath and change of clothes, they were ready to turn their attention to the evening. Even in Maitland the roller skate reigned, with the night at Galton's Skating Rink dedicated to a celebration and welcome to the Britishers. "Inside, the place was beautifully decorated with red, white and blue, and 'Welcomes' (banners) hanging all about the place," described Seddon.

The following morning Seddon spent some time in his room at the Royal Hotel, completing another letter home. He then went down to the river with his teammates; he was a good swimmer and enjoyed rowing but on this occasion was happy to stand on the water's edge watching the others enjoy themselves at the 'floating baths' next to the Maitland Rowing Club's boathouse. Banks tried his hand at rowing in a 'stump outrigger', a short sculling race boat. It is normally an easy craft to handle but somehow he managed to capsize it.

After an hour so of fun and exercise, everyone returned to their hotel rooms to pack and get ready for their departure to Newcastle on the early afternoon train. Stoddart and Anderton announced they preferred to do some more boating on the river and would catch the early evening train instead. Seddon in the meantime had told Lillywhite he was going stay for the later train as well, wanting to use the time to write last minute letters for the mail ship that was leaving Newcastle that night for England.

"We left him standing outside his hotel at Maitland," said Shrewsbury, "with no hat upon his head and a cigarette in his mouth, in the very best of health and spirits. It was a most beautiful day, the sun shining out in full splendour and Bob stood looking the very impersonation of perfect happiness and contentment."

The Great Game of Life Itself

"Then came the gloom upon our enjoyment."
Jack Anderton, British Rugby team, Maitland, August 15, 1888

———

Tom Haslam came hurrying into the hotel, tears in his eyes: "Bob Seddon is drowned!"

"At first no one could realise the possibility of such an event occurring, as only an hour and a half previous we had seen him," said Shrewsbury. The team had left Maitland railway station at 1.50pm and arrived in Newcastle at 2.50pm. "We had only taken up our quarters at the hotel about a quarter of an hour when in rushed Tom."

"His death was so sudden," said Dr. Brooks. They had left Seddon "quite jolly, and when we got to Newcastle an hour and a half afterwards, we received a telegram announcing his death. It was a terrible shook to us all."

What the telegram to the team said—and who sent it—is not known. It is unlikely to have been any more informative than the news cable that went out shortly after:

Mr. Seddon, the captain of the English football team, was

drowned in the Hunter River at Maitland this afternoon. He had gone out rowing in an outrigger, which capsized with him and before assistance could be rendered, he sank.

Dr. Smith spoke of "the grief that has fallen upon us all, and no amount of pleasure that we may derive from the rest of our tour will eradicate from our memories the shock the tidings gave us this afternoon. Were it not that our promoters' interests are at stake, we would one and all prefer, under the circumstances, to disband and return home at once."

Harry Eagles, Seddon's friend for more than 20 years, and himself having saved people from drowning, was particularly distraught. Each of the team would say they would willingly have dived into the river and given assistance but Eagles undoubtedly and unhesitatingly would have. So too many of the tens of thousands of Australians and New Zealanders that had come in contact with the team and the numberless admirers of its captain. Instead, at that moment when he most needed help, Seddon was entirely alone.

With the departure of the mail ship for England imminent, Shrewsbury hurriedly prepared a letter to the *Athletic News*, which in part said:

It is a cruel blow for the team, by whom he was very much liked and respected, and what must it be for his own relations in England? I don't know that I ever met a more straightforward, honourable, and honest young fellow in my life and I don't think I am likely to. A meeting of the team was at once convened, and our match with Newcastle, which was to have taken place to-morrow, broken off. From what I have already been able to gather—which must not yet be taken for truth—it would appear that his feet were fastened by straps in the boat and although he nearly succeeded in reaching the bank, the struggle was too severe, as he would have the weight of the boat to drag after him, which would be a terrible handicap. You will have seen the account of his death cabled from here a long time before you receive this and at the present time it is not necessary to go into the question as to whether he acted foolishly in going out by himself or having his feet fastened, or if he had done this or that he might have been saved. A letter of condolence, signed by all the team, is being sent Home to his brother. The mail leaves here tonight and I am only sending you a few particulars which have from different sources come to hand. In fact, I don't feel like writing or anything else. The very life appears to be taken out of me. I can't believe it is true and keep thinking he is sure to come here tonight, as arranged. He was indeed a fine fellow was Bob Seddon and the more you knew of him the more you would appreciate his nobleness of character. As captain of the team it would be impossible to find his superior, or even his equal, and the players fully recognised this when they elected him for that post. His heart and soul was in all kinds of sports and in practising or playing under the Victorian rules he showed the same eagerness to win as if playing his own Rugby game— which he was passionately fond of. He was always the first to propose practice; and he would study the rules and detect faults, if any, that other players would never notice. In fact, you could not give him too much work in connection with football.

The letter from the team to Seddon's family:

August 15,1888. To the Brothers and Sisters of the late Mr. R.L. Seddon, captain first Anglo-Australian Football Team.

We, the members of the Anglo-Australian Football Team now in Australia, beg to offer you our most heartfelt condolence in the very great loss you have sustained this day by the drowning of your much-esteemed brother and our captain, the late Mr. R.L. Seddon. Boating on the Hunter River, Maitland, New South Wales, he has met, while still in the full prime of his vigorous manhood, an untimely death far distant from you all at Home, and out of the reach even of the helping hand that would have been so willingly held out by any of his companion football players. Since we have been comrades together here he has, by the conscientious discharge of his duties as captain, his genial disposition and his largeness of heart, evoked a tender memory that will long live in the minds of us all. Our hearts are too full of sorrow to give an adequate expression to the feelings of deep sympathy which we have towards you but we take the earliest opportunity of conveying to you how sincerely we sympathise with you in your great and sudden bereavement. His memory will long live, not alone with his friends at Home, nor merely with us his touring companions in this colony, but with hundreds who have come in contact with him here and have thus been drawn within the influence of his manly and upright character.

It would be a month before those letters arrived in England. Shrewsbury and Lillywhite opted to rely upon the news cables to inform the dreadful news to the people at Home.

The cable that was flashed around the colonies, appeared in Sydney's evening newspapers that same day, and caused great distress when the terrible news reached the teams at half-time in the game in Melbourne between Tom Scarborough's Victorian XV and the 'New Zealand Natives' party that Maori footballer Joe Warbrick was about to take to England.

Charlie Mathers, a forward from the Bramley club in Yorkshire, who had played with and against Seddon many times over the past decade, wrote in his tour diary:

August 15: A telegram came saying your captain is drowned. We were all amazed and decided to cancel the match with Newcastle the following day. The effect on the team when the news arrived by telegram was devastating. At night everyone very quiet and discussing the matter.

Piecing together the various accounts, it seems that after lunch, as Stoddart and Anderton were heading out of the hotel to go down to the river, Seddon said he would join them. He reportedly was wearing his football clothing, which suggests he had made his mind up before leaving the hotel that he intended to have a row. In any event, the three men got into an "ordinary pleasure boat" and when opposite the floating baths, saw the outrigger that Banks had been tipped out of earlier in the day. Seddon said he would like to have a row in it, adding it was a boat he was familiar with, though he hadn't been in one for two years. He got into the craft and told his colleagues he would follow them.

Stoddart and Anderton headed up the river, and were soon out of sight. Some witnesses on the shore would later say that almost immediately it was apparent Seddon was unaccustomed to handling such a boat. However, Shrewsbury, presumably having obtained it from Stoddart and Anderton, gave a different account, saying Seddon "went down the river some distance and then pulled back, passing the place where Stoddart and Anderton were seated on the bank. After going about 200 yards beyond them, he disappeared round a bend in the river. About 25 minutes afterwards a boy came along and told Stoddart and Anderton that Seddon had been drowned (or was drowning). The boy said he saw him (Seddon) turn on his back in the water and make for the bank, which was distant about 15 or 16 yards, but he went down before he reached it."

"The boy informed them that a man was drowning," said Eagles in his version, "and though Stoddart and Anderton pulled hard and fast, when they had turned the bend of the river and reached the place where the accident occurred, nothing was to be seen but the upturned skiff in which Seddon had passed them some short time before laughing and joking."

Town & Country reported: "The river was not above 50 yards wide at the point where he was rowing; though it was from about 15 feet to 20 feet deep. The first that was known of the accident by his friends was obtained from a boy named Wesley Richards, who came running along the bank to them with the news that their comrade was in the water. They rowed back and observed the outrigger floating bottom upward and Seddon's cap; but nothing of their companion was to be seen."

The Newcastle Morning Herald stated his boat capsized, he was thrown out, and "two men saw him swimming and encouraged him by shouting, but could render no assistance as no boat was available". Seddon made a last desperate effort to reach the shore and safety. He "swam about 15 yards on his back and then sank twice, the last time for good".

Mathers said that a witness told him "his feet were stuck in the straps and when he struck out, he dragged the boat after him. In his death struggles he must have tried to loosen the straps under water because they were found partly unbuckled when the boat was found."

The "drags" were sent for and the alarm spread rapidly. About half an hour elapsed before the body was recovered. "Stoddart and I got him out of the water and the shock of that sight will ever remain with me," said Anderton. "We could scarcely believe our own eyes. Poor Seddon."

Medical aid was at hand and the town's doctor and others resorted to every possible means for nearly an hour to restore life, but without avail. It finally became evident to all that Seddon was gone. "The doctor who examined the body said he had died instantly and without pain, from cramp on the chest," said Anderton.

News quickly moved through the township and all of Maitland was soon in mourning. As the sun went down on that fateful day and with their teammates in Newcastle struggling to comprehend the news, Stoddart and Anderton were called to give their testimony at a hurriedly convened inquest before the coroner and a jury panel.

The evidence presented provides nothing to add to the events other than a claim that Seddon "went in the boat with odd sculls, which may have caused the accident". However, even if that were so, it doesn't explain why Seddon drowned. The rowing columnist for *The Sydney Mail* wrote that "it is difficult to solve the causes of this most unfortunate and melancholy occurrence" and that a stump rigger is a "class of boat considered very safe, easily managed, and buoyant—the accident took place on placid water and Mr. Seddon had some time previously had a practical knowledge of similar boats".

Seddon would have known to stay with the boat. "It may not be out of place to point out how easily a person can help themselves when similarly placed. When a man finds he has capsized his boat, or by any other means has been thrown into the water, his first idea is to cling to the craft. He is then quite safe, even if he cannot swim, as the boat will float lightly. It is not a difficult matter to hold on and the boat can be easily propelled, even by a weak swimmer. Accidents very seldom happen which terminate fatally but upsets and swampings are by no means rare. The most experienced men are liable at times to be thrown into the water. Several of our prominent rowers cannot swim but so little do they consider the danger that they fearlessly row in all classes of racing boats, knowing that while they retain a hold of the boat they are comparatively safe from harm."

At the inquest's conclusion "a verdict was returned that deceased met his death by asphyxia from drowning and no blame could be attributed to anyone".

"To my mind it is clear that he met his death through being seized with cramp," Shrewsbury said a few days later. "Seddon was a fairly good swimmer but there was a nasty undercurrent in the river which made swimming difficult. He would, I think, have stuck to the boat if he had not been seized with cramp and his turning over on to his back also strengthens my opinion that he was seized with it, probably through making a strong effort when he was first in the water. I do not agree with the suggestions made by several newspapers that his feet were caught in the leathers of the footboard."

The Bulletin had suggested Seddon drowned as he was unable to release his feet and that he was racing to catch up to Stoddart and Anderton, and despite the latter's account, he had not gone past them at all:

> It appears that he went with his feet strapped into the stretcher in his own boots, instead of being inserted naked (bare-footed) into big shoes strapped to the stretcher. He had not been in an outrigger for some time and was out of practice, so lost time at the start and Stoddart and Anderton got away from him.

He started to spurt after them, and not sitting his boat well and she being cranky, he drove her under. A little girl who saw him capsize says that his feet stuck in the straps, and when he struck out he actually towed the boat after him, and, of course was dragged head under and drowned. His feet must have slipped out during his death struggles and he must also have tried to loosen the straps under water, for they were found partly unbuckled when the boat was recovered. What a fearful struggle for life his must have been.

Eagles was never convinced by any of it, saying when the team returned home to England, "no adequate explanation can be given of the accident which resulted in Mr. Seddon's death". Unfortunately Stoddart, as he had done all tour, remained aloof from the press and despite the gravity of the events, never spoke about what happened on the river that day.

The sadness which came over the town as word passed from one to another that Seddon was drowned was palpable. *The Maitland Mercury* said solemnly:

The dark cloud of sorrow and the heavy pall of sadness have seldom lain more heavily upon Maitlanders in their direst calamities than on Wednesday afternoon when the news was spread that Mr. R.L. Seddon, the captain of the English team of footballers, had been drowned in the Hunter River whilst boating. The excitement evinced by the shocked community was sufficient to show the poor fellow's companions that the public of the colonies can bear their full share in sympathy.

I am not a fatalist, but death is indeed a strange, incomprehensible thing, which I suppose we will all have to undergo to understand; still it is queer to ponder over the fact that the big, strong gallant young Englishman had braved death by flood and field in his own land for years and then met his doom so tragically in a river in such an out-of-the-way corner as Maitland, a place he probably never heard of until a few short months ago. Perhaps it was poor Seddon's destiny; who knows.

The body was taken to the Royal Hotel, placed in the care of "good motherly Mrs. Hodgson, who was as deeply grieved, shocked, and put about as if the deceased had been her own son, and the body could not, or would not, have been treated with greater respect and womanly devotion if such had been the case". The funeral would be held the next day.

Anderton went to Seddon's room to collect up his belongings; searching his jacket he came upon a letter, addressed to the editor of the *Manchester Courier*. He forwarded the letter on:

> Sir,
>
> The enclosed letter, addressed to you, was, among other things, found in Mr. R.L. Seddon's breast pocket immediately after his death and had evidently been written this morning, just previous to the unfortunate circumstance, by which he lost his life, occurred, and I thought it advisable to forward same on to you.

In what the newspaper headlined 'Captain Seddon's Last Letter', he had chronicled for readers at home the kangaroo hunt in Bathurst, the final games in Sydney, sailing the Hawkesbury under moonlight, their football match in Maitland and setting out the final itinerary before the team would sail for England. He had added, "Today all of the team are going out 'driving and boating.' The rowing party will also enjoy themselves by stripping and having about an hour's fun in the water." Though the cabled news of Seddon's death spread across Britain's newspapers within two to three days, the letters he had written and posted detailing their expedition through the colonies would continue to arrive from Australia on mail ships and be posthumously published in England over the ensuing six weeks.

While the corpse lay at the Royal Hotel later that night and early the next morning, it was viewed by hundreds of deeply-affected Maitlanders, who smothered the polished cedar coffin with great numbers of wreaths and flowers, mostly violets and orange blossoms; also left were many memorial cards with kind words and fitting mottos.

"He had made a host of sterling friends, in Sydney, Melbourne, Adelaide, and all through New Zealand," wrote the *Australian Star*. "Never in the annals of our football career has so sad an occasion commanded our sympathies." A delivery brought two magnificent wreaths on behalf of the Geelong and Fitzroy football clubs in Melbourne. Telegrams to the team expressing the deepest sympathy came from football clubs and associations from across the colonies, including from Hobart where the tourists first landed back in April. *The West Australian* in Perth wrote: "All footballers will read with regret in our telegraphic intelligence of the sad accident which has befallen the skipper of the first English football team that visited the colonies."

Mid-morning the rest of the Lions team arrived back in Maitland with hundreds of other mourners on a specially chartered train organised by Newcastle footballers. The injured men, Penketh and Bumby, apparently would not have sufficient time to arrive from Sydney to attend, while Clowes, dealing with the sad news on his own, was even further away. Mathers' diary noted:

> August 16: In morning went from Newcastle to Maitland, 20 miles to bury our poor, unfortunate captain, Mr. Seddon. When we got there we found him laid in his coffin. They all broke down but me.

John Gillies, the town mayor, told the team: "It had been my pleasure to see him (Seddon) marshalling and commanding his men in the field on the occasion of the match with our local team on the day previous, and I was much gratified with his manly, generous bearing, highly indicative of genuine British generosity and gentlemanly characteristics. Little did I think at the time that within a few hours his fine active form would be passive and silent in death and in such sad circumstances. As a lover of the game, especially when carried out in that manly spirit displayed by your team in this colony, I cannot say how sorry I am at your loss."

"I should not care to live through another day like that on which poor Bob Seddon was buried," said Dr. Brooks speaking about it a few weeks later. "It was touching. The sympathy extended to us was something wonderful."

The funeral procession started from the Royal Hotel at 3pm. In the 30 minutes or so before that, Reverend Warner met the members of the Lions team in the room where the body lay. He offered a few words of sympathy, read a portion of scripture and prayed with them.

The funeral was one of the largest ever known in the Maitland district. "As a testimonial of public sympathy it could not be surpassed," reported *Town & Country*. It was estimated between 2000 to 3000 people were present. "He might have been one of the oldest and most respected residents, judging by the sincere and universal condolence that was shown on that lamentable occasion," said Anderton. A Maitland newspaper clipping stated: "That his melancholy end was keenly felt, not only by his comrades but by the whole population was plainly shown by the splendid turn out. Almost every business place in Maitland closed out of respect to the memory of the deceased."

The players placed a wreath on the coffin, then eight of them lifted and carried it on their shoulders outside the hotel, carefully placing it in the waiting hearse—the carriage was drawn by four black horses, plumed and dressed entirely in sable. It was a sad and solemn spectacle as the train of mourners moved out on its path to St. Paul's Church. The procession was headed by 300 footballers of the Maitland and Newcastle districts, wearing their club colours in crape on their breast; then came the hearse, flanked on its sides by officials from the local football clubs. Behind the hearse walked all the British footballers with Shrewsbury and Lillywhite, followed by four mourning coaches, the mayor and other public officials, then 60 other vehicles, mostly buggies, and hundreds more on foot and horseback completed the tail.

"They had a beautiful choral service in the church," said Brooks. The funeral was conducted by Reverend Warner. "The scene in the church—the coffin completely covered with flowers; strong men, his companions from home, weeping like children," one local noted. "The surpliced (white gowns) choir had been got together and when the solemn hymn *Brief Life Is Here*

Our Portion was sung, many a stout heart gave way to tears and the grief that was outwardly shown by the numerous congregations assembled to join in the solemn service was doubtless nothing by comparison with what was inwardly felt."

As the congregation left the church, the organist played Handel's *Dead March in Saul*. The cortege then moved to the cemetery, passing through the town along the way. All of the shops and businesses were closed, thousands of people "who had come to do honour to dead" and give consolation to the grieving, stood quietly along the route, many ladies wiping away tears, men bare headed; nothing to be heard but the shuffle of feet and horses' hooves, the whirr of slowly moving vehicles, and above it all the sombre tolling over and over of the large bell of St. Mary's Church. Mr. Galton's skating rink now coming into view, its doors shut, all its rooftop flags at half-mast, fluttering in the now cold, late-afternoon breeze.

Nearing the cemetery it could be seen the approaches to the grave were lined thick with mourners. Reverend Canon Tyrell joined Reverend Warner in officiating at the burial. The coffin was borne to the grave by members of the team, the rest gathering all round. All looked very distressed, and when the coffin "was lowered scarcely a dry eye could be discerned among the vast assemblage".

Before the team boarded the train to recommence their tour, they prepared and left the following letter:

> The promoters and members of the Anglo-Australian football team beg to express their heartfelt gratitude and thanks to the inhabitants of West Maitland and district—particularly those who took an active part in the funeral of the late Mr. R.L. Seddon—for the many sympathies were displayed by them on the sad event becoming known and to say that the many kindnesses which have been shown to them in their sad bereavement will never be forgotten. West Maitland and its sympathetic inhabitants will always remain foremost in

> our memories and we shall convey Home to the friends and relatives of our late respected captain a faithful account of your kind and Christianlike behaviour at this sad period of our tour, which up to now has been full of happy and pleasant recollections of the colonies.
>
> Royal Hotel, West Maitland, August 16, 1888

Speaking on behalf of the team, Dr. Smith also particularly thanked "Mrs. Hodgson, the genial proprietress of the Royal Hotel, for her noble conduct during the last two days in connection with the funeral arrangements. That lady, whose kindness of heart, had manifested true womanly sympathy and affection. Mrs. Hodgson could not have shown more consideration if it had been her own relative who was lying dead."

In the evening a meeting of local footballers was held, where it was resolved to raise donations from footballers and their supporters throughout Australasia, to erect a memorial over the grave, and to place a tablet on a wall in St. Paul's Church. Just on a year later, both objectives had been achieved:

> This tablet is erected by sympathising friends and comrades in memory of Robert L. Seddon, Captain of the English Footballers, drowned in the River Hunter, at West Maitland, August 15th, 1888, aged 28 years. The funeral service was held in this church August 16th. 'Death took him in the morning of his days. Or e'er he reached the goal.'
>
> A fine monument has been placed over the grave in the Church of England cemetery, Campbell's Hill. It has a bluestone base, above which is a white marble pedestal, and on the side of which has been carved a scroll with flowers. Bound to a marble broken column, emblematic of a shortened life, is a rustic cross, with a circlet of flowers, significant of faith. The whole is enclosed with bluestone, having cast iron railing of neat design. The monument is some eleven feet high. 'By kindly hands thy humble grave adorned, By strangers honoured and by strangers mourned'.

THE GREAT GAME OF LIFE ITSELF

In late 2012 St. Paul's Church was deconsecrated; while the tablet remains in its place on the wall, it now overlooks the building's new use as a childcare centre. Though the gravesite and headstone could do with repairs, the cemetery and monument can still be visited today.

Some in Australia suggested the blow the news of his death would deliver in England would be less severe as Seddon's parents were already deceased, he was not married and had no children. Restoring some logic and sensibility, an unattributed letter spoke of the pain the news must have caused Seddon's relatives and friends at home, particularly his fiancé:

> Ere this the cable will have flashed the news to the Mother Country, where the grief of old friends will be o'ershadowed by the sorrow of one whose once fair face, now pale and careworn, bespeaks too plainly that life has lost much of its brightness for her. How empty is the sorrow of others when placed beside such bitter pain as she must feel at the loss of him, who was all-in-all to her, and who left her looking hopefully forward to their next meeting. It was well known that Mr. Seddon was to be married on his return to England, and now he sleeps his last sleep in a strange land, to which the thoughts of her he loved will ever be turning, with a heart beating sadly at the thought that there are no loving hands to keep the weeds from encroaching upon his earthy couch or twining their foul arms round the headstone which marks the spot where lie the mortal remains of R.L. SEDDON, a true footballer, a genial comrade, and real good fellow, liked by all, disliked by none. In his time he saw many goals won, won by earnest and devoted work. Let us fondly trust that he who rests in that sacred ground at Maitland, has gained a higher and greater victory than any secured on earth, and has achieved that goal for which all of us are striving.

Relatives in England began to hear about and see for themselves the newspaper headlines and the very brief telegraphed reports of the tragedy, but dismissed them as false. "Naturally the poor folk," wrote an English newspaper, "willing to persuade themselves against the truth of such a disaster, argued that that the wire must be a mistake because, said they, we would be the first to know. Surely if Lillywhite and Shrewsbury could not have been at the trouble to wire to his relatives, some of the team might have done so. Not a word was cabled and the first and only intimation his family received was through a *Sporting Life* telegram."

"How terrible the suspense was can scarcely be imagined," said James Seddon, Robert's brother. "I wrote to Shaw and Shrewsbury's place at Nottingham (Henry Turner) and was informed they had no definite news. Not much consolation to a family distracted with grief. At the least they might have wired out for confirmation or offered to do so. I had just arranged with the Swinton club to wire out to Australia, when we saw the announcement of his funeral on the *News* placard, and at once gave up all further hope.

"Amidst all our trouble we must not forget the universal sympathy that has been shown towards us, and especially thankful ought we to be to those good people of Maitland, who so thoughtfully and well did the last honours to what remained of our beloved brother. I don't know if I shall ever get as far as the grave, but should much like to, and the first opportunity that presents itself I am off."

The Melbourne *Argus* concluded its report on the funeral by writing:

> His end was truly sad. He left Home a few short months ago, full of life and manly vigour, to seek pleasure and enjoyment, and to uphold the prestige of his country in the football field and has found a grave in a strange land, far removed from relatives and friends.

IN MEMORIAM.
ROBERT L. SEDDON

CAPTAIN ENGLISH FOOTBALL TEAM.

His manly form lies stiff in death's calm hush;
* Never again upon his men he'll call;*
No more across the turf he'll lead the rush
* Of forwards, ever playing "On the ball."*

No more we'll grip his honest English hand,
* Nor hear his cheery greeting as of yore;*
And they, his comrades in that sea-girt land,
Will watch in vain. They'll meet him nevermore.

Brother and sister, in that far-off home,
* Grieve not; he is at rest. His spirit free*
Calleth so tenderly across the foam,
"Brother, I am but sleeping; sister, comfort ye."

"It may seem hard to you who cannot see
* Beyond the veil—a bitter cruel lot.*
God knoweth best in all things. All that ye
Can know or do is this—Forget me not."
  —'Tackle Low' in *The Referee*

Three Hearty Cheers and a Tiger

*"As anticipated Queensland, to a man, played
a splendid dashing game throughout, giving their
opponents all their work to do to defend their citadel."*
Queensland Figaro and Punch, September 1, 1888

Understandably a tiring three days on a steam train did nothing to lift the gloom naturally resting upon the tour party. At a mayoral reception inside the Brisbane Town Hall to welcome the team to the Queensland capital, a "visibly affected" Stoddart pushed back tears as he made a return speech of thanks. "It is very trying to speak on such an occasion, knowing well that I would not be doing so if our late lamented captain had still been alive." The mayor said he was certain their stay would "be made pleasant, although the serious loss which the team had sustained in the loss of their captain could not but throw a damper on the members during the remainder of their tour in the colonies".

Mercifully perhaps, the Lions' first game was that afternoon. *The Queenslander* called it "a red-letter day in the annals of the Northern RU (now QRU), and one to be long remembered by all who had the good fortune to witness the great game played at the Exhibition Ground between the representatives of the Mother Country and this young colony". The now usual pomp was followed, the team colours bountiful around the ground, on clothes and vehicles. A brass band provided musical pieces before and during the game.

The home side turned out in all white jerseys and knickerbockers, dark maroon stockings and a short, silk necktie. An impressive sporting gentleman's attire, indeed. The Queenslanders normally wore dark blue jerseys and switched to their now traditional deep red or maroon in 1895. Their captain, Bob Wilson, was a teammate of current NSW player Henry Braddon in the New Zealand team of 1884.

Queensland Figaro noted: "Both teams wore black bands on their arms out of respect to the memory of the late Mr. Seddon" (something the Lions continued to do both on and off the field for the remainder of the tour) and were photographed at the back of the grandstand. In a touching scene, the British players gathered in the usual setting, but where the captain holding a football would normally sit in the centre they left an empty seat, placing the ball on the ground in front of his ghostly feet. Stoddart would be their field captain but Seddon would remain the tour captain. It may have just been the glare of the bright Queensland sun, but looking into the photo none have the gleaming eyes of young men ready to play football.

As was the tradition before all Rugby games the opposing sides exchanged three cheers. Here though, in their first game without their captain, the Lions gave tribute by "three cheers and a tiger"—possibly 18th-century British naval in origin, it was a style of cheering popularised in the United States during the Civil War, and reserved to mark or honour an extra special dignitary or event. In some instances the added "tiger" was an "Huzzah!" while others extended it into a short war cry of some sort, that usually ended "Rah! Rah! Rah!" Some, as the name suggests, simply unleashed a loud tiger growl or roar. Whatever it was here in Brisbane, the crowd recognised the significance of it to the tourists and showed this by giving an extra round of applause.

At the kick-off there must have been 10,000 spectators, already the largest to gather at a football game in Queensland, but continued to increase until near half-time. The scoring system reverted back to the English and New Zealand system (even though Queensland normally used the same method as NSW), but this information hadn't been widely made known to the public, and the ground had no scoreboard. The Lions crossed for seven tries (three converted) in a 13-6 victory, but many locals left the ground thinking the end result was 23-9.

Queensland's Jimmy Exton kicked the second 'flying goal' seen against the visitors during the tour (the first was in the tour opener in Dunedin). *The Brisbane Courier* said the game was "exceedingly fast, the play travelling all over the ground with great rapidity and as previously predicted, the match was undoubtedly the finest ever witnessed here". The Lions replacement captain gained most plaudits. *The Queenslander* said: "Stoddart played a most brilliant game as centre three-quarter back and it is well worth a long journey to see this fine exponent of the game play. He was well supported in the back division by Nolan, Speakman, Anderton, and Haslam. The forwards all played a hard and fast game, Eagles, Williams, and Kent being always prominent."

The Capricornian summarised the game:

> Their play (Queensland) was far more brilliant and dashing than that of their opponents but there was too much individual and too little combined effort. On the other hand, the Englishmen, though slow in their play—and, I thought, somewhat cumbrous—compared to the more dashing colonials, were certainly all there in every part of the game. When a man got away with the ball, he was invariably accompanied by two or more of his mates, and the passing was a treat to see. There was no necessity for him to look to whom he was to pass the ball and they scarcely ever did so, but when pushed simply threw the ball back a little and there was sure to be some fellow to take it. This, to my mind, was just where the other fellows failed.

THREE HEARTY CHEERS AND A TIGER

Looking forward to the Queenslanders coming back stronger in the return game, *The Brisbane Courier* wrote: "When it is considered who they had opposed to them ... it is only hoped that they may have learnt enough from the Englishmen to make even a better fight next Saturday". The tourists were finding it a bit hard to adapt to the 'winter' conditions enjoyed by Queenslanders. "At Brisbane we found it excessively hot sometimes, more like the cricket weather at home in July," said Shrewsbury.

Away from the hosted engagements, the players were free to avail themselves at any of Brisbane's four skating rinks (a fifth was set to open within days). The round of entertainment then began: first a visit with the Queensland team to the Opera House that evening. Another night the tourists were guests of honour at a banquet and ball held by "the Lancashire Association", who arranged for the players to be collected by a fleet of hansom cabs and had "very great pleasure in tendering a very hearty welcome not only to the Lancashire men but to all the gentlemen of the English football team". A special toast was made to the memory of Bob Seddon, who, being from Lancashire, meant all gave it an especially heart-felt touch.

In the first of two mid-week games, the Lions were pitted against "18 Combined Juniors of Queensland." *Queensland Figaro* suggested the visitors did as "they jolly well liked" with the Juniors in an 11-3 victory. *The Queenslander* added: "There is no doubt that the boys were quite overmatched; still they played up pluckily and well, showing at times some very creditable play. The Englishmen played a very gentle game, scarcely ever throwing any of the boys, and it is to be hoped the juniors have picked up a few of the fine points in the Englishmen's play."

The following game was in Ipswich, a major inland port and centre of a mining district, some 40km to the south-west of Brisbane on the Bremmer River. A short train journey brought the Lions to Ipswich on the morning of the match and a large crowd had gathered at the railway platform to welcome them.

Naturally, all then headed to the pub, the team carried on wagons and carriages to White's Australian Hotel. The mayor made a nice speech of welcome and Stoddart returned in kind, eulogising "the sporting spirit displayed to them since their advent to Queensland".

One of the speakers said: "The Englishmen would, no doubt, notice that there was a spirit of Australian nationality growing up among them, but they still held out the right hand of fellowship to their visitors."

After a generous luncheon ended with a rollicking rendition of *For They Are Jolly Good Fellows*, the teams were taken via carriages on a tour of the city and surrounding lands. They then walked from the hotel to the North Ipswich Reserve, followed by a convoy of horse-drawn drags, men on horseback and pedestrians. At the ground a marquee had been erected, allowing the players to change into their football togs. The Lions were out of resources and carried to Brisbane two 'ring-ins' for the day, Deacon Wadsworth (a crack half-back of the Union Harriers club and the Queensland team) and Tom Bryce (forward from the Fireflies club). The Ipswich Rangers included four players who had appeared for Queensland.

A crowd of more than 3000 locals were left disappointed at the start made by their team. Almost all of the play in the first half was near the Ipswich goal line, enabling the visitors to amass an 11 to nil lead. "In the second half," said the *Queensland Figaro* report, "the Englishmen easing off somewhat enabled Ipswich to put on more steam, which they did, and their play in the second half was of a much more dashing description than that shown in the first half of the game." The result in the finish was 12 (7 tries, 1 conversion, 1 drop goal) to two.

In Rockhampton's *Morning Bulletin* in 1929, a "grey beard" recalled the Lions match and the local excitement it caused among the boys at Ipswich Grammar School:

> The first impetus to Rugby football was the visit of the English team in 1888 ... Stoddart was a slick mover on the field and he scored a try after Steve Welsh, the Ipswich full-back, tore his pants off. The head at the Grammar had so little time for Rugby that he declined to take half-an-hour off in the dinner hour and let us out at 3pm. We had to stay in until half-past three. There

was a helter skelter rush from the school to the North Ipswich grounds and some records were broken. The heads (team captains) were sympathetic and they delayed the kick-off till 3.45. We saw all the game and Ipswich got a hiding. That English team was a very fine one; it was before the North of England cut adrift and started what is now known as the League game.

The opposition to the Rugby game can be imagined when I mention that the head of the Grammar School, Mr. Donald Cameron, M.A. of Edinburgh University, would not allow a change from the Victorian game to Rugby. Brought up in that [Edinburgh] atmosphere of Rugby, where I doubt the Victorian code had then been heard of, one would have expected a Scotsman to stand up for the national [Empire] game. But he was its bitterest opponent. We used to indulge in surreptitious games of Rugby and once, after a scratch match one Saturday afternoon in which I got rather badly gravel rashed on the face, I was carpeted by him on the Monday morning and asked to explain. When I told him I had been playing Rugby his wrath knew no bounds and I thought I was in for a hiding.

Ipswich Grammar changed to Rugby from Australian Rules the first season after the Lions visit, joining the only other two high schools in Queensland—Toowoomba Grammar and Brisbane Grammar—both of which had switched to Rugby in 1886. The change of codes had been demanded by the boys themselves, in the wake of fellow schoolboy Fred O'Rourke (Brisbane Grammar) starring for Queensland in their first victory in Sydney over the NSW reps.

The switch in allegiance by the three schools mirrored the trend throughout the colony, with the QRU boasting 25 clubs as the 1888 season neared. It was rapid growth given the QRU had only been founded in 1883 with just two informal teams (Wasps and Fireflies). Football in the Brisbane and Ipswich region in the 1870s saw clubs playing either of the two English codes, Australian Rules, or locally devised rules. In 1880 the Queensland Football Association (now AFLQ) was formed, and its six clubs played

Australian Rules, but also set aside specific Saturdays for playing games under Rugby. Modern claims there were 300 clubs playing Australian Rules in Queensland in the early 1880s simply defy all sense when one ponders for a brief moment just how many players that would have required.

"The Rugby game is running out the Victorian in Brisbane," Shrewsbury wrote home. During the Lions stay *Queensland Figaro* stated "as far as Melbourne rules are concerned, to say the least of it, the past season has been a very sick one as regards this game" and "Jim Kelly ... swears he will make the Victorian game hum is this city next season, or die in the attempt. You will have to work very hard, Kelly, old man, to make the dry bones live; take it from me."

The final game was the return fixture against Queensland. A crowd as large as the preceding Saturday welcomed both teams to the arena. The play at the start was fast and furious, with Queensland putting in a much better effort all round, and no longer fell for the Britishers' feinting to pass and other ruses. "The game up to half-time being most interesting and of a nature that will not again be seen in Queensland for some time to come," wrote *The Queenslander*. The tourists had a 1-0 lead thanks to a runaway try from Stoddart, but it went unconverted. The same paper continued:

> During the second half Stoddart unfortunately had to play with a bad shoulder but after a short spell at full-back he returned manfully to his post as centre three-quarter and played a wonderfully plucky game, tackling time after time with one arm. During this half Stoddart and R. Burnett both secured tries for England, which Paul converted into goals, although the general opinion of those who were in a position to see is that both these tries should have been disallowed—one because the ball was put in one side of a scrummage and went right through to Speakman [on the opposite side of the scrum] without being played, and the other because it is asserted that Burnett was off-side when he took the pass; however, the two umpires agreed, and their decision was final. The Queensland team played very hard during the last quarter

of an hour and certainly deserved to score, but they were unable to do so, and when time was called victory rested with the Englishmen, who scored seven points to Queensland's nil.

Queensland Figaro, with some local bravado perhaps, felt the visit of the Lions would pay dividends, writing: "The play shown by the Queensland team in the late contest will do a vast amount of good to the Rugby game in this colony and I am safe in asserting that Queensland will, in the course of another season or two, have a football team worthy to contend with any in Australia, New Zealand, yes, or even the Old World."

The Queenslander agreed: "Our boys deserve every credit for the fine and plucky game they played against such redoubtable opponents and when they better understand the finer points of the game they will be able to more than hold their own against any team in Australia. The Northern RU (QRU) are to be congratulated upon their enterprise in going to the heavy undertaking of bringing the English team to Queensland and certainly deserve the best thanks of the sport-loving members of the community for showing them true Rugby Union football."

As the decade came to a close, *Queensland Figaro* summed up the state of play in the colony as "Rugby, an unbounded success; Melbourne (Australian) Rules very sick indeed, in fact on their last legs; British Association Rules (soccer), also in a sickly state, but if anything showing more life than the Victorian game." Speaking at the QRU annual meeting in 1894, J.E. Stevens, the QRU president, reflected upon how far the code had come: "Some years ago one or two clubs played Rugby but it was now played throughout the colony and the football game of Queensland was undoubtedly Rugby. There were no signs that any other game was likely to become so popular as it."

Following the win over Queensland, the Lions had two more days in Brisbane and surrounds, before they had the sad task of re-visiting Newcastle to play the game called off when news of Bob Seddon's drowning reached them. From there they would go on to Sydney and take the steamer to New Zealand.

255

The tour party arrived in Newcastle early on the day of match, and were taken to the Great Northern Hotel on Scott Street (which still trades today, though not the original building) for a reception from officials and players from the local Rugby clubs. Some kind words were given in remembrance of their captain and good wishes for the team. The contest received scant newspaper coverage in what became a very low-key departure from Australia for the tourists. The brief mention in *Town & Country* said, in passing: "In Newcastle the weight of the visitors beside our light Northerners was very noticeable and although our lads played a plucky uphill game, they had no show at all against their heavy opponents, who simply brushed them out of their way when necessity required it." The final result was a 14-7 win to the Lions.

Only *The Sydney Mail* gave any mention at all of the tourists' departure from Australia and that was meagre: "Hardly a soul turned up to say goodbye to the British footballers when they left for New Zealand by the *Manapouri* the other day."

One who was there on the dock waving the team off was Clowes. Shrewsbury had again arranged lodgings for him, so he could leave the young footballer behind while the tourists worked their way through New Zealand over the course of September. The treatment of Clowes seems unnecessarily harsh and petty, merely for the sake of saving a few pounds. He would rendezvous with the tourists in Wellington in early October, in time to board the *Kaikoura* for the voyage home.

A Trip Through Maori Land

"Before many seasons have gone by a New Zealand team is certain to come over and a good one it will be."
Arthur Shrewsbury (on the prospect of a New Zealand team playing in Britain), Auckland, September 1888

———

The Lions players could see from their vantage on the *Manapouri* deck on their approach to Auckland's Queen Street wharf there were some 200 people waiting. By the time the steamer pulled alongside, the footballers had been greeted three boisterous cheers of welcome and they returned the cheer in kind. As soon as the gangway was put out many of the gathered local footballers and friends of the team swarmed on board the ship, hand-shaking and hugging the men once more to New Zealand shores. A few of the team carried football injuries but they were all in good health and spirits, though the black band round the arm or hat of each man showed that they were mourning an absent friend.

No one seemed to be wishing the tour over or regretting a second visit to the colony. "It will be quite a treat to play on soft ground, after the hard fields of Australia," said Stoddart. Though now captain, he was no more inclined to speak to newspaper men then he had been all tour. The Lions were to spend a month traversing New Zealand, playing a further 10 games before boarding the *Kaikoura* for the return voyage home. Again it was a tight schedule of playing and travelling; an uneventful five-day sea voyage from Sydney had provided welcome respite and refreshed the players but after such a long campaign, fatigue lurked very close to the surface.

In Auckland two games were played, though not without some difficulty in arranging a second match. Initially contests were to be against Auckland representatives and then a combined North Island team (or another against Auckland), but the Auckland RU demanded too high a percentage for Shrewsbury's liking. The first game against Auckland was confirmed, but for the second, as had happened in Wellington during the first visit, an unofficial team would have to be raised after the Auckland RU refused to be involved. The public supported both games well, drawing a combined total near 17,000.

The teams were again taken to the ground in a procession of heavily decorated carriages along with a brass band, flag waving and the usual pageantry. The Lions, out of respect for Seddon, chose not to hoist any flags in their vehicle. The contest itself was hard fought but did not reach any spectacular heights, the only score of the day being a rather easy but nevertheless smartly kicked drop goal by Speakman, taking advantage of an opportunity close to the posts in the second half.

For the second game a meeting was held at the Imperial Hotel to finalise the home team and elect a captain; in this case they appointed Timothy O'Connor, a member of the 1884 New Zealand team that visited Sydney, and who later won titles in shot put and hammer throw at Australasian athletic championships. Bob Whiteside, thought to have been consigned to retirement after his lengthy farewell from the field during the contest against the Lions back in May, revived his unintentionally comic "a soldier of the Queen" routine by demanding, and obtaining, a fitness test so as to have another tussle with the Britishers. "The crack three-quarter showed good form while he lasted," wrote the *Auckland Star*, "but after about 15 minutes play he declared that he could feel his knee getting weak and that he had better not play tomorrow, a decision that everybody will agree with."

Of the game *Press* said "the football match today was one of the hardest that has been fought out here and a deal of very rough play was indulged in on both sides. The team Auckland put in the field played much better than our representatives did on Saturday. In the line-out play, the Aucklanders showed an improvement, but in dodgy [evasive] runs, following up and drop-kicking, three of the strongest points for the Englishmen, they were sadly deficient."

The Lions scored an unconverted try in the opening half—from a line-out win "Stoddart again secured the ball from a neat pass from Bumby and got in with a grand dodgy run". In the second half Stoddart got over the line but a tackler took the ball from him, and after Braund for Auckland got an unconverted try the match soon ended in a tie.

Press did offer one criticism of the Britishers: "The visitors made themselves notorious for their off-side play today, which was very conspicuous, and against all fairness". A letter writer to the *Auckland Star* was equally frustrated, stating, the team played "with an inveterate predisposition for off-side play". Eagles later claimed that he was "presented by a number of Aucklanders, in solemn, ceremonious fashion, with a huge leather medal bearing the words: 'To the boss off-side player of the world!' inscribed in gilt letters on both sides! Now I reckon those jokers were rather hard on me, because I would have had to blossom into a champion indeed to equal some of the off-side artists I played against in sunny Auckland about that time!"

Leaving Auckland by an overnight steamer, the tour party moved further down the Pacific Coast of the North Island, landing at Napier in Hawke's Bay, where a game would be played against the combined local RU's representatives that afternoon. Still hampered by his shoulder injury, Stoddart announced he would play, but as full-back. A beautifully fine day, as the hour for the match approached every avenue to the Recreation Ground became thronged with would-be spectators. When the ball was kicked-off the playing area was walled with a sea of faces, ropes around the touch-lines doing their silent best to keep the crowd back.

The Marlborough Express reported: "Hawke's Bay (black and white jerseys) had the best of the first spell but Nolan intercepted his opponent's pass and scored. In the second spell the play was very fast. Trotten and Swan secured a try each for Hawke's Bay from forward rushes. The Englishmen tried hard to score and the Napier full-back kicking badly twice, Nolan got two more tries. England won by three points to two." The local men were denied two points, that ultimately would have meant victory for them, when a brilliant touch-line conversion goal from the team's Maori back Taku, was ruled by the Lions' umpire to have missed and the Hawke's Bay umpire hadn't arrived behind the posts in time to see. The tourists admitted the goal appeared good but Stoddart, as captain, made no move to override the umpires and allow the goal to count.

The Hawke's Bay XV had at least two other backs of Maori blood: Wi Hape (who played this game bootless) and Jack Taiaroa (the team's captain). It would have been four Maori in the team had the outstanding forward, Te Whatu, not been inexplicably left out. Taiaroa was by 1888 already recognised as among the very best of the footballers in New Zealand and was certainly the first Maori player to come to international prominence. After playing a leading role for Otago in their 1882 defeat of NSW, an account of the match found its way to London's *The Sporting Life* who speculated that "it is quite within the bounds of possibility that in course of time we may have to chronicle the doings of a New Zealand football team on English grounds".

In 1884 he came to Australia as *the* star player of the first New Zealand team; in the days leading up the final tour game against NSW, poster size placards were struck up all over Sydney, proclaiming: "Last Great Match. Final Appearance of Taiaroa."

By 1888 he had settled in Hawke's Bay, practising as a solicitor. In 1901 "someone well versed in the history of the game" in New Zealand wrote in Sydney's *The Daily Telegraph* of the on-field battle in wits between Stoddart and Taiaroa in the Napier match:

> There has been no other player like Taiaroa. He threw his assailants off with his hips as a steamer hurls the waves back from her bows. It was fascinating, said the men on his side, to see him glide and bump his way through a knot of exponents; a distinctly opposite view was held by his opponents. Taiaroa made himself famous with the first English team. He was then playing for Hawke's Bay and after crashing into a scrummage there were pieces of the pride of Yorkshire and Lancashire scattered all over the turf. "My goodness," said Nolan, the stumpy Rochdale Hornet, "'e do bump 'un!"
>
> The game was remarkable for proving the aptitude of the Maori at picking up the points of the game. One of the Englishmen successfully did what so many players try to do and fail—correctly bounced the ball back into play after being run into touch and scored. Taiaroa's ancestors had not put him up to the dodge. Snorting with indignation, he came up the field, yelling, "Here, you English; what game this?" Stoddart, the great cricketer, who captained the Britishers, always an obliging gentleman explained to Jack what game it was. Taiaroa said nothing and the game went on. Presently the big Maori got a chance, and he bounced the ball in, jumped into the field, took the ball and slid over the line. "Is that all right?" he nervously inquired. It was "all right according to Cocker" (conformed to the game's laws) and the referee allowed the score. There was a smile on Taiaroa's face that lit up the whole ground, he rolled the whites of his great eyes and observed: "My word, that's a great game. I play it some more."

After a post-game dinner and songs at the Criterion Hotel, where there was nowhere near enough seats to cope with the numbers that wanted to get in, the team walked outside and found the surrounding streets were blocked with a dense mass of people waiting to see them. Boarding carriages they were driven to the wharf to take the steamer south to Wellington, then a train on to Masterton. Not all the team though had managed to arrive before the ship sailed and were soon seen in a fast-moving launch with some Napier footballers, hurrying across the water in pursuit. The boat caught up to the large steamer and with both vessels still moving, the players were hauled onboard by the crew using ropes.

The *Wanganui Chronicle* wrote after the team's arrival in Masterton: "The visitors are reported to be somewhat out of condition and have confessed that they feel decidedly 'stale' and far from being as fresh as they would like to be. Those of the visitors who were not going to take part in the contest (Stoddart, Mathers, Burnett and Stuart) went straight on to Christchurch."

The second tour of New Zealand did not include any matches in Wellington.

In Stoddart's absence, Arthur Paul was elected captain for the game against Wairarapa. The green-jerseyed locals were unable to match this depleted Lions side and Paul landed a conversion from one of the Britons' three tries to give them a 5-1 win.

The matches now came with increasing frequency. Shrewsbury and Lillywhite must have reckoned the players could have all the rest they wanted at sea; in the meantime efforts to boost the tour's finances saw six games played over the final fortnight.

The first was at Christchurch's Lancaster Park against Canterbury. It was getting very late though in what had been an already long and eventful football season for not just the Lions, but footballers everywhere. Drawing an impressively large 10,000 crowd for a week-day, the Red-White-and-Blue proved far too formidable, particularly in defence, winning a game that didn't reach any great heights 8-0. Stoddart re-took his normal place, scoring two tries and kicking a conversion goal. A correspondent for the *Auckland Star* claimed despite the big audience and beautifully grassed field "there was very little fast play seen during the afternoon, both teams showing unmistakable signs of staleness. At times, the players seemed to 'spell' by mutual consent and then the play was of a most tedious description."

The team would play once more in Christchurch but for the moment they boarded the train for the long journey down the coast to Dunedin, where the Lions had opened their tour and received such a friendly and generous welcome to New Zealand and, in particular, to Otago. At the reception Dr. Coughtry (Otago RU President) offered some kindly words to the team: "There was one reminiscence to which I might refer, namely the loss of your captain. I had come a good deal in contact with poor Seddon during the visit of the team to Otago and was struck with his modesty of character and temperateness of life and with the zeal with which he entered into the game of football. We are sure that the sympathy which was felt among the members of Mr. Seddon's team was equally felt by footballers throughout New Zealand concerning his sad loss. We hope that the memorial which is to be erected over his grave will show his loss was felt as much in New Zealand as in the colony where his death occurred."

Perhaps it was Stoddart's captaincy, maybe it was fatigue and laziness, but the Lions were increasingly forsaking "that spirit of manliness and fair play" that had underpinned the style of their first visit.

Of the nil-all draw against Otago, once again at the Caledonian Ground, the *Timaru Herald* observed: "As an exposition of the Rugby rules the game was not satisfactory. Instead of depending on scientific play in the open field, the visitors displayed a strong tendency to little dodges on the line-out, off-side play and various other smart practices quite foreign to the game usually played here. These trumpery little advantages were very irritating and cries of 'Play the game, England!' were frequently raised."

The *Otago Daily Times* added: "It is greatly to be regretted, however, that some of the English team indulged in what is known among footballers as 'pointing' (sharp practice), that is they are a little inclined to take unfair advantages in violation both of the spirit and letter of the rules. This is admitted by some members of the team themselves and noticed even by the spectators, who are now very well up even in the finer points of the game. It is only a few who are guilty, and their conduct no doubt does not meet with the approval of the majority. Therefore it is all the more pity that the unfairness should prevail, for it certainly detracts from the prestige which otherwise the team have so justly earned."

The next two games were against the combined representatives of the South Island; first in Dunedin, then back at Christchurch. Two days before the Dunedin contest Shrewsbury and Stoddart led a coterie of willow-wielding footballers in a little cricket practice on the Caledonian Ground and a number of the South Island team took part. The following day members of both teams agreed to take a scenic drive along Brighton Beach, some 20km away from Dunedin. The convoy included various vehicles, with most of the Lions in one of "Mr. Taggart's four-in-hand brakes". The trip out was leisurely, scenic and enjoyable. After picnicing on the seashore at Brighton, a start was made on the return journey shortly before 4pm.

The *Star* gives an account of what happened next:

> In returning, coming down the pinch into Green Island, the brake failed to hold and the result was that the vehicle was capsized over the bank, smashing through the fence and rolling into the adjoining paddock. A number of the occupants jumped out but others were unable to get clear and were thrown heavily on the ground; but fortunately all escaped with slight injuries, though the escapes were almost miraculous. Harper, of Nelson, sprained his wrist. Haslam, an English player, had his hand cut. Lillywhite was pitched fully 10 yards and received a severe shaking. The harness was a good deal broken and one of the four horses received a severe wound in crashing through the fence.

The *Otago Daily Times* further explained:

> Mr. Harper, of Dunedin, who was walking behind at the time, watching the action of the brake, saw the danger, and called

A TRIP THROUGH MAORI LAND

out to the occupants of the trap to jump out. Most of the footballers acted on his advice but some remained in the vehicle and were thrown heavily to the ground. Fortunately no one was seriously hurt, though several seem to have had a most miraculous escape.

The driver really saved a bad situation from becoming far worse; sticking to his seat until thrown out into the paddock and even then he held on to the reins of his horses, preventing them from bolting. Remarkably, he escaped without a scratch. After everyone checked their bones and limbs were all still in the correct places, the footballers walked into nearby Green Island. Following a calming cup of tea (or maybe something stronger), they caught the express train back to the safety of Dunedin.

The Combined South Island team was led onto the Caledonian Ground by Edward Morrison, the Otago captain and man who had scored the opening points of the tour against the Lions. Though wearing Otago's blue jerseys, the side included three from Canterbury, two from Southland and one from Nelson. *Press* recorded: "The attendance was large, probably about 4000 being present. The weather was fine and cool, with a breeze blowing off the bay and fair up the ground. There was a mist on the hills and this blowing over the ground caused almost a drizzle."

The home side got off to a great start, landing a place-kicked goal from a mark taken about the half-way line. That certainly got the Lions' attention, particularly their forwards, who began playing much more determinedly. A feature of the game was Dr. Smith, having been forced into playing more often than not in the latter stages of the tour, he was now coming into his own, bringing some real threat and territory by applying his adroit ball dribbling expertise and shouldering away defenders. In one instance he broke clear at the half-way line with the ball at his toe and could only be stopped from scoring a try when the South Island full-back came racing across and riskily fly-kicked the ball away just as the big Scot was about to fall on it.

Deep into the second half the visitors were still behind 3-1. Suddenly, in the midst of an exchange of kicks up and down field between the teams, Mathers secured the ball and bolted away down the touch-line and crossed for a runaway try. *Press* noted "the Englishmen were jubilant". This was a victory they wanted badly. Under enormous pressure, Paul kicked the very difficult conversion from the sideline, leaving Britain ahead 4-3. Now they had the lead, the Lions played with even greater vigour than before. Near time Mathers got the ball from a heeled-back scrum win and after another great run, secured his second try and the final score of a 5-3 win.

Mathers had a great day out scoring the two tries but, as the crowd's response after the game would confirm, across the whole 90 minutes the stand-in captain was again the standout. The *Southland Times* wrote: "Stoddart was the hero of the match. He has played well heretofore but never such a game as today's. He was everywhere and once he got started on a run it was impossible to stop him till he was grassed with two or three sitting on him."

Press concurred: "The feature of the game was the wonderful play of Stoddart. He was ubiquitous. One second he would be on the wing of a scrum and then he would be back in a favourable position to get a pass, after which he would be seen careering away towards the goal. It seemed impossible to stop him unless he was fairly grassed, as with even three players hanging to him he still kept moving. Next to Stoddart, Dr. Brooks was the best, but of the others all played so hard and well that none can be individualised, except that Dr. Smith showed how effective and hard to stop a good dribbler is."

As recounted earlier, after the two teams were accompanied by cheering supporters all the way back into the city, many gathered outside the Lions' hotel and refused to leave until Stoddart came out and took one more bow. In the evening both sides attended the Palace Skating Rink where a footballers' race was run: despite all those months of skating, none of the tourists were in the contest near the finish line. The Britishers left the next morning, a large crowd assembling at the railway station to see them off.

Once back in Christchurch, some relief from the tediousness of playing the same game was found in cricket. Held on Lancaster Park, an invitational

'Canterbury XI' met the "Lillywhite and Shrewsbury's Football Team XI"—a beautiful day, it did not attract a crowd, and no one seemed to mind that at all. The match was not played out, but was greatly in favour of the Lions, who made 88 runs in each of their innings, while Canterbury made 54 in one. The local newspapers reported: "The principal feature of the match was the splendid batting of Shrewsbury, who made nearly half the runs gained by the Englishmen. He gave few chances and hit hard. Stoddart also played in very good form. The fielding of the Englishmen was exceedingly good." The impromptu 'Lions XI' boasted the three Test cricketers in Lillywhite, Shrewsbury, and Stoddart, in addition to Paul who in 1889 made his county cricket debut for Lancashire. The rest of the team was comprised of Haslam, Dr. Smith, Burnett, Penketh, Thomas, Anderton and Mathers.

The second meeting against the South Island representatives was a "severe contest" on the players, with fast-pace action mirrored by resolute defence. Though the final score of six points to nil in favour of the Lions might suggest they had the better of the battle, it was really two flashes from that man again, Stoddart, that provided the difference.

The *Press* wrote: "The spectators were doomed to disappointment, as attack after attack of the Red-and-Blacks (South Island played in Canterbury's colours) were repulsed with success. Stoddart was the hero of the day and he gained the Englishmen's win. Others of the Colours (Britain) tried hard to score but they were well matched. Stoddart was the stumbling block to the South Islanders, as his peculiar method of evading their arms was extremely tantalising." *The Grey River Argus* added: "Stoddart was the hero of the match, his grand runs being heartily cheered. In the first spell he wound up a run by drop-kicking at goal, the ball going just inside the post. In the early part of the second spell he scored a try close to the corner flag, after a fine run. Paul, who took the kick against the wind, made a magnificent long shot, the ball hitting on the bar and dropping over."

The tour wound down with two minor games; the first was a 7-1 win over Taranaki, gaining some revenge for the loss during the team's first visit. Kent, who spent nearly 12 weeks of the campaign on the injured list, suffered a shoulder injury against Taranaki, but backed up the following day against Wanganui, where "he played full-back with his arm in a sling, and received general congratulations from the local press for his excellent play". Salford's Harry Eagles completed the remarkable feat of having played in every game on tour—all 54 of them. This final outing appeared certain to end with the Lions being defeated, but in the dying moments the desperate visitors won a scrum near the Wanganui goal line. "The local team was leading by a try," recalled Jack Anderton. "Just as we were giving up hopes of scoring, Sam Williams gave me a pass, and you may bet I just galloped for all I was worth, and managed to scramble over the line and gain a try. Paul took the place-kick and failed. The whistle then blew, and our game and tour was at an end."

Lots of Kangaroo Tales to Tell

"Starting out as they did in disobedience to a parental authority ... they returned with glory."
Birmingham Daily Post, England, November 20, 1888
(referring to the Lions touring team)

"Not one of the football teamsters returning from Australia can be classed as anything but willing professors [of professionalism]," wrote London's *Referee* when the Lions on board the *Kaikoura* docked at Gravesend on the Thames. In the north of England there was high anticipation for the team's return, but there was far wider interest across Britain, and indeed in the Australasian colonies, at whether the RFU would stick to its pre-tour threats. "The Rugby Union talked about wholesale inquiry into the terms of the arrangement with the then amateur footballers and delivered itself specifically in one retail instance (Clowes) with most damaging effect. None of the salient features of the contract has been varied by its performance; and I shall therefore watch with great curiosity to see what this, generally speaking, most robust institution, which is decidedly the best back-boned of all the associations, will do with the difficulty."

Three of the players had preferred to be left behind on the wharf at Wellington and waved goodbye to their teammates, rather than return home and face almost certain sanction from the RFU. Instead Harry Speakman, Angus Stuart and Robbie Burnett had chosen to explore opportunities in the colonies. A number of reports in New Zealand newspapers stated that the footballer-cricketer Arthur Paul had remained on the dock too, having signed terms with a Melbourne cricket club. However, he seemingly changed his mind at the last moment, and left with the team on the *Kaikoura*.

Speakman was a machinist (metal), and he stayed the 1888/89 summer in Wellington, employed helping to erect cranes on the wharf for the Harbour Board. At the beginning of the next football season he suddenly left for Brisbane, where a better paying job in the government railways had been found for him. The Englishman took a prominent role in local Rugby, playing for and captaining the Queensland team against NSW in three series between 1889 and 1891. He then moved to Charters Towers in the far north of the colony, believing he could make his fortune from a gold mining boom. *The Brisbane Courier* wrote in 1929 that "he imparted a lot of his genius to local players, and raised the game to a high standard. 'Speakie' has been rightly described as the 'Father of Towers Football.'"

His gold riches never came, and alcoholism soon took hold. Speakman died alone in a Townsville hotel room in January 1915, one of the city's victims of a dire heat wave that summer. In the 1950s an old acquaintance recalled: "He offered to train and coach our junior Rugby Union teams for a mere 25s a week. His 'board money' as he put it. He had reached the derelict stage by now, and was a pitiful sight. From member of a touring English team to a 'washed-up wreck' in the faraway Gulf of Carpentaria! Speakman, however, was still an idol with the sporting men of the time, all eager to hear him talk of his football career. Even then his physique had not quite deserted him and when he stripped for coaching it was evident what a grand footballer he must have been in his 'salad days'."

Robbie Burnett too made a new home in the northern colony, becoming a farmer in western Queensland. His first move had been to Melbourne, where he played Rugby for the North Melbourne club in 1889, but that seems to have been his last association with the sport. Meanwhile Angus Stuart had remained in Wellington, where he added to his already varied Rugby résumé by playing with the Poneke FC. He became a regular in Wellington reps XV, and in 1893, at the age of 35, was in New Zealand team that visited Australia. In the early 1900s he returned to Britain, re-joining his old club Dewsbury (which had moved to rugby league) as team trainer.

As with the Lions departure in early March, the team's return to London caused little interest. From that point all of the players and promoters took their leave of each other, and headed off to their home destinations.

The progress of the tour had been followed closely by many Rugby enthusiasts in Britain, and the team found the tone from the newspapers had switched from disdain to praise. The *Birmingham Daily Post* suggested: "The travellers show points of similarity with the Prodigal Son, starting out as they did in disobedience to a parental authority; but unlike him, they returned with glory," and that "amity and forgiveness" should be shown to them.

Sporting Life wrote: "It will be universally admitted that the promoters deserve the highest credit for the enterprising manner in which they have carried out from first to last one of the most, if not the most, responsible undertakings which have ever been recorded in connection with athletic sports. As far as one can judge, the tour throughout seems to have been conducted in the most business-like as well as liberal spirit, and Shrewsbury and Lillywhite, who have been mainly, if not entirely, instrumental in this first visit of an English football team to the colonies, have thoroughly deserved the thanks of football players in both hemispheres."

Shrewsbury was asked by the *Nottingham Evening Post* as to how profitable the venture had been: "The financial result was much more satisfactory than that of the cricket venture. It had hardly answered expectations, but still there would be no loss, he and his partners having cleared their expenses. During his travels in the Colonies he had advanced the business interests of the concern, and returned with some very considerable orders from leading

Australian houses. We must not forget to remark that the Melbourne Cricket Club did all they could to thwart the scheme in many little annoying ways."

Though all the contemporary reports indicate the tour managed to break-even or produced a small profit, it has been suggested the promoters were not willing to admit the true result, and that the project ended anything up to £1000 in debt. This latter figure was stated at the time, but in regard to the 1887/88 cricket tour. In any event, for Shrewsbury and Shaw at least, such losses were easily offset by the extra income the tours brought to their sporting goods business.

The largest celebrations for the returning players were centred around Manchester, with the two clubs that had the largest contingents in the tour party, Salford and Swinton. Enormous crowds and local brass bands accompanied the footballers from Central Station to their club's home ground, where hundreds more supporters were waiting. Each of the men was swamped with hand-shaking, smiling faces and relentless stream of questions about how they were feeling and about the tour.

The Athletic News reported that the welcome home dinner for the Salford tourists (Eagles, Kent, Williams and Anderton) "was a massive affair." In a long and jovial evening, the players each in turn gave a speech about the tour. Anderton was the last to speak, and finished up by saying: "There is one thing we are unanimous about, and that is we had a high old time, and we are glad to be back. We were feasted and fêted wherever we went, invited and received by the best society, even public bodies had vied with one another in their efforts to do us honour. Magnificent was the only word to express our reception along the whole line. It was a privileged experience, and one that will live in the memory as long as reason holds its sway."

The Swinton club gave a banquet of a similar scale and merriment in honour of the return of Bumby, Banks, and Paul, though it had its sad moment when everyone paused to reflect upon the tragic loss of Seddon. The club presented the Seddon family with "a beautiful 'illuminated address' of sympathy" (a poster size custom letter and artwork).

The same newspaper reported that "Bumby, the Swinton half-back, has brought home quite a houseful of curiosities from Australia, and his residence now has the appearance of a miniature Peel Park Museum." Asked what souvenirs he had returned with, Anderton told the reporter: "No, I did not bring any stuffed kangaroos over, but I've got lots of kangaroo tales to tell. Yes they would be better told in a dark room. Then you wouldn't see me blush!"

What money the returned tourists now had was less certain, publicly at least. The *Birmingham Daily Post* believed it was a "substantial, if fleeting, reward of their efforts," while *The Athletic News* stated "Most of the players brought over little money, and if they are professionals they are very, very poor ones." The body of evidence firmly suggests the *Post* was closer to the truth.

A few days after the Lions arrived home the Rugby Union authorities in the north of England issued a circular to clubs "warning all not to play with or against any members of the team until the RFU shall have made up its official mind upon the subject of their amateur status". It appeared the footballers worst fears about their playing career prospects were about to be realised.

However, at the same time, Stoddart was selected by the RFU in a composite team from the London clubs, and played for them against the combined Oxford-Cambridge Universities side. When news of this reached the clubs in Yorkshire and Lancashire, the so-called warning appeared inconsequential.

This was confirmed two days later at a meeting in London of the RFU. In view of what had transpired with the team's preparation in February and March, and in regard to its stated pursuit to rid the game of professionalism, the RFU delivered two astonishing resolutions. The first was to immediately reinstate Jack Clowes, and allow him to again play with Halifax. The second was to take no action against any member of the Lions, provided each made "an affidavit that they received nothing beyond hotel and travelling expenses."

The players immediately began appearing again for their clubs, and though few seemed to rush to fall in with the RFU's demand, by the end of January all had complied, bar one man—Andrew Stoddart. Despite his recalcitrance, the RFU did not pursue him. Their fear was that if Stoddart, the biggest star in British Rugby, had been outed as a professional, then a wholesale rebellion would have ensued to allow professionalism—either by overthrowing the RFU from within, or by starting a rival Rugby organisation.

The latter of course came to reality just seven years later—a process that began when Captain Bell of the Halifax club, who had fought a lone hand for the reinstatement of Clowes, in February 1889 formally put forward a proposal to a RFU meeting that players be given "broken time" payments "to give compensation for loss of time" from work. It wasn't accepted and became the issue upon which Rugby's existence as a single code irrevocably foundered. On 29 August 1895 a meeting of 21 Rugby clubs at the George Hotel in Huddersfield voted in favour of founding the Northern RFU (rugby league).

Eight of the clubs that contributed players to the 1888 Lions tour had by 1898 joined the new body. Though a few of the tourists' contemporaries would play rugby league, and early records are scant, it seems none of the British team were still playing at that time. Some though were involved through the management committees of their clubs, including Harry Eagles at Salford (he also spent three seasons as a referee).

In 1891 Eagles' Salford and Lions teammate Tom Kent won selection for England, and the following season was ever-present in the side that not only won the Triple Crown, but did so without conceding a single point to Scotland, Ireland or Wales. Willie Thomas (Wales) and Stoddart (England) continued their international careers after the tour, and both went on to captain their national team.

Arthur Paul pursued his cricket career, appearing for Lancashire and other teams until the early 1900s. He twice played against touring Australian XIs. In 1895 Paul was in the Lancashire side against Somerset that scored 801 runs in one innings. Paul contributed 177 runs, and shared in a partnership of 363 with Archie MacLaren (424). Usually a wicket-keeper, he not only had proved himself adept at handling a Rugby ball, but in 1899, at the age of 35, had a brief stint in the round-ball code as goal-keeper for Blackburn Rovers.

Of the promoters that accompanied the Lions, Lillywhite continued to be involved in cricket, umpiring first class matches until 1901, including an England-Australia Test at Old Trafford in 1899. For a time he operated the Wheatsheaf pub in Chichester (Sussex), and was still a resident of the town when he passed away in 1929 at the age of 87.

Shrewsbury too returned to cricket, playing with Nottinghamshire. He was selected in the next two Ashes series against visiting Australian teams (1890 and 1893). In the latter series he opened the batting alongside Stoddart, and with his 106 runs in the Test at Lord's, Shrewsbury became the first batsman to score three Test centuries and 1000 runs.

Heading towards the cricket season of 1903, the now 46-year-old Shrewsbury had become worried that his eyesight had deteriorated, and it began to prey on his mind that he would no longer be able to play cricket for his beloved Nottinghamshire. Also suffering back pain, he was certain he had the early signs of kidney disease. His doctor carried out investigations, and tried to reassure Shrewsbury there was no internal disease. The famous cricketer, now hypochondriacal, was not convinced. His friends began to worry about him. Harry Turner, who had sought out and signed-up the players for the Lions tour, said: "He became so strange in his manner that it seemed probable he would either have to be sent to an asylum or would commit suicide. His depression was very great, and his brain seemed to be upset. The pains in his head were acute."

Shrewsbury told his fiancé, Gertrude Scott: "I shall be in the churchyard before many days are over." She begged him not to think that way, but he replied, "It's quite correct". Unbeknown to her or to any of his friends, he went to a gun shop and purchased a revolver. Finding he had the wrong size bullets, Shrewsbury returned to the shop, exchanged them for the correct size, and was shown by the assistant how to properly load the weapon.

Sitting in his bedroom a few evenings latter, Shrewsbury asked Gertrude to go downstairs and make a cup of hot cocoa for him. She went to prepare it, and then shortly afterwards heard a loud noise. Not knowing what is was, she cried out, "What are you doing?" Shrewsbury replied, "Nothing". A minute later she heard a second bang, and having immediately recognised it as a gun shot, raced up the stairs. She found him bleeding from a wound in his head. He had put the first bullet into his lung, then placed the gun up to his temple, and fired again. Help was called for, but within half an hour he was dead. The autopsy confirmed Shrewsbury had not been suffering from any serious physical ailments.

Four years later, Rochdale Hornets' tourist Johnny Nolan was working on building extensions to the Atlas Mill, a large cotton factory in Waterloo district of Greater Manchester. The 43-year-old Nolan was caught in a scaffolding collapse, and suffered fatal injuries. As the decades rolled by the rest of the team quietly passed into history. Into the 1940s the tourists had been reduced to three. Of the last survivors Willie Burnett died in 1944, Arthur Paul in 1947, while Harry Eagles proved to the end he was the team's iron man, reported in a 1949 history of the Salford club as still enjoying life at the age of 87 in the Lancashire seaside town of Cleveleys.

There is no record of the first Lions team ever regathering after the tour. The closest reunion came in February 1889 when many of the party once again donned their red-white-and-blue jerseys, taking part in a "Robert Seddon Memorial Match" that doubled as a fund-raiser for his younger brother's education costs.

The game was played against Seddon's club, Swinton, at their Chorley Road Ground. Banks, Bumby and Paul opted to play for the tourists instead of their own club. Displaying the regard that he continued to hold for Seddon, Stoddart travelled up from London to add his star-billing to the drawcard and help aid the cause. The home side was led by James Valentine, who went on to play for England four times from 1890-96, then captained Swinton's first rugby league Challenge Cup final victory in the 1899/1900 season. It is interesting to note that Swinton's nickname since the mid 1870s had been 'The Lions', attributed to the White Lion hotel where the players changed into their royal blue football kit before home games at nearby Stoneacre Field.

Jack Clowes was announced as being in the British XV, but on match day declined to play—it isn't known whether he was injured, or perhaps, more likely, didn't feel he had the right to join the team given he made no appearances during the tour.

"The Anglo-Australian Team": Arthur Paul, Andrew Stoddart(c), Tommy Haslam, Jack Anderton, Walter Bumby, Johnny Nolan, Harry Eagles, Tom Kent, Alf Penketh, Sam Williams, Charlie Mathers, Willie Burnett, Alex Laing, Tom Banks (+ 1 non-member).

A crowd of over 6000 were on hand when Stoddart kicked-off. The game was very fast throughout, and it was only some hard luck that stopped the British representatives from scoring several tries. Deep into the second half the score was still nil-all, until Stoddart broke into space, and put in a run that mesmerised the Swinton defence and brought the crowd to their feet. Following up his captain, Anderton got possession, and just as he was being tackled he passed back, the ball rebounding off a Swintonian into the hands of Kent, who crossed for what proved to be the only points of what the Manchester press called "an exceedingly well contested game".

At the final whistle the players from both teams rushed to shake hands with friend and foe alike, the crowd generously applauded, and the brass band stationed near the grandstand closed the proceedings with the customary playing of the Great Britain national anthem, *God Save the Queen*.

APPENDIX I
A Record of the 1888 Tour

During the tour through the Australasian colonies the team played 54 matches, of which they won 33, lost 14 and drew seven. The following is list of all matches played. (RU = Rugby Union game; AR = Australian Rules game.)

RU—April 28: Beat Otago reps 8 to 3. Caledonian Grd, Dunedin, NZ.
RU—May 2: Beat Otago reps 4 to 3. Caledonian Grd, Dunedin, NZ.
RU—May 5: Beat Canterbury reps 11 to 6. Lancaster Park, Christchurch, NZ.
RU—May 9: Beat Canterbury reps 4 to 0. Lancaster Park, Christchurch, NZ.
RU—May 13: Drew w/ Wellington reps 3-all. Basin Reserve, Wellington, NZ.
RU—May 14: Beat 'Mr. Roberts' XV' 4 to 1. Basin Reserve, Wellington, NZ.
RU—May 16: Lost to Taranaki reps 1 to 0. New Plymouth Racecourse, NZ.
RU—May 19: Beat Auckland reps 6 to 3. Potter's Park, Auckland, NZ.
RU—May 24: Lost to Auckland reps 4 to 0. Potter's Park, Auckland, NZ.
RU—June 2: Beat New South Wales 18 to 2. Sydney Cricket Grd, NSW.
RU—June 6: Beat Bathurst reps 13 to 6. Bathurst Cricket Grd, NSW.
RU—June 9: Beat New South Wales 18 to 6. Sydney Cricket Grd, NSW.
RU—June 11: Beat 'Eighteen Sydney Juniors' 11 to 0. Sydney Cricket Grd, NSW.
RU—June 13: Drew w/ King's School (Past & Present) 10-all. Parramatta Cricket Grd, NSW.
AR—June 16: Lost to Carlton FC 14 goals (14-17) to 3 (3-8). Melbourne Cricket Grd, VIC.
AR—June 20: Beat Bendigo FC 5 goals (5-16) to 1 (1-14). Back Creek Cricket Grd, Bendigo, VIC.
AR—June 21: Drew w/ Castlemaine reps 1-all (GB 1-2, C'M 1-4). Camp Res. Grd, Castlemaine, VIC.
AR—June 23: Lost to South Melbourne FC 7 goals (7-20) to 3 (3-7). South Melb Cricket Grd, VIC.

APPENDICES

AR—June 27: Lost to Maryborough 4 goals (4-12) to 3 (3-11). Prince's Park, Maryborough, VIC.
AR—June 29: Lost to South Ballarat FC 7 goals (7-18) to 3 (3-7). Eastern Oval, Ballarat, VIC.
AR—June 30: Lost to Fitzroy FC 12 goals (12-20) to 3 (3-4). Fitzroy Cricket Grd, VIC.
AR—July 3: Lost to Port Melbourne 7 goals (7-15) to 6 (6-11). East Melb Cricket Grd, VIC.
AR—July 7: Lost to South Adelaide FC 8 goals (8-9) to 5 (5-9). Adelaide Oval, SA.
AR—July 10: Beat Port Adelaide FC 8 goals (8-8) to 7 (7-8). Adelaide Oval, SA.
AR—July 12: Lost to Adelaide FC 6 goals (6-13) to 3 (3-5). Adelaide Oval, SA.
AR—July 14: Lost to Norwood 5 goals (5-8) to 3 (3-1). Adelaide Oval, SA.
RU—July 16: Beat 'Twenty of South Australia' 28 to 3. Adelaide Oval, SA.
AR—July 18: Beat Horsham FC 6 goals (6-5) to 0 (0-2). Recreation Reserve, Horsham, VIC.
AR—July 20: Lost to Ballarat Imperial FC 4 goals (4-15) to 1 (1-2). Saxon Paddock, Ballarat, VIC.
AR—July 21: Beat Ballarat FC 5 goals (5-8) to 4 (4-8). Saxon Paddock, Ballarat, VIC.
AR—July 25: Beat Sandhurst FC 3 goals (3-3) to 2 (2-10). Back Creek Cricket Grd, Bendigo, VIC.
AR—July 27: Beat Kyneton FC 2 goals (2-7) to 1 (1-5). Kyneton Racecourse, VIC.
AR—July 28: Lost to Essendon FC 7 goals (7-16) to 3 (3-5). East Melb Cricket Grd, VIC.
RU—August 1: Beat Melbourne RFC 9 to 3. East Melb Cricket Grd, VIC.
RU—August 4: Beat New South Wales 16 to 2. Sydney Cricket Grd, NSW.
RU—August 6: Drew w/ Sydney Grammar (Past & Present;16 players) 2-all. Sydney Cricket Grd, NSW.
RU—August 8: Beat Bathurst reps 20 to 10. Bathurst Cricket Grd, NSW.
RU—August 11: Beat Sydney University FC Club by 8 to 4. Sydney Showground, NSW.
AR—August 14: Lost to Northern Districts reps 9 goals (9-19) to 4 (4-5). Albion Grd, Maitland, NSW.

RU—August 18: Beat Queensland 13 to 6. Exhibition Grd, Brisbane, QLD.

RU—August 21: Beat 'Eighteen Combined Juniors of QLD' 11 to 3. Exhibition Grd, Brisbane, QLD.

RU—August 23: Beat Ipswich Rangers FC 12 to 1. North Ipswich Reserve, QLD.

RU—August 25: Beat Queensland 7 to 0. Exhibition Grd, Brisbane, QLD.

RU—August 29: Beat Northern Districts reps 14 to 7. Newcastle Cricket Grd, NSW.

RU—September 8: Beat Auckland reps 3 to 0. Potter's Park, Auckland, NZ.

RU—September 12: Drew w/ "Mr. O'Connor's XV" 1-all. Potter's Park, Auckland, NZ.

RU—September 15: Beat Hawke's Bay reps 3 to 2. Napier Recreation Ground, NZ.

RU—September 17: Beat Wairarapa reps 5 to 1. Masterton Ground, NZ.

RU—September 20: Beat Canterbury reps 8 to 0. Lancaster Park, Christchurch, NZ.

RU—September 22: Drew w/ Otago reps 0-all. Caledonian Grd, Dunedin, NZ.

RU—September 28: Beat Combined South Island 5 to 3. Caledonian Grd, Dunedin, NZ.

RU—September 30: Beat Combined South Island 6 to 0. Lancaster Park, Christchurch, NZ.

RU—October 2: Beat Taranaki reps 7 to 1. Hawera Racecourse, NZ.

RU—October 3: Drew w/ Wanganui reps 1-all. Victoria Park, St John's Hill, Wanganui, NZ.

POINTS VALUES

Australian Rules: Goals only are counted. 'Behinds' are recorded only.

Rugby Union: The RFU's values were used for all games (except in NSW) as follows: three points for all goals from the field; two points for a conversion goal; one point for a try. In NSW four points for all goals from the field; three points for a conversion goal; two points for a try.

APPENDIX II
Post-tour Timeline

August 24, 1889: The 'New Zealand Native Football Team' plays the final game of its monumental 107-match Rugby tour of Great Britain, Australia and New Zealand. The side loses to Auckland reps 7-2 at Potter's Paddock.

March 15, 1890: After the RFU agrees to join IRB, England returns to playing against other Home nations, starting with 1-0 loss to Wales at Crown Flatt, Dewsbury.

June 21, 1891: London Scottish RFC's Bill Maclagan leads the second British Lions team, this time to South Africa (British colonies). The RFU sanctioned the tour, and the majority of the players were from Cambridge and Oxford Universities. The tourists returned undefeated in their 20 games.

April 16, 1892: The New Zealand Rugby Football Union is founded at a meeting of provincial RUs in Wellington.

January 27, 1893: The RFU bans brothers David and Evan James for professionalism after they moved from the Swansea club in Wales to Broughton Rangers in Lancashire. Unable to prove payment was received, the RFU found them guilty on basis they had asked for a signing-on fee.

September 20, 1893: At the RFU annual meeting held at the Westminster Palace Hotel, James Miller of the Yorkshire RU moved "players be allowed compensation for bona-fide loss of time". Mark Newsome of Dewsbury seconded the motion. The motion was defeated 282 to 136.

November 21, 1894: Meeting of 21 leading Rugby clubs from Yorkshire and Lancashire resolve to object to RFU proposal to implement stricter laws against professionalism, whereby clubs found guilty are to suffer expulsion, and onus placed on club to prove innocence. RFU subsequently reaffirmed its commitment to implementing the powers at start of 1895/96 season.

August 29, 1895: At The George Hotel in Huddersfield the 'Northern Rugby Football Union' (later Rugby League) is founded "to push forward, without delay, its establishment on the principle of payment for bona-fide broken-time only". The founding clubs: Batley, Bradford, Brighouse Rangers, Broughton Rangers, Halifax, Huddersfield, Hull, Hunslet, Leeds, Leigh, Liversedge, Manningham, Oldham, Rochdale Hornets, Runcorn, Stockport, St Helens, Tyldesley, Wakefield Trinity, Warrington, Widnes, Wigan.

June 20, 1896: Under Blackheath FC's Johnny Hammond, the third British Lions touring squad is formed, and undertake the second visit to the South African colonies. The tourists were undefeated in all but the last of their 21 games, losing the Fourth Test to South Africa.

October 2, 1896: In Melbourne eight Australian Rules clubs breakaway from the VFA, establishing an elite league. The inaugural Victorian Football League (now AFL) season in 1897 comprised: Carlton, Collingwood, Essendon, Fitzroy, Geelong, Melbourne, South Melbourne and St. Kilda. Points values introduced: 6 for a goal, 1 for a behind. In 1899 teams in the VFL were reduced from 20 players to 18.

June 14, 1899: The fourth British Lions team—and the second to visit Australia—play their first game, defeating Central Southern RU reps at Goulburn 11-3. Organised and led by Cambridge University player, Reverend Matthew Mullinuex, the team plays in NSW, Queensland, and Melbourne, but not New Zealand. They win a four-Test series against the first Australian Rugby team.

October 28, 1900: France defeats Great Britain (represented by Moseley Wanderers) at the Vélodrome de Vincennes to win the gold medal in the Paris Olympic Games.

July 9, 1903: Under the captaincy of Scotland's Mark Morrison the fifth British Lions open their tour of South Africa. With the first two Tests drawn, the home team takes the series after victory in the deciding Test.

August 15, 1903: Australia and New Zealand play each other for the first time in Rugby Union. Held at the Sydney Cricket Ground, the visitors win 22-3.

June 15, 1904: The sixth British Lions arrive in Sydney to start their tour of Australasia. Led by Scotland's David Bedell-Sivright the tourists twice defeat Australia, but are beaten by New Zealand in a one-off Test in Wellington.

July 30, 1905: The first 'All Blacks' sail from Wellington to undertake a 35-game tour of the British Isles, Paris and San Francisco. Captained by Dave Gallaher, the New Zealanders defeat all opposition, apart from a controversial 3-0 loss to Wales at Cardiff.

June 12, 1906: A meeting of the Northern Union (Rugby League) reduces teams from 15 players to 13 and adopts the play-the-ball rule. (The line-out was abolished in 1897).

September 22, 1906: The first 'Springboks' arrive in England to commence their 29-match visit to the British Isles and Paris. The South Africans achieved 26 wins, but lost to Scotland and Cardiff, and were held to a draw by England.

August 8, 1907: In Sydney a meeting resolves to establish the NSW Rugby League and adopts the playing and professionalism rules of the Northern Union. In early 1908 a club competition (now NRL) is established comprising: Glebe, Newtown, South Sydney, Balmain, Eastern Suburbs, Western Suburbs, North Sydney, Newcastle and Cumberland.

August 9, 1907: A 'Professional All Blacks' (aka 'All Golds') team leaves Wellington bound for Sydney to start a 10-month tour playing Rugby League against 13-a-side teams in England, Wales, NSW and Queensland.

September 12, 1907: The 'All Golds' play against the Ceylon RFU during a stop-over in Colombo, Sri Lanka. Played under RU laws, the visitors win 33-6. The English RFU subsequently bans the Ceylon RFU as professionals, despite claims the hosts had no idea their opponents were not a RU team, and that all gate-money was donated to charities.

February 28, 1908: In Brisbane a meeting resolves to form the Queensland Rugby Association to play Rugby League under amateur restrictions. The body is later renamed the Queensland Rugby League.

May 23, 1908: The seventh British Lions begins its 26-game tour of Australasia. The tour party includes only English and Welsh players, the result of the Scottish and Irish RUs' stance that international tours were proving so profitable it was encouraging professionalism. The only Tests played were against New Zealand—the tourists lost twice and the other game drawn.

August 10, 1908: The first 'Wallabies' defeat Victoria at the MCG, then embark on a 10-month tour to Britain and North America. The Australians defeat England and are beaten by Wales, while Ireland and Scotland decline to play them, claiming the team's 3s per day allowance is professionalism. In October the tourists defeat Cornwall (representing Great Britain) to claim the gold medal at the London Olympic Games.

October 3, 1908: The first 'Kangaroos' open their 45-match Rugby League tour of England and Wales with a win over Mid-Rhondda at Tonypandy. After the final game many of the players sign contracts to join English clubs.

September 4, 1909: Fourteen of the 31 members of the recently returned Australian RU team agree to lucrative financial terms to play in a four-game "Kangaroos v Wallabies" series under Rugby League rules in Sydney. The players are immediately banned for life by the NSWRU. Eight go on to have significant careers in the rival code.

January 1, 1910: The 'Five Nations Championship' begins with France joining England, Scotland, Ireland and Wales. The debutants lose all four games.

April 25, 1910: At a meeting in Auckland the New Zealand Rugby League is founded.

June 4, 1910: Led by Salford's James Lomas, Rugby League's first British Lions play NSW in the opening game of their tour of Australia and New Zealand. The 26-man team, primarily from Yorkshire and Lancashire, also included seven from Wales and one Scot. The visitors won all Tests, but were unable to defeat a combined Australasian team (one game drawn).

June 11, 1910: Captained by Ireland's Tommy Smyth, the British Lions play the first game of their 24-match tour of South Africa. The following day another British Lions party led by England's John Raphael defeats Argentina in Buenos Aires near the close of its six-game visit. These would be the last Lions tour until 1924.

APPENDICES

APPENDIX III
The First Anglo-Australian Football Team

FULL-BACKS
Tommy HASLAM (Batley); Arthur PAUL (Swinton).

THREE-QUARTER BACKS
Jack ANDERTON (Salford); Dr Herbert BROOKS (Edinburgh University); Harry SPEAKMAN (Runcorn); Andrew STODDART (Blackheath).

HALF-BACKS
Walter BUMBY (Swinton); Willie BURNETT (Hawick); Johnny NOLAN (Rochdale Hornets).

FORWARDS
Tom BANKS (Swinton); Robbie BURNETT (Hawick); Jack CLOWES (Halifax); Harry EAGLES (Salford); Tom KENT (Salford); Alex LAING (Hawick); Charlie MATHERS (Bramley); Alf PENKETH (Douglas FC); Robert SEDDON (Swinton) (captain); Dr. John SMITH (unattached); Angus STUART (Dewsbury); Willie THOMAS (London Welsh & Cambridge University); Sam WILLIAMS (Salford).

SUPPLEMENTARY PLAYERS
RUGBY UNION: Tom BRYCE (Fireflies RFC); Deacon WADSWORTH (Union Harriers RFC). AUSTRALIAN RULES: Charles CHAPMAN (Melbourne RFC, ex Southampton Trojans FC); P. KENNEDY (Northumberland FC); Jack LAWLOR (ex Essendon FC); Fred McSHANE (ex Fitzroy FC); R. NORMAN (Northumberland FC); Tom SCARBOROUGH (Melbourne RFC, ex Halifax RFC).

TOUR MANAGERS/PROMOTERS
James LILLYWHITE; Alfred SHAW; Arthur SHREWSBURY.

CLUBS
Batley (Yorkshire): Tommy Haslam.

Blackheath (London): Andrew Stoddart.
Bramley (Yorkshire): Charlie Mathers.
Dewsbury (Yorkshire): Angus Stuart.
Douglas FC (Isle of Man): Alf Penketh.
Halifax (Yorkshire): Jack Clowes.
Hawick (Scotland): Robbie Burnett; Willie Burnett, Alex Laing.
London Welsh (London): Willie Thomas.
Rochdale Hornets (Lancashire): Johnny Nolan.
Runcorn (Cheshire): Harry Speakman.
Salford (Lancashire): Jack Anderton; Harry Eagles; Tom Kent; Sam Williams.
Swinton (Lancashire): Tom Banks; Walter Bumby; Robert Seddon (c); Arthur Paul.

UNIVERSITIES
Edinburgh University: Dr Herbert Brooks; Dr. John Smith.
Cambridge University: Willie Thomas.

CLUBS
Represented in 1888 touring team that switched to Rugby League (Northern Union) in 1895-1898: Batley, Bramley, Dewsbury, Halifax, Rochdale Hornets, Runcorn, Salford, Swinton.

APPENDIX IV
British & Irish Lions Tours

1888 AUSTRALIA & NEW ZEALAND
1891 SOUTH AFRICA
1896 SOUTH AFRICA
1899 AUSTRALIA
1903 SOUTH AFRICA
1904 AUSTRALIA & NEW ZEALAND
1908 AUSTRALIA & NEW ZEALAND
1910 ARGENTINA
1910 SOUTH AFRICA
1924 SOUTH AFRICA
1927 ARGENTINA
1930 AUSTRALIA & NEW ZEALAND
1936 ARGENTINA
1938 SOUTH AFRICA
1950 AUSTRALIA & NEW ZEALAND
1955 SOUTH AFRICA
1959 AUSTRALIA, NEW ZEALAND & CANADA
1962 SOUTH AFRICA
1966 AUSTRALIA, NEW ZEALAND & CANADA
1968 SOUTH AFRICA
1971 AUSTRALIA & NEW ZEALAND
1974 SOUTH AFRICA
1977 NEW ZEALAND
1980 SOUTH AFRICA
1983 NEW ZEALAND
1989 AUSTRALIA
1993 NEW ZEALAND
1997 SOUTH AFRICA
2001 AUSTRALIA
2005 NEW ZEALAND
2009 SOUTH AFRICA
2013 AUSTRALIA

APPENDIX V

The Two Games Explained

Unlike other ball sports, such as cricket, baseball or golf, each of the football codes has continued to evolve over time as each generation has sought to shape the game to their modern needs and changes have occurred in regard to the players, spectators, administrators and technology.

If we could travel back in time to the 1880s to watch our favourite football code, great sections of the play would be familiar, however, much would also make little sense on first appearance. For such reasons, it was not uncommon for football writers in newspapers and journals to attempt to explain and illustrate for the benefit of their readers how a rival football code was played and regulated. Such articles are a valuable window into how our football codes were once played, providing an insight that reading the rules and laws alone could never accurately nor fully provide.

Following are two such descriptions from 1888-89 that describe how the Australian Rules and Rugby codes were played at that time.

AUSTRALIAN FOOTBALL
(per 1888 laws)

The goal posts shall be seven yards apart, of not less than 20 feet in height. The ball to be used shall be No.2 size Rugby (26in. in circumference.) The size of the ground generally used is 170 yards x 120 yards, and is oval in shape.

Twenty men are required to constitute a team, 15 of whom have stated positions on the field, four are supposed to always be on the ball, and are called "followers", the remaining one is termed a "rover", to whom the followers are instructed to play.

The 15 place men are ranged five up the centre and five along each wing.

Sketches at the football match, Melbourne v Carlton: Scenes of a game in Melbourne in 1880, captioned as 'A good shot' (top left), 'A run for goal' (top right), and 'A little mark' (bottom). The latter, which awarded a mark if the ball travelled as little as two yards from a kick, greatly perturbed the Lions captain Bob Seddon and his players during the 1888 tour. 'Little-marking' was effectively abolished after the minimum distance for the taking of a mark was raised to 10 yards in 1897.

THE AUSTRALIAN PICTORIAL WEEKLY, PUBLISHED 1880; SOURCE: STATE LIBRARY OF VICTORIA

The names of the different places are as follow: Centre back, right wing back, left wing back; half-back in centre, right wing half-back, left wing half-back; centre, right wing centre, left wing centre; half forward in centre, right wing half-forward, left wing half-forward; centre forward, right wing forward, left wing forward. Each man in a team has one of his opponents to watch; for instance, the centre forward of one side is watched by the full-back of the other, and so on. There is no off-side.

A brief description of the play will prove of interest to those who do not understand it. The game is divided into four quarters. At the conclusion of the first and third quarters the players simply change ends and at half-time, or the conclusion of the second quarter, besides changing ends, a spell of 10 minutes is allowed. At the commencement of each quarter the field umpire bounces the ball in the centre of the ground.

The game is begun by one of the side which has lost the toss kicking-off from the centre of the ground, back men on each side having previously taken up their positions (something akin to kick-off to a soccer match). As soon as the ball is kicked-off the forwards of each side, who have all been lined up in the centre, race forward and take up their positions alongside of their opponents' backs and the followers of each side, accompanied by the rover, pursue the leather.

The ball may be taken in hand at any time, but not carried further than is necessary for a kick, unless the player strikes it against the ground at least once in every seven yards. In the event of a player with the ball in hand trying to pass an adversary and being held by him, he must at once drop the ball.

Any player catching the ball directly from the foot of another player, be he opponent or one of his own side, may call 'mark'. He then has a free kick in any direction, from any spot behind his mark and in a line with it and his opponents' goal posts, no player being allowed to come within the spot marked, or within five yards in any other direction.

The 'little-marking', as this is called, is one of the prettiest features of the game and the dexterity with which it is done is often incomprehensible to the uninitiated. To make sure of being picked in a first class team, a player must be able to not only perform a really good long punt and drop-kick with great precision, but also to catch, or, as it is called, mark the ball from the punt or drop-kick.

A team whose members play an unselfish game can frequently carry the ball with great rapidity from one end of the long ground to the other by three or four judicious kicks. The way the players of this game jump in the air and mark the ball with their hands above their heads is a treat to witness. Place-kicking is seldom indulged in, except when there is a strong wind blowing, and then only for a shot at goal.

When the ball goes out of bounds, it is brought back to the spot where it crossed the boundary line and thrown in by the field umpire at right angles with that line, but is not playable until it touches the ground within bounds. Under no circumstances can the ball while in play be thrown or handed to a player (it can be punched or fisted). Open and fast play is the characteristic feature of the game. All attempts at scrummages are stopped by the field umpire, who stops the play and then bounces the ball.

The game is won by the side kicking the greatest number of goals. A goal must be kicked by one of the side playing for goal, kicking the ball between the posts without touching either of them (flags excepted) or any player after being kicked. The goal line only extends 10 yards on each side of the goal posts. In cases where the ball is kicked behind the goal line by one of the opposite side (which is called a "behind" and behinds are always counted but do not affect the result of the game), anyone of the side behind whose goal it is kicked may bring it 10 yards in front of any portion of the space within the goal and shall kick it towards the opposite goal; except when a a goal is kicked, in which case the ball is kicked off from the centre of the ground.

One of the best features of the game is that rough play is prohibited. Law 14 says: "Tripping, hacking, rabbiting, slinging, unfairly interfering with a player after he has made a mark or catching hold of a player below the knee are prohibited; pushing with the hands or body is allowed only when a player is running within five or six yards of the ball. Pushing from behind shall not be allowed under any circumstances. An infringement of this rule will result in a free kick being awarded to an opponent."

Originally the only interval was at half-time, but so many matches being lost and won through the wind frequently dropping and greatly favouring one side, ends are changed now when one-fourth, one-half and, three-fourths of the time arranged for play have expired. At half-time only there is an interval of 10 minutes limit and on resuming play after each change of ends the ball is bounced by the field umpire. At quarter-, half-, and three-quarter time, and at time, a bell is rung to command cessation of play, and immediately it rings the ball is dead, even though it be in the air after being kicked. So strictly is this enforced that "no goal" has often been the umpire's verdict when the bell has rung while the ball was travelling from the foot to the goal, through which it has subsequently passed.

The Maitland Mercury & Hunter River General Advertiser August 24, 1889; final paragraph *Otago Witness* October 12, 1888.

RUGBY FOOTBALL
(per 1888 laws)

So little is known of the game by the public that a detailed description of the play would be unintelligible. A few points may, however, be referred to. The ground, to begin with, is oblong, 110 yards long yards king and 75 yards broad and a white mark being placed all round. At each end the goal posts are placed, the goal consisting of two uprights, across which, about 12 feet from the ground, a bar is placed. [A No. 2 size Rugby ball is used].

The sides consist of a full-back, two half-backs, and three three-quarter backs, the remainder being called 'forward', but a better appellation would be 'followers'. The object of game, of course, is so score goals, which have to be kicked over the bar.

If a player carries the ball over a line stretching across the ground at one end [the goal line], and places it on the ground, a 'try' is scored. That entitles any player of the side—usually the best kicker—to a [place-kick] shot for goal from a spot in a straight line from where the ball was placed on the ground.

North v South at Manchester, 1893: First played in 1874 the annual 'North v South' game was a fiercely contested selection trial for choosing the England representative team. By the late 1880s the North had the [gr]eater number and quality of players to choose from, but often fell to the South as their footballers, drawn from [a] smaller pool of clubs, were more familiar with each others play. Of the English players in the first Lions tour party the majority were from the North, with only Andrew Stoddart having played for the South.

ILLUSTRATED SPORTING AND DRAMATIC NEWS, PUBLISHED 1893; SOURCE: FRÉDÉRIC HUMBERT

A goal—which may also be scored from a running [drop-kick] shot—counts three points; if the goal is not kicked the 'try' secures one point. [A player catching the ball on the full from an opponent's kick may claim a 'mark', which allows him to drop-kick for goal, or hold the ball on the ground for a teammate to place-kick for goal—both of these score three points if successful.]

Almost as soon as the ball is kicked-off a scrimmage is formed. Such a peculiar sight has seldom been seen on a South Australian football field. The forwards of either side assume a bent position and locked together one behind the other they set to work to get the ball out of the scrimmage. The most scientific play is to heel it out backwards.

As soon as it is clear of the scrum one of the 'back' men, who are always speedy, rushes in and getting the ball under his arm tries to work it forward. Then an opponent tackles him and he has to get rid of the ball unless he can get through his [opposing] men.

The most effective way of working the ball is to pass it—by throwing—to a comrade, who must not, however, be in front of the passer. Off he dashes until he is collared. Any amount of license is allowed in tackling. A player may be collared round the neck, tripped, pushed, or pulled, in fact well-nigh any means may be used to put him over. Of course dodging (stepping) is a feature of the game.

When a man makes a breach of the rules a scrimmage is formed. If the ball goes out of bounds all the forwards get in a line opposite each other at right angles from the spot where it goes out, and a player has to throw it straight in.

There is, however, a good deal of scope for scientific play and all the men on the field are kept hard at work; but one must come to the conclusion, that weight is the great essential.

—*South Australian Register,* July 17, 1888

BIBLIOGRAPHY

Blainey, Geoffrey; *A Game of Our Own—The Origins of Australian Football*, Black Inc (2003)

Collins, Tony; *Rugby's Great Split*, Cass (1998)

Diehm, Ian; *Red! Red! Red! The Story of Queensland Rugby*, Playright Publishing (1997)

Ellison, Tom; *The Art of Rugby Football*, Geddis & Blomfield (1902)

Fagan, Sean; *The Rugby Rebellion—The Divide of League and Union*, author (2005)

Frith, David; *"My Dear Victorious Stod": A Biography of A.E. Stoddart*, Richard Smart Publishing (1997)

Gallaher, Dave & Stead, William; *The Complete Rugby Footballer*, Methuen & Co. (1906)

Grainger, Ron; *Rugby Union in Victoria: The Early Years*, author (2010)

Griffiths, John; *British Lions (History)*, Crowood (1990)

Hughes, Thomas; *Tom Brown's Schooldays*, Macmillan & Co. (1857)

Jackson, Ian; *Pocket-money Professionals*, (*Rugby League Review No.2*) London League Publications (2008)

Mancini, A. & Hibbins, G.M.; *Running With The Ball: Football's Foster Father*, Lynedoch Publications (1987)

Morris, Graham; *100 Greats: Salford Rugby League Club*, Tempus Publishing (2001)

RFU, *The Laws of the Game of Football as Played by the RFU*, (var. editions from 1871–1914)

Ryan, Greg; *Forerunners of the All Blacks*, Canterbury University Press (1993)

Sewell, E.H.D.; *The Book of Football*, J.M. Dent & Sons (1911)

Thomas, C.&G.; *125 Years of the British & Irish Lions: The Official History*, Mainstream Publishing (2013)

Thomson, A.A.; *Rugger My Pleasure*, Sportsman's Book Club (1957)

Twain, Mark; *Following the Equator*, American Publishing Company (1897)

Wild, Stephen; *Swinton Rugby League Football Club*, Tempus Publishing (2002)

Williamson, John; *Football's Forgotten Tour: The Story of the British Australian Rules Venture of 1888*, (2003)

OTHER SOURCES

Contemporary newspapers, journals & books as noted in narrative.

- Staff & archives of the ARU/NSWRU, NZRU, RFU
- *AustralianFootball.com*
- *JottingsOnRugby.com*
- *Rugby-Pioneers.com*
- *espncricinfo.com*
- *paperspast.natlib.govt.nz* National Library of New Zealand
- *trove.nla.gov.au/newspaper* National Library of Australia
- *britishnewspaperarchive.co.uk* The British Library

ACKNOWLEDGEMENTS

Geoff Slattery (for making it happen), Luanne Fagan (transcribing newspapers/letters), Frédéric Humbert, John Griffiths, Ron Grainger, David Thomas (Clowes v RFU), Graham Morris, Tony Collins, Ian Heads, ARU Archives, RFU Museum of Rugby, Rugby Museum of NZ, Michael O'Malley, Annelise Fagan, Matthew Fagan.